Ivy Global

SSAT
ENGLISH
1ST EDITION

IVY GLOBAL, NEW YORK

This publication was written and edited by the team at Ivy Global.

Editor: Laurel Perkins
Layout Editor: Sacha Azor
Producers: Lloyd Min and Junho Suh

About Ivy Global

Ivy Global is a pioneering education company that provides a wide range of educational services.

E-mail: info@ivyglobal.com
Website: http://www.ivyglobal.com

CONTENTS

INTRODUCTION
CHAPTER 1

HOW TO USE THIS BOOK

Welcome, students and parents! This book is intended for students preparing for the Verbal, Reading, and Writing sections of the Middle or Upper Level Secondary School Admission Test (SSAT). For students applying to many top private and independent schools in North America, the SSAT is a crucial and sometimes daunting step in the admissions process. By leading you step-by-step through the fundamental content and most effective strategies for the SSAT, Ivy Global will help you build your confidence and maximize your score on this important exam.

This book is right for you if:

- you are applying to a private or independent school that requires the SSAT for admission
- you will be in Grades 5-7 (Middle Level) or 8-11 (Upper Level) when you write the SSAT
- you would like to learn and practice the best strategies for the Verbal, Reading, and Writing sections of the SSAT
- you are a parent, family member, or tutor looking for new ways to help your Middle or Upper-Level SSAT student

We know that no two students are exactly alike—each student brings a unique combination of personal strengths and weaknesses to his or her test preparation. For this reason, we've tailored our preparation materials to help students with a specific subject area or goal. Ivy Global's *SSAT English* walks students through the best strategies for the SSAT Reading and Verbal sections, plus a step-by-step approach to the Writing Sample and a thorough vocabulary and writing skills review. This book includes:

- an up-to-date introduction to the SSAT's administration, format, and scoring practices, including the changes that took effect in fall 2012
- targeted strategies for students new to standardized tests, including study schedules, pacing, and stress management
- a complete introduction to the SSAT Reading and Verbal sections, explaining in detail what concepts are tested and what types of questions are asked

- the most effective strategies to approach each type of question on these sections, including advanced strategies for Upper Level students
- a step-by-step approach for the Writing Sample, preparing students to write short stories and essays that will stand out in the admissions process
- a thorough review of all of the fundamental concepts you will need to know for the SSAT, including vocabulary, grammar, and literary terminology
- 500 core vocabulary words to prepare for the level of vocabulary tested by the SSAT, plus innovative and fun strategies to make vocabulary building part of your daily life
- close to 900 practice questions and drills, grouped into targeted practice sets for each concept and difficulty level

Work through the material that is appropriate to your level. If you are a Middle Level student, work through all of the material except any content marked "Upper Level." If you are an Upper Level student, review all of the basic material before you look at the "Upper Level" content. The two exams have the same basic format, so both younger and older students will benefit from learning the same basic strategies.

Finally, keep in mind that every student has a different learning style. If you come across a strategy or a concept that you find challenging, circle it and move on. You might find that some of the other strategies work better for you, and that is okay! Pick the strategies that are the best fit for your learning style and add them to your toolkit for writing the SSAT. You can always come back to more difficult material with the help of a trusted adult or tutor.

To get started, continue reading for an overview of the SSAT and some general test-taking advice. Good luck in this exciting new step for your education!

ABOUT THE SSAT

The **SSAT (Secondary School Admission Test)** is a standardized test administered to students in grades 3-11 to help determine placement into certain private and independent schools. Many secondary schools worldwide use the SSAT as an integral part of their admissions process. The SSAT is owned, published, and developed by the Secondary School Admission Test Board. All tests are printed in English.

You will register for one of three SSAT tests, depending on your grade level:

- The **Elementary Level** exam (new in 2012) is for students currently in grades 3-4.
- The **Middle Level** exam (formerly Lower Level) is for students currently in grades 5-7.
- The **Upper Level** exam is for students currently in grades 8-11.

All levels have the same basic format but vary in difficulty and length. The Elementary Level is shorter than the Middle and Upper Levels.

WHEN IS THE TEST ADMINISTERED?

The SSAT is administered at national test centers on "**Standard**" dates eight times during the academic year. In some locations, regional private schools and organizations also have the option of administering the test independently on non-standard dates. These independent dates are called "**Flex**" test dates, and they are listed by region on the SSAT website at www.ssat.org. It does not matter whether you take the exam on a Standard or Flex test date if this is offered in your location.

HOW MANY TIMES CAN I TAKE THE TEST?

In most locations, a student can register for a Standard test as often as desired, up to eight times per academic year. However, a student can only register for a Flex test once per academic year. For students applying to schools in Ontario, the Ontario Testing Consortium allows students to register for only one SSAT test per academic year. Any subsequent attempts to write the exam will be considered invalid and will not be reported to schools.

HOW DO I REGISTER?

The easiest and fastest way to register is to complete the **online application**. Visit www.ssat.org to register for an exam in your location. The other alternative is to mail/fax a completed form to SSAT by the regular registration deadline.

Important! Make sure to print off and keep the **Admission Ticket** that is obtainable only after SSAT has received and processed your registration and payment. This ticket both serves as a confirmation for your test registration, and includes important details of your pending test: date, location of scheduled test, specific instructions regarding taking the SSAT, and your list of schools and consultants chosen to receive your SSAT scores.

WHAT IS THE FORMAT OF THE SSAT?

The SSAT consists of three main sections (**Verbal**, **Math**, and **Reading**), plus a **Writing Sample** that either takes the form of a creative writing assignment or an essay. The format of the test differs based on the level of the exam:

ELEMENTARY LEVEL			
Section	**Questions**	**Length**	**Topics Covered**
Math	30 questions	30 min	Arithmetic, geometry, word problems
Verbal	30 questions	20 min	Vocabulary: synonyms and analogies
15-minute break			
Reading	28 questions	30 min	Short passages: fiction, non-fiction, poetry
Writing	One prompt	15 min	Creative writing assignment (not scored)
Total testing time: 1 hour, 50 minutes			

MIDDLE AND UPPER LEVELS			
Section	**Questions**	**Length**	**Topics Covered**
Writing	One prompt	25 min	Creative writing assignment or essay (not scored)
5-minute break			
Math I	25 questions	30 min	Arithmetic, algebra, geometry, word problems
Reading	40 questions	40 min	Short passages: fiction, non-fiction, poetry
10-minute break			
Verbal	60 questions	30 min	Vocabulary: synonyms and analogies
Math II	25 questions	30 min	Arithmetic, algebra, geometry, word problems
Experimental Section	16 questions	15 min	Varies: this section is testing out questions for upcoming years and is not scored
Total testing time: 3 hours, 5 minutes			

Except for the Writing Sample, all questions are **multiple choice** (A) to (E). You are not allowed to use calculators, rulers, dictionaries, or other aids during the exam.

HOW IS THE SSAT SCORED?

All of the multiple-choice questions on the SSAT are equal in value, and your **raw score** for these sections is calculated as follows:

- One mark is given for every question answered correctly.
- ¼ mark is deducted for every question answered incorrectly.
- No marks are awarded or deducted for questions left blank.

Therefore, your raw score is based on the number of questions correctly answered subtracted by one quarter point for each question you answer incorrectly.

Your raw score is then converted into a **scaled score** for each section (Verbal, Math, and Reading) that represents how well you did in comparison with other students taking the same exam:

- Elementary Level scaled score: 300-600 for each section, 900-1800 total
- Middle Level scaled score: 440-710 for each section, 1320-2130 total
- Upper Level scaled score: 500-800 for each section, 1500-2400 total

The **Writing Sample** is not scored, but is sent to the schools you are applying to as a sample of your writing skills. Admissions officers may use your essay or story to evaluate your writing ability when they are making admissions decisions.

The **Experimental Section** on the Middle and Upper Levels is the SSAT's method of testing out new questions for upcoming years. The section is not scored, but students should try to complete it to the best of their ability. The section may include any mixture of Verbal, Reading, or Math questions.

Scores are released to families, and to the schools that families have designated as recipients, within two weeks after the test date. Schools receive a printed report by mail and an electronic copy online. Families receive an electronic copy and can request a printed report for an extra fee. You may designate certain schools as recipients during registration, or at any time before or after testing, through your online account at www.ssat.org.

WHAT ARE THE SSAT PERCENTILES?

The SSAT score report also provides **SSAT percentile** rankings for each category, comparing your performance to that of other students in the same grade who have taken the test in the past three years. If you score in the 60th percentile, this means you are scoring higher than 60% of other students in your grade taking the exam.

These percentile rankings provide a more accurate way of evaluating student performance at each grade level. However, the SSAT percentiles are a comparison against only other students who have taken the SSAT, and these tend to be very high-achieving students. Students should not be discouraged if their percentile rankings appear low.

Because the Elementary Level exam is new in 2012, percentile data for this test has not yet been released.

MEDIAN SCORES (SSAT 50TH PERCENTILE)				
	Grade	Reading	Verbal	Math
Middle Level	5	569	584	563
	6	593	614	593
	7	611	638	614
Upper Level	8	629	662	647
	9	644	683	668
	10	656	695	686

The SSAT also publishes an Estimated National Percentile Ranking for test takers in grades 5-9, which provides an estimated comparison of student performance against the entire national student population, not just the set of students taking the SSAT. The test also provides a projected SAT score for test-takers in grades 7-10.

HOW DO SCHOOLS USE THE SSAT?

Schools use the SSAT as one way to assess potential applicants, but it is by no means the only tool that they are using. Schools also pay very close attention to the rest of the student's application—academic record, teacher recommendations, extracurricular activities, writing samples, and interviews—in order to determine which students might be the best fit for their program. The personal components of a student's application sometimes give schools a lot more information about the student's personality and potential contributions to the school's overall community. Different schools place a different amount of importance on SSAT and other test scores within this process, and admissions offices are good places to find how much your schools of interest will weight the SSAT.

TEST-TAKING STRATEGIES

CHAPTER 2

APPROACHING THE SSAT

Before you worry about the content covered on the SSAT, you need to focus on *how* you take the SSAT. If you approach the SSAT *thoughtfully* and *strategically*, you will avoid common traps and tricks planted in the SSAT by the test makers. Think of the SSAT as a timed maze—you need to make every turn cleverly and quickly so that you avoid getting stuck at a dead end with no time to spare.

In this section, you will learn about the SSAT's format and structure; this awareness will help you avoid any surprises or shocks on test day. A very predictable exam, the SSAT will seem less challenging once you understand what it looks like and how it works. By learning strategies and techniques for best test-taking practice, you will discover how to work as quickly and intelligently as possible. Once you know what to expect, you can refine your knowledge of the actual material tested on the SSAT, such as the verbal and math skills that are based on your grade level in school.

This section on SSAT strategies will answer your **major questions**:

1. How does the SSAT differ from a test you take in school?
2. What preparation strategies can you learn before you take the SSAT?
3. What strategies can you learn to use during the SSAT?
4. How can you manage stress before and during the SSAT?

In the process of answering your big questions, this section will also highlight key facts about smart test-taking:

- Your answer choice matters—your process does not. Grid your answer choices correctly and carefully to earn points. You have a set amount of time per section, so spend it wisely.
- The SSAT's format and directions do not change, so learn them now.
- All questions have the same value.
- Each level of the SSAT corresponds to a range of grades, and score expectations differ based on your grade level.
- Identify your areas of strength and weakness, and review any content that feels unfamiliar.

- Apply universal strategies—prediction-making, Process of Elimination, back-solving, and educated guessing—to the multiple-choice sections.
- Stay calm and be confident in your abilities as you prepare for and take the SSAT.

HOW DOES THE SSAT DIFFER FROM A TEST YOU TAKE IN SCHOOL?

The SSAT differs from assessments you take in school in four major ways:

1. It is not concerned with the process behind your answers. Your answer is either right or wrong: there is no partial credit.
2. You have a set amount of time per section (and for the exam as a whole).
3. It is divided into three levels that correspond to three grade ranges of students.
4. It is extremely predictable given that its format, structure, and directions never vary.

NO PARTIAL CREDIT

At this point in your school career, you have probably heard your teacher remark, "Be sure to show your work on the test!" You are most likely familiar with almost every teacher's policy of "No work, no credit." However, the SSAT completely ignores this guideline. The machine that grades your exam does not care that you penciled brilliant logic in the margins of the test booklet—the machine only looks at your gridded answer choice. Your answer choice is either right or wrong; **there is no partial credit**.

SET AMOUNT OF TIME

You have a **set amount of time per section**, so spend it wisely. The SSAT test proctors will never award you extra time after a test section has ended because you spent half of one section struggling valiantly on a single problem. Instead, you must learn to work within each section's time constraints.

You also must view the questions as equal because **each question is worth the same number of points** (one). Even though some questions are more challenging than others, they all carry the same weight. Rather than dwell on a problem, you should skip it, work through the rest of the section, and come back to it if you have time.

THREE LEVELS

There are three levels of the SSAT—Elementary, Middle, and Upper—each of which is administered to a specific range of students. The Elementary Level is given to students in grades 3 and 4; the Middle Level is given to students in grades 5, 6, and 7; and the Upper Level is given to students in grades 8, 9, 10, and 11. While you might be used to taking tests in school that are completely tailored to your grade, the SSAT is different: each test level covers content from a specific range of grade levels.

Score expectations differ based on your grade level. You are not expected to answer as many questions correctly on a Middle Level exam if you are only in fifth grade. Conversely, if you are in seventh grade, you are expected to answer the most questions correctly on the Middle Level exam because you are one of the oldest students taking that exam.

STANDARD FORMAT

The SSAT is, by definition, a **standardized test**, which means that its format and directions are standard and predictable. While your teachers might change formats and directions for every assessment they administer, you can expect to see the same format and directions on every SSAT.

WHAT PREPARATION STRATEGIES CAN YOU LEARN BEFORE YOU TAKE THE SSAT?

Now that you are familiar with how the SSAT differs from the tests you take in school, you are ready to learn some test tips. You can prepare for the SSAT by following these three steps:

1. Learn the format and directions of the test.
2. Identify your areas of strength and weakness.
3. Create a study schedule to review and practice test content.

LEARN THE FORMAT AND DIRECTIONS

The structure of the SSAT is entirely predictable, so learn this now. Rather than wasting precious time reading the directions and understanding the format on test day, take the time now to familiarize yourself with the test's format and directions.

Refer to the tables on page 6 and 7 for an overview of the SSAT's format. Continue reading for specific directions for the Verbal, Reading, and Writing sections. Specific directions for the Math section can be found in Ivy Global's *SSAT Math*.

IDENTIFY YOUR STRENGTHS AND WEAKNESSES

To determine your areas of strength and weakness and to get an idea of which concepts you need to review, take a full-length, accurate practice exam to serve as a diagnostic test. Practice exams for the SSAT can be found in Ivy Global's *SSAT Practice*.

Make sure you simulate test day conditions by timing yourself. Then, check your answers against the correct answers. Write down how many questions you missed in each section, and note the topics or types of questions you found most challenging (e.g. analogies, fiction passages, geometry, or data analysis). What was hard about the test? What did you feel good about? Did you leave a lot of questions blank because of timing issues, or did you leave questions blank because you did not know how to solve them? Reflecting on these questions, in addition to looking at your score breakdown, will help you determine your strengths, weaknesses, and areas for improvement.

CREATE A STUDY SCHEDULE

After determining your areas of strength and weakness, create a study plan and schedule for your SSAT preparation to review content. Work backward from your test date until you arrive at your starting point for studying. The number of weeks you have until your exam will determine how much time you can (and should) devote to your preparation. Remember, practice is the most important!

To begin, try using this sample study plan as a model for your own personalized study schedule.

SAMPLE STUDY PLAN

My test date is: _____.

I have ____ weeks to study. I will make an effort to study ____ minutes/hours each

night, and I will set aside extra time on _____ to take timed sections.

I plan to take ____ full-length tests between now and my test date. I will study for ____

weeks and then take a practice test. My goal for this test is to improve my score in the

following sections:

_____

_____

_____

_____

_____

_____

_____

If I do not make this goal, then I will spend more time studying.

Ivy Global

STUDY SCHEDULE				
Date	Plan of Study	Time Allotted	Time Spent	Goal Reached?
1/1/2013	Learn 5 words and review perimeter of polygons	1 hour	44 minutes	Yes, I know 5 new words and can calculate perimeter!
1/3/2013	Learn 5 words and review area of triangles	1 hour	1 hour	I know 5 new words, but I'm still confused about the area of triangles. I'll review this again next time and ask a teacher, tutor, or parent for help.

WHAT STRATEGIES CAN YOU LEARN TO USE DURING THE TEST?

Once you have grown accustomed to the SSAT through practice, you are ready to learn strategies to use during the SSAT. The following points will prepare you to take the test as cleverly and efficiently as possible:

1. Grid your answer choices correctly and carefully.
2. Pace yourself to manage your time effectively.
3. Learn a strategic approach for multiple-choice questions.

GRIDDING ANSWER CHOICES

For the Middle and Upper Level exams, you must enter your answers on a separate answer sheet. In school you probably take tests that, for the most part, do not ask you to transfer your answers to a separate sheet. However, the SSAT streamlines the grading process by only reviewing your answer sheet. You must grid in your multiple-choice answers onto this sheet using an HB pencil to fill in the circle that corresponds to your answer. This sheet is scanned and scored by a highly sensitive computer. You will also write your Writing Sample in separate lined pages of this answer sheet.

Since you have to take an additional step to record your answers, it is important that you avoid making gridding mistakes. Sadly, many students get confused and mismark their answer sheets. Remember, even if you arrive at the right answer, it is only correct and counted in your favor if you grid correctly on your answer sheet.

To grid correctly and carefully to maximize your points, consider the following tips:

Keep your answer sheet neat. Since your answer sheet is graded by a machine, your score is calculated based on what your marks look like. The machine cannot know what you really meant if you picked the wrong bubble. Stray marks can harm your score, especially if you darken the correct answer but accidentally make a mark that confuses the machine! Avoid this and other errors by consulting the following image, which shows the difference between answers that are properly shaded and those that are not.

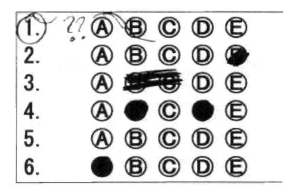

- *Answer 1 is wrong because no answer is selected and there are stray marks.*
- *Answer 2 is wrong because choice E has not been darkened completely.*
- *Answer 3 is wrong because two answers have been selected.*
- *Answer 4 is wrong because two answers have been selected.*
- *Answer 5 is neither right nor wrong because it was left blank.*
- *Answer 6 is right because choice A has been darkened properly.*

Train yourself to **circle your answer choice in your test booklet**. If you have time to go back and check your answers, you can easily check your circled answers against your gridded ones.

You should also **create a system for marking questions that you skipped** or that you found confusing (see the next section for more information about skipping around). Try circling those question numbers in your test booklet only so that you can find them later if you want to solve them later or check your work. Be aware of these questions when gridding answers on your answer sheet.

Finally, **grid your answers in batches of four, five, or six answer choices.** That way, you do not have to go back and forth between your test booklet and your answer sheet every minute. If you choose to use this strategy, keep an eye on the clock—you do not want to get to the end of the section and find you have not gridded any answers. Depending on how much time you have left to check your work (if you happen to finish early), you can either review every problem or spot-check a series of questions on your answer sheet against your test booklet.

TIME MANAGEMENT (PACING)

Manage your time effectively to boost your score. Just as effective gridding contributes to time management, other strategies enable you to work efficiently and maximize the number of problems you answer. Specifically, skipping questions is particularly important because you need to learn to keep moving on the exam rather than wasting your time on any single question.

You can skip questions within each section of the SSAT. In fact, you might find the freedom to skip questions to be helpful, especially since each question is worth one point. If you are stuck on a problem, you should move on after a minute or two and try to answer another problem. It makes more sense to answer as many questions as possible (and get as many points as possible) rather than spending all your time on one question. If you come across a question you want to skip, mark it in your question booklet (by circling it, underlining it, etc.) and move to the next question. Just be sure to skip the corresponding number on your answer sheet if you choose to skip questions. Remember not to make any stray marks on your answer sheet.

There is a benefit to skipping questions. By moving quickly through each question of the section, you will ensure that: 1) you see every question in the section; 2) you gain points on questions that are easy for you; 3) you return to more challenging problems and hopefully answer as many as you can with your remaining time. It is also important to note that you might not be able to answer several questions in each section if you are on the younger end of the testing group for your particular test level. In that case, you should skip those questions unless you can eliminate one or more answer choices. Also, think about the value of skipping in terms of the guessing penalty. If you cannot make a clever guess on a hard problem, then you should skip it and move on because choosing a random answer will most likely cause you to lose one quarter of a point.

Continue reading for more detailed information about the guessing penalty and guessing strategies.

Follow this step-by-step process to decide when to skip questions:

1. Look through the section and first answer the questions that are easy for you. Circle any questions that you are not sure about or seem harder.
2. After answering all the easier questions, go back to the questions you have circled and spend some time working on ones that you think you might be able to solve.
3. Skip any questions that you have no idea how to solve.

STRATEGIES FOR MULTIPLE-CHOICE QUESTIONS

Apply universal strategies— prediction-making, Process of Elimination, back-solving, and educated guessing—to the multiple-choice sections. To illustrate the value of these strategies, read through the following example of a synonym question from the Verbal Section:

HAPPY:

    (A) delighted

    (B) unhappy

    (C) crazy

    (D) nice

    (E) depressed

Answer: (A). "Delighted" is the correct answer because it is the word that most nearly means "happy."

Regardless of whether the answer choices are easy, difficult, or somewhere in between, you can use certain tricks and tips to your advantage. To approach SSAT questions effectively, you need to step into the test makers' minds and learn to use their traps against them.

Make predictions. When you see a question, try to come up with an answer on your own before looking at the answer choices. You can literally cover the answer choices with your hand so that you must rely on your own intelligence to predict an answer instead of being swayed by answer choices that you see. If you look at the answer choices first, you might be tempted to circle a choice without thinking about the other options and what the question is asking you. Instead, make a prediction so that you understand the question fully and get a clear sense of what to look for in the answers. In the synonym example above, you could predict that a possible synonym for "happy" would be something like "glad."

Use the **Process of Elimination**. For each multiple-choice question, you must realize that the answer is right in front of you. To narrow down your answer choices, think about the potential incorrect answers and actively identify those to eliminate them. Even if you can eliminate just one answer, you will set yourself up for better odds if you decide to guess. For the synonym example above, test your prediction of "glad" against the answer choices and immediately eliminate "unhappy" and "depressed" since they are nearly opposite in meaning. You can also probably eliminate "crazy" and "nice" since those words do not match your prediction as well as "delighted," which is the correct answer.

Try back-solving. This strategy is most useful on the math sections, especially when you are given a complicated, multi-step word problem. Instead of writing an equation, try plugging in the answer choices to the word problem. Take a look at the following question:

Catherine has a basket of candy. On Monday, she eats ½ of all the candy. On Tuesday, she eats 2 pieces. On Wednesday, she eats twice the amount of candy that she consumed on Tuesday. If she only has 4 pieces left on Thursday, how many pieces did she initially have?

(A) 12

(B) 14

(C) 16

(D) 20

(E) 22

To use back-solving, start with answer choice (C) and plug it into the word problem. If (C) is the correct answer, you are done. If not, you will then know whether you should test (B) or (D). When we start with 16 pieces of candy, we subtract 8 on Monday, then 4 more for Tuesday, and then 2 more for Wednesday. By Thursday, Catherine only has two pieces of candy left, which is less than the amount we wanted. Therefore, we know our answer has to be bigger, so we eliminate choices (A), (B), and (C) and try (D), which works.

(*Fun Fact:* If you think about it, you will have to plug in three answer choices at most to determine the right answer.)

Use educated guessing. Before taking any test, it is important to understand the test's grading rules for correct answers, incorrect answers, and blank answers. The SSAT has a **wrong-answer penalty** for each level, which means:

- You lose one quarter of a point from your total score for each question you answer incorrectly.
- You receive one point for every question you answer correctly.
- If you leave a question blank, you do not lose points—but you do not gain points either (so your score will not reach the highest possible range).

The SSAT's penalty is often referred to as a guessing penalty since its purpose is to discourage random guessing. If you did not lose points for guessing, then you could possibly pick the same answer choice for an entire section and get twenty percent of the questions—or more—correct. Thus, the guessing penalty is important because it keeps your score on the same level as other students' scores.

Guessing cleverly can certainly improve your score. If you can rule out one or two choices for a tricky question, then you should guess because your chances for guessing correctly are above average. However, if you cannot eliminate any of the answer choices, then guessing is not worth the risk of a quarter-point penalty. In that case, leave the answer blank and move on quickly to gain points on other questions.

Armed with these strategies, you might feel that SSAT is starting to look more manageable because you now have shortcuts that will help you navigate the maze of questions quickly and cleverly.

Take a look at this example to practice using the strategies you just read about.

Doll is to toy as pasta is to

    (A) mall
    (B) Italy
    (C) America
    (D) dessert
    (E) food

1. Assess the question and recognize what it is testing. In this case, the question tests whether you can complete the analogy.
2. Make a prediction. A doll is a type of toy, so pasta must be a type of something. How about "dinner"?
3. Look for inaccurate answer choices and eliminate them. "Mall" does not make sense. "Italy" and "America" both make pasta, but they are not examples of food or dinner. Dessert is a type of food, but pasta is not a dessert. "Food" is the only possible answer in this case.
4. Make an educated guess, or choose the best answer if you feel confident about the answer. Since you made a fantastic prediction and used Process of Elimination, you only have one choice left: (E). "Food" is the correct answer—you just earned yourself a point!

HOW CAN YOU MANAGE YOUR STRESS?

If you have ever had a big test before, or an important sports match, play, or presentation, then you know what anxiety feels like. Even if you are excited for an approaching event, you might feel nervous. You might begin to doubt yourself, and you might feel as if your mind is racing while butterflies flutter in your stomach!

When it comes to preparing for the SSAT, the good news is that a little anxiety (or adrenaline) goes a long way. Anxiety is a natural, motivating force that will help you study hard in the days leading up to your test. And, that anxiety will also help you stay alert and work efficiently during the test.

Sometimes, however, anxiety might become larger than life and start to get the best of you. To prevent anxiety and nerves from clouding your ability to work effectively and believe in yourself, you should try some of the suggestions below. Many of these suggestions are good ideas to use in everyday life, but they become especially important in the final week before your test and on test day itself.

- **Relax and slow down.** To center yourself and ease your anxiety, take a big, deep breath. Slowly inhale for a few seconds and then slowly exhale for a few seconds. Shut your eyes and relax. Stretch your arms, roll your neck gently, crack your knuckles—get in the zone of Zen! Continue to breathe deeply and slowly until you can literally feel your body calm down.
- **Picture your goals.** Close your eyes or just pause to reflect on what you want to achieve on test day. Visualize your success, whether that means simply answering all the math questions or getting a top score and gaining acceptance into the school of your dreams. Acknowledge your former successes and abilities, and believe in yourself.
- **Break it down.** Instead of trying to study a whole section at once, break up your studying into small and manageable chunks. Outline your study goals before you start. For example, instead of trying to master the entire Reading Section at once, you might want to work on one type of passage at a time.
- **Sleep.** Make sure you get plenty of rest and sleep, especially the two nights leading up to your exam!
- **Fuel up.** Eat healthy, filling meals that fuel your brain. Also, drink lots of water to stay hydrated.
- **Take a break.** Put down the books and go play outside, read, listen to music, exercise, or talk to a trusted friend or family member. A good break can be just as restful as a nap. However, watching television will provide minimal relaxation.

On the night before the exam, study only lightly. Make a list of your three biggest fears and work on them, but don't try to learn anything new. Pick out what you are going to wear to the exam—try wearing layers in case the exam room is hotter or colder than you expect. Organize everything you need to bring, including your Admissions Ticket. Know where the test center is located and how long it will take to get there. Have a nutritious meal and get plenty of sleep!

On the morning of the exam, let your adrenaline kick in naturally. Eat a good breakfast and stay hydrated; your body needs fuel to endure the test. Bring along several pencils and a good eraser. Listen carefully to the test proctor's instructions and let the proctor know if you are left-handed so you can sit in an appropriate desk. Take a deep breath and remember: you are smart and accomplished! Believe in yourself and you will do just fine.

THE VERBAL SECTION

CHAPTER 3

INTRODUCTION

The SSAT Verbal Section tests your ability to recognize word meanings and logically relate words to each other. In this section, you will have 30 minutes to complete 60 questions: 30 synonym questions and 30 analogy questions. **Synonyms** are words with similar or same meanings; these questions will give you a word in capital letters and ask you to find another word that means the same thing. **Analogies** are statements that ask you to find a relationship between two words, and then find another pair of words that demonstrates the same relationship.

HOW TO APPROACH THE VERBAL SECTION

Review the following test-taking strategies and study methods to help you prepare for the Verbal Section as a whole. Then, turn to the following sections on specific strategies for the synonym and analogy questions.

TIME MANAGEMENT

You have 30 minutes to complete the section, so you only have half a minute to spend on each question! In this section, as in every section on the SSAT, it is important to pace yourself and be smart about which questions you answer and in what order. First, skim the section and answer questions with words you know immediately. Then, go back and try to tackle the words you are less familiar with.

SKIPPING QUESTIONS

You aren't expected to be able to answer every question on the section, and often you will earn a better score by skipping questions you really don't know instead of guessing. Remember, you lose a quarter-point for every incorrect answer. If you really don't know a word, it is probably best to skip that question rather than trying to guess. Only guess if you are sure that you can eliminate at least one answer choice.

PROCESS OF ELIMINATION

Use the Process of Elimination to narrow down your answer choices by crossing out the obviously wrong answers, and make your best guess among the answers that could be right.

VOCABULARY BUILDING

Vocabulary building is the best long-term way to improve your Verbal score. Work your way through the vocabulary building chapter and word list included in this book. Test yourself regularly on your vocabulary, making sure you are reviewing old words as you learn new ones.

Ivy Global

SYNONYMS

PART 1

SYNONYM STRATEGIES

The first 30 questions of the SSAT Verbal Section take the form of synonyms. In this section, read about the best strategies for approaching the SSAT's synonym questions.

WHAT ARE SYNONYMS?

Synonyms are words with similar or same meanings. On the SSAT, you will see a word in capital letters and will be asked to find another word that is closest in meaning. Here is an example:

CAUTIOUS:

    (A) different

    (B) careful

    (C) angry

    (D) together

    (E) worthwhile

The question is asking you to pick which word among the answer options most nearly means the same thing as CAUTIOUS.

How would you define the word "cautious"? To be cautious means to display caution, or to be careful.

"Different" means "unlike," so (A) is incorrect. "Angry" means characterized by anger, so (C) is incorrect. "Together" can mean "in a group" or "composed and calm," so (D) is incorrect. "Worthwhile" means sufficiently important or rewarding, so (E) is incorrect.

Therefore, the only correct answer for this question is (B) careful.

Even though this example is a bit easier than some of the questions you will see on the SSAT, you can rest assured that every synonym question will have only **one correct answer**. Before moving onto the next question, be sure to look through all 5 answer choices to make sure you have really selected the correct answer. If multiple answers seem possible, it is your job to test out each answer choice to find which one is the best synonym for the word in capital letters. Be careful—the test will try to trick you by including many words that sound like possible synonyms! Continue reading for some strategies to help you avoid these misleading answer choices and select the best synonym every time.

APPROACHING SYNONYMS

Start by covering up the answer choices and thinking of your own definition for the word in capital letters. If it helps, write your definition down. If you can define the word easily, look for an answer that matches your definition. Try this with the example below:

CHARGE: (YOUR DEFINITION: _____)

 (A) release

 (B) accuse

 (C) belittle

 (D) conspire

 (E) prevent

If no answer choice fits the definition you chose, you might need to look for a different definition of the word.

CHARGE can mean "price" or "fee" (as in the phrase "free of charge"), but here there is no answer choice like "price" or "fee" or "cost."

To find other definitions of a word, come up with many **contexts**—phrases where you might have heard the word before. A word's context is everything in a phrase or sentence that might influence the word's meaning. The word CHARGE can have many different meanings, depending on its context.

It might be helpful to make yourself a bubble chart and think of as many phrases as you can:

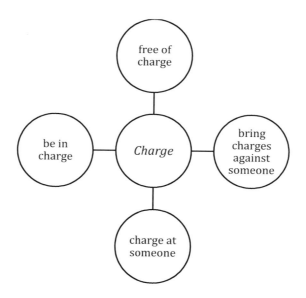

What does CHARGE mean in each of these contexts? To be "in charge" means to have power or be in control; to "charge at someone" means to attack suddenly or assault; and to "bring charges against someone" means to accuse or blame. The correct answer here is (B) accuse.

Exercise #1: For each of the following words, try to come up with three different contexts and write them in the bubble charts. If you run out of room, use a separate sheet of paper. The first word has been filled in for you. If you can think of more than three contexts, draw a new bubble! To check your work for this exercise, look up each word in a good dictionary and see if your contexts related to all of the word's possible meanings.

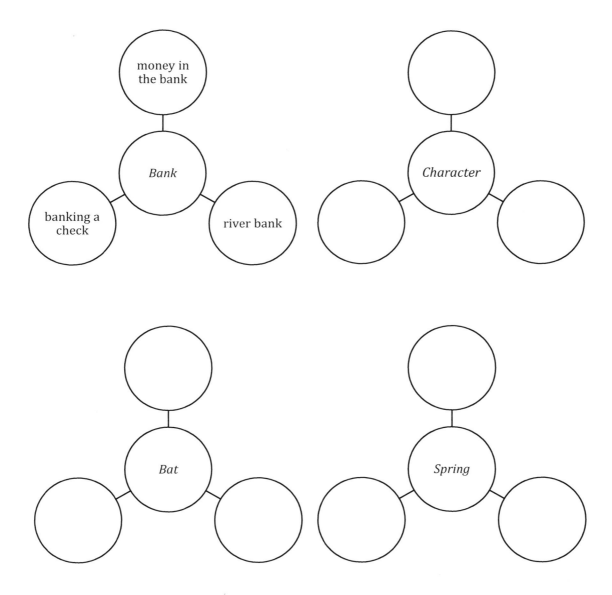

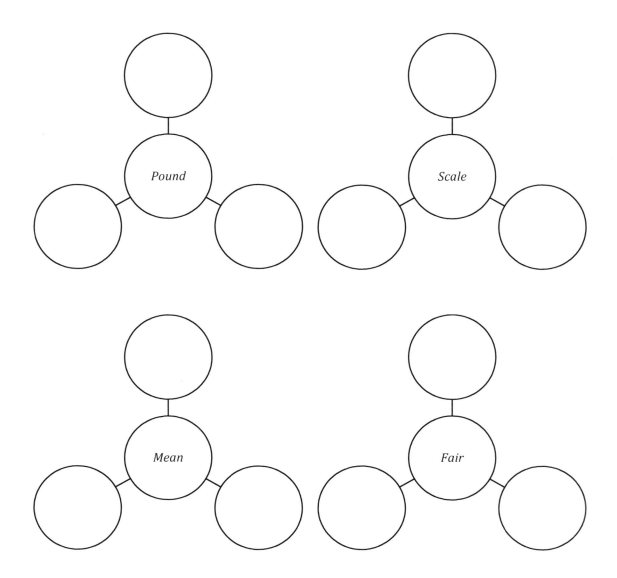

Looking for more words to try out? On a separate piece of paper, try drawing bubble charts for FINE, ROLL, FIGURE, LIE, SOLE, FAST, EXPRESS, and DRIVE. Not all of these words will have three different meanings, and some might have more than three.

USING CONTEXT TO DEFINE UNFAMILIAR WORDS

Coming up with **contexts** can also help you define a word that you only sort of know, or at least match it with an answer choice that makes sense. Look at the following example:

CONSENSUS:

> (A) difference
>
> (B) survey
>
> (C) agreement
>
> (D) dispute
>
> (E) cooperation

Do you know the meaning of CONSENSUS? If not, can you think of a context in which you may have heard it used? Perhaps you have heard it in the context of "come to a consensus" or "arrive at a consensus."

What answer choices make sense in these contexts? Let's test: "come to a difference," "come to a survey," "come to an agreement," "come to a dispute," and "come to a cooperation." The answer that makes the most sense is (C) agreement.

Exercise #2: See if you can come up with a context for each of the following words by writing a sentence where you have heard the word used. Then, try to guess a definition of the word based on its context. When you are finished, use a dictionary to check your answers. The first question has been filled out for you.

1. ADVANCE

   Context: advance to the front of the line

   Definition: to move forward. Other definitions: a forward movement ("the advance of civilization"), sent beforehand ("in advance").

2. PROMOTE

   Context:

   Definition:

3. AUTHENTIC

   Context:

Definition:

4. NARRATE

    Context:

    Definition:

5. ESTABLISH

    Context:

    Definition:

Have you mastered the words above? Try your hand at these more challenging words:

6. LOFTY

    Context:

    Definition:

7. ALLEGIANCE

    Context:

    Definition:

8. SYMPATHETIC

    Context:

    Definition:

9. TESTIMONY

    Context:

    Definition:

10. AILMENT

Ivy Global

Context:

Definition:

WORD CONNOTATIONS

A word's **connotation** is its secondary meaning, or the feeling we get from the word. A word can have a positive (+) connotation if it means something good, a negative (-) if it means something bad, or a neutral connotation if it is neither good nor bad. For example, the word "horrible" has a negative connotation, whereas "joyous" has a positive connotation. If you can remember that a word means something positive or negative, you can eliminate answer choices with the opposite connotation. Your context can also help you remember if the word has a positive, negative, or neutral connotation.

Exercise #3: Try to come up with a context for the following words, and use this information to decide whether they have a positive, negative, or neutral connotation. Then, check your connotation with the following answer key. The first question has been filled out for you.

1. TRAGEDY

    Context: coping with the tragedy of Hurricane Sandy

    Connotation: negative

2. IRRITABLE

    Context:

    Connotation:

3. RADIANT

    Context:

    Connotation:

4. HAIL

    Context:

Connotation:

5. BLEAK

    Context:

    Connotation:

6. INADEQUATE

    Context:

    Connotation:

7. ADMIRATION

    Context:

    Connotation:

Have you mastered the words above? Try your hand at these more challenging words:

8. DILAPIDATED

    Context:

    Connotation:

9. EXEMPLARY

    Context:

    Connotation:

10. TURMOIL

    Context:

    Connotation:

11. ECSTASY

Context:

Connotation:

12. ABJECT

Context:

Connotation:

SYNONYM PRACTICE QUESTIONS

In this section, you will find 246 practice questions to prepare you for the types of synonym questions you might find on the SSAT. There are 6 sets of questions, grouped by difficulty. Pay attention to the difficulty of each set to determine which questions are appropriate for the Middle and Upper Levels.

WARM-UP QUESTIONS

Use these questions to test your familiarity with basic synonym strategies for both the Middle and Upper Levels.

1. ERROR:

    (A) edit
    (B) fear
    (C) mistake
    (D) frustration
    (E) pause

2. EXIT:

    (A) open
    (B) leave
    (C) wave
    (D) undo
    (E) experience

3. CREATE:

    (A) find
    (B) glimpse
    (C) adore
    (D) break
    (E) make

4. REPLACEMENT:

    (A) mission
    (B) stand-in
    (C) pretense
    (D) move
    (E) location

5. BOLD:

   (A) old

   (B) nasty

   (C) daring

   (D) weak

   (E) submissive

6. TRY:

   (A) attempt

   (B) hold

   (C) plow

   (D) desire

   (E) put

7. EMBRACE:

   (A) laugh

   (B) spoil

   (C) hug

   (D) scold

   (E) lug

8. SCARE:

   (A) cry

   (B) frighten

   (C) scold

   (D) shove

   (E) lose

9. BOTHER:

   (A) tickle

   (B) snuggle

   (C) snap at

   (D) ignore

   (E) annoy

10. STUMBLE:

   (A) hum

   (B) chatter

   (C) trip

   (D) rage

   (E) throw

BASIC QUESTIONS

Use these questions to practice the most basic difficulty level you might see in both the Middle and Upper Level synonym sections. The Middle Level exam will include more basic questions than the Upper Level exam.

1. DEMAND:
   (A) employ
   (B) punish
   (C) give to
   (D) ask for
   (E) yell

2. SHRIEK:
   (A) ghost
   (B) prince
   (C) screech
   (D) whistle
   (E) song

3. CASUAL:
   (A) unnecessary
   (B) traditional
   (C) disrespectful
   (D) resulting
   (E) informal

4. HAZY:
   (A) sad
   (B) unclear
   (C) sloppy
   (D) laughable
   (E) harmful

5. MIRACLE:
   (A) gift
   (B) fortune
   (C) life
   (D) wonder
   (E) symbol

6. TECHNIQUE:
   (A) point
   (B) engineer
   (C) detail
   (D) direction
   (E) method

7. INSPECT:
   (A) answer
   (B) plan
   (C) examine
   (D) ignore
   (E) require

8. ATTRACT:
   (A) fight
   (B) annoy
   (C) refuse
   (D) interest
   (E) surprise

9. REALITY:

   (A) vision

   (B) theory

   (C) truth

   (D) sorrow

   (E) persistence

10. DECEIVE:

    (A) clarify

    (B) unwrap

    (C) predict

    (D) control

    (E) lie to

11. REGRETFUL:

    (A) enraged

    (B) sorry

    (C) stubborn

    (D) gleeful

    (E) homesick

12. DETACH:

    (A) curse

    (B) separate

    (C) attack

    (D) torture

    (E) knock down

13. CRATER:

    (A) cavity

    (B) lake

    (C) mountain

    (D) sphere

    (E) moon

14. FERTILE:

    (A) productive

    (B) deserted

    (C) warm

    (D) sympathetic

    (E) girlish

15. REFRESH:

    (A) polish

    (B) caress

    (C) practice

    (D) renew

    (E) retreat

16. COMBINE:

    (A) join

    (B) whisk

    (C) list

    (D) braid

    (E) visit

17. CONSTRUCT:

    (A) carry

    (B) withdraw

    (C) explain

    (D) destroy

    (E) build

18. VILE:

    (A) tasty

    (B) disgusting

    (C) strong

    (D) syrupy

    (E) unknown

19. DEFINITE:

   (A) certain

   (B) endless

   (C) tight

   (D) likely

   (E) formal

20. ATTEND:

   (A) learn from

   (B) be present

   (C) flee from

   (D) hold

   (E) simplify

21. ENCOUNTER:

   (A) number

   (B) betrayal

   (C) meeting

   (D) story

   (E) celebration

22. CATEGORIZE:

   (A) replace

   (B) classify

   (C) recount

   (D) found

   (E) bless

23. COMPROMISE:

   (A) bargain

   (B) possibility

   (C) ending

   (D) trick

   (E) failure

24. SOLITUDE:

   (A) weariness

   (B) forgetfulness

   (C) isolation

   (D) concern

   (E) brightness

25. FRAIL:

   (A) shy

   (B) imaginary

   (C) insulting

   (D) expensive

   (E) weak

26. FASCINATE:

   (A) pacify

   (B) imitate

   (C) avoid

   (D) amuse

   (E) interest

27. APPROACH:

   (A) scare away

   (B) come near

   (C) observe

   (D) wave at

   (E) criticize

28. HUMOROUS:

   (A) comic

   (B) plump

   (C) good

   (D) ill

   (E) forgetful

29. HUMBLE:

    (A) boastful

    (B) hungry

    (C) quiet

    (D) modest

    (E) resentful

30. PREDICT:

    (A) relate

    (B) confuse

    (C) maneuver

    (D) foretell

    (E) return

31. CONFESS:

    (A) disappoint

    (B) imprison

    (C) admit

    (D) understand

    (E) reject

32. TRIUMPH:

    (A) happiness

    (B) truth

    (C) obstacle

    (D) wound

    (E) victory

MEDIUM QUESTIONS

Use these questions to practice the medium difficulty level you might see in both the Middle and Upper Level synonym sections. Questions like these will make up a majority of the Middle Level synonym section, and a smaller portion of the Upper Level section.

1. FATIGUE:
   (A) service
   (B) outfit
   (C) exhaustion
   (D) relief
   (E) excitement

2. ADMIRING:
   (A) appreciative
   (B) wonderful
   (C) secretive
   (D) worthwhile
   (E) memorable

3. DREAD:
   (A) permit
   (B) fear
   (C) animation
   (D) wish
   (E) fog

4. CLARITY:
   (A) desire
   (B) error
   (C) disgust
   (D) clearness
   (E) shine

5. AGENDA:
   (A) plan
   (B) effect
   (C) compass
   (D) invitation
   (E) unit

6. PACT:
   (A) hymn
   (B) agreement
   (C) angle
   (D) family
   (E) interest

7. HUE:
   (A) idea
   (B) interval
   (C) shade
   (D) shift
   (E) costume

8. ERA:
   (A) extent
   (B) period
   (C) character
   (D) measurement
   (E) clock

Ivy Global

9. ASSIST:

    (A) need

    (B) prevent

    (C) score

    (D) support

    (E) create

10. REBEL:

    (A) prolong

    (B) invent

    (C) agree

    (D) destroy

    (E) disobey

11. DEVOUR:

    (A) obey

    (B) consume

    (C) insist

    (D) collect

    (E) expand

12. MANUAL:

    (A) boundary

    (B) guide

    (C) machine

    (D) heavy

    (E) human

13. POSTPONE:

    (A) annoy

    (B) consider

    (C) delay

    (D) confuse

    (E) mention

14. VOCAL:

    (A) patient

    (B) intriguing

    (C) likeable

    (D) calm

    (E) outspoken

15. UNIFIED:

    (A) important

    (B) created

    (C) inspiring

    (D) together

    (E) national

16. RATIONAL:

    (A) generous

    (B) cold

    (C) peaceful

    (D) strict

    (E) reasonable

17. BENEFIT:

    (A) energize

    (B) enhance

    (C) compose

    (D) lessen

    (E) worship

18. ABUSE:

    (A) buoy

    (B) care

    (C) harm

    (D) partake

    (E) soften

19. CONFIDE:

    (A) hide

    (B) rescue

    (C) ruin

    (D) entrust

    (E) develop

20. UTILIZE:

    (A) correct

    (B) bargain

    (C) invent

    (D) use

    (E) alter

21. PRODUCE:

    (A) create

    (B) affect

    (C) expand

    (D) protect

    (E) impact

22. INQUIRE:

    (A) discover

    (B) question

    (C) reply

    (D) amuse

    (E) command

23. EXTINCT:

    (A) joyous

    (B) dull

    (C) short

    (D) completed

    (E) dead

24. OPTIMISTIC:

    (A) hopeful

    (B) upset

    (C) cheerless

    (D) flawless

    (E) excellent

25. SACRIFICE:

    (A) complain

    (B) give up

    (C) refuse

    (D) pray

    (E) set fire

26. BOUND:

    (A) unrestricted

    (B) restrained

    (C) confident

    (D) deep

    (E) quick

27. THRILL:

    (A) worry

    (B) surprise

    (C) excite

    (D) satisfy

    (E) annoy

28. NEUTRAL:

    (A) mental

    (B) unbiased

    (C) passionate

    (D) untrue

    (E) conservative

29. HORRID:

    (A) honorable

    (B) moist

    (C) massive

    (D) terrible

    (E) wasteful

30. BASHFUL:

    (A) sunken

    (B) confident

    (C) cruel

    (D) hurtful

    (E) shy

31. LIMITATION:

    (A) fabric

    (B) constraint

    (C) range

    (D) speed

    (E) minimum

32. THOROUGH:

    (A) thoughtful

    (B) physical

    (C) complete

    (D) partial

    (E) inefficient

33. HESITATION:

    (A) pause

    (B) moment

    (C) surge

    (D) boredom

    (E) evidence

34. RENEW:

    (A) sparkle

    (B) finish

    (C) dampen

    (D) clean

    (E) regenerate

35. REVEAL:

    (A) repair

    (B) expose

    (C) intersect

    (D) seek

    (E) attempt

36. ABSTRACT:

    (A) conceptual

    (B) healthy

    (C) unintentional

    (D) loose

    (E) inferior

37. FUNDAMENTAL:

    (A) accidental

    (B) additional

    (C) joyful

    (D) basic

    (E) hilarious

38. INSTINCTIVE:

    (A) detestable

    (B) favorable

    (C) intuitive

    (D) varied

    (E) forgiving

39. CHUCKLE:

    (A) laugh

    (B) deride

    (C) incline

    (D) grin

    (E) daydream

40. RARE:

    (A) old

    (B) uncommon

    (C) best

    (D) flawed

    (E) early

41. WRITHE:

    (A) enliven

    (B) wriggle

    (C) digress

    (D) grumble

    (E) circle

42. ELDERLY:

    (A) fresh

    (B) employed

    (C) senior

    (D) detached

    (E) decent

43. BIZARRE:

    (A) treasured

    (B) unhealthy

    (C) magical

    (D) unusual

    (E) symphony

44. LINGER:

    (A) tickle

    (B) remain

    (C) depart

    (D) select

    (E) vibrate

45. ALTER:

    (A) sustain

    (B) savor

    (C) offer

    (D) preserve

    (E) adjust

46. REVOLVE:

    (A) rotate

    (B) block

    (C) rethink

    (D) guide

    (E) discard

47. EXHAUSTED:

    (A) odorous

    (B) serene

    (C) depleted

    (D) disappointed

    (E) confused

48. SERIOUS:

    (A) unfortunate

    (B) important

    (C) evil

    (D) irresponsible

    (E) angry

49. PARADE:

   (A) procession
   (B) holiday
   (C) festival
   (D) dance
   (E) umbrella

50. CURRENT:

   (A) antique
   (B) contemporary
   (C) useful
   (D) electric
   (E) foolish

51. PURPOSE:

   (A) finding
   (B) expectation
   (C) realization
   (D) accident
   (E) intent

52. REPOSE:

   (A) death
   (B) silence
   (C) pomp
   (D) rest
   (E) delight

53. MATURE:

   (A) capable
   (B) knowledgeable
   (C) developing
   (D) adult
   (E) decayed

54. CLARIFY:

   (A) describe
   (B) confuse
   (C) orate
   (D) explain
   (E) aid

55. SYNOPSIS:

   (A) letter
   (B) dialogue
   (C) diagnosis
   (D) summary
   (E) argument

56. SURLY:

   (A) unfriendly
   (B) mournful
   (C) hopeful
   (D) nostalgic
   (E) amused

57. REMOTE:

   (A) sophisticated
   (B) respectful
   (C) distant
   (D) convenient
   (E) unimportant

58. EJECT:

   (A) expel
   (B) forgive
   (C) ignore
   (D) measure
   (E) question

59. NURTURE:

   (A) commence

   (B) follow

   (C) soil

   (D) nourish

   (E) please

60. IMPACT:

   (A) problem

   (B) understanding

   (C) argument

   (D) consequence

   (E) conclusion

DIFFICULT QUESTIONS

Use these questions to practice the more advanced questions you might see in both the Middle and Upper Level synonym sections. The Upper Level exam will include more difficult questions than the Middle Level exam.

1. VIVID:

   (A) beneficial

   (B) intense

   (C) living

   (D) wide

   (E) upbeat

2. ELATED:

   (A) curious

   (B) delayed

   (C) delighted

   (D) blown up

   (E) grieving

3. CONVENTIONAL:

   (A) assembled

   (B) constructive

   (C) representative

   (D) customary

   (E) irregular

4. CONVERGE:

   (A) visit

   (B) overlook

   (C) align

   (D) scatter

   (E) unite

5. COUNSEL:

   (A) treasure

   (B) restraint

   (C) assembly

   (D) advice

   (E) committee

6. SKEPTICAL:

   (A) prejudiced

   (B) doubtful

   (C) intriguing

   (D) sneaky

   (E) certain

7. RECREATION:

   (A) regulation

   (B) gathering

   (C) production

   (D) reviewing

   (E) amusement

8. ALLEVIATE:

   (A) injure

   (B) relieve

   (C) leave

   (D) remove

   (E) believe

9. AGGRAVATE:

    (A) improve

    (B) dismiss

    (C) harvest

    (D) agitate

    (E) cultivate

10. IMPLY:

    (A) suggest

    (B) concern

    (C) shun

    (D) define

    (E) suppress

11. ECCENTRIC:

    (A) perceptible

    (B) uniform

    (C) exciting

    (D) unusual

    (E) annoying

12. AMPLIFY:

    (A) indulge

    (B) intensify

    (C) hinder

    (D) compress

    (E) reunite

13. ILLUMINATE:

    (A) brighten

    (B) distort

    (C) nauseate

    (D) flicker

    (E) glance

14. VEND:

    (A) acquire

    (B) sell

    (C) twist

    (D) influence

    (E) catch

15. COMPOSURE:

    (A) lapse

    (B) arrangement

    (C) collectedness

    (D) harmony

    (E) symphony

16. INVERT:

    (A) reunite

    (B) reverse

    (C) transmute

    (D) consult

    (E) calculate

17. GULLIBLE:

    (A) naive

    (B) deceptive

    (C) discerning

    (D) birdlike

    (E) edible

18. QUIVER:

    (A) convulsion

    (B) inquiry

    (C) target

    (D) tremble

    (E) provoke

19. PONDER:

    (A) consider

    (B) dabble

    (C) ascertain

    (D) misconstrue

    (E) propose

20. MOURN:

    (A) torment

    (B) devastate

    (C) conjecture

    (D) awaken

    (E) grieve

21. JUVENILE:

    (A) childish

    (B) criminal

    (C) delicate

    (D) jovial

    (E) compassionate

22. FUSION:

    (A) electricity

    (B) mixture

    (C) disorientation

    (D) duration

    (E) decision

23. PROPORTION:

    (A) expanse

    (B) category

    (C) ratio

    (D) quality

    (E) continuation

24. SILKEN:

    (A) snide

    (B) inaudible

    (C) bright

    (D) valuable

    (E) smooth

25. ROUT:

    (A) trip

    (B) perish

    (C) defeat

    (D) exhibit

    (E) conspire

26. CONSENSUS:

    (A) restriction

    (B) agreement

    (C) proposition

    (D) nuisance

    (E) attitude

27. ASSESS:

    (A) interrogate

    (B) determine

    (C) speculate

    (D) nominate

    (E) regress

28. NULL:

    (A) veritable

    (B) mundane

    (C) nonexistent

    (D) corresponding

    (E) calculated

29. DISCLOSE:

    (A) insult

    (B) estimate

    (C) refrain

    (D) shut

    (E) reveal

30. CONCISE:

    (A) contrary

    (B) decisive

    (C) specific

    (D) terse

    (E) gracious

31. CONTRACT:

    (A) shorten

    (B) dilute

    (C) uphold

    (D) extend

    (E) absorb

32. FRINGE:

    (A) interior

    (B) edge

    (C) minimum

    (D) skirt

    (E) conclusion

33. CREVICE:

    (A) closure

    (B) fissure

    (C) insight

    (D) culmination

    (E) warning

34. AIL:

    (A) afflict

    (B) soothe

    (C) interfere

    (D) aid

    (E) whine

35. EMBELLISH:

    (A) cleanse

    (B) resonate

    (C) decorate

    (D) individualize

    (E) belittle

36. ROTATION:

    (A) cycle

    (B) system

    (C) teamwork

    (D) quantity

    (E) formation

37. SERIAL:

    (A) granular

    (B) vicious

    (C) flying

    (D) recurring

    (E) usual

38. MAKESHIFT:

    (A) dingy

    (B) valueless

    (C) improvised

    (D) unreliable

    (E) unpredictable

39. ANIMATE:

   (A) discourage

   (B) enliven

   (C) bewilder

   (D) hypnotize

   (E) organize

40. ADAMANT:

   (A) flexible

   (B) demonstrative

   (C) evident

   (D) obstinate

   (E) encouraging

41. DISPERSE:

   (A) flourish

   (B) contribute

   (C) scatter

   (D) deduce

   (E) garner

42. IMMORAL:

   (A) dishonest

   (B) absurd

   (C) farcical

   (D) chaste

   (E) unwavering

43. CHRONICLE:

   (A) dream

   (B) prospect

   (C) exhibit

   (D) narrative

   (E) lie

44. SUBSIDE:

   (A) diminish

   (B) advance

   (C) descend

   (D) immerse

   (E) humiliate

45. FAVOR:

   (A) dislike

   (B) except

   (C) halt

   (D) prefer

   (E) agree

46. INNOVATE:

   (A) jumble

   (B) pioneer

   (C) standardize

   (D) associate

   (E) categorize

47. INTRICATE:

   (A) confusing

   (B) systematic

   (C) distinctive

   (D) elaborate

   (E) elementary

48. INTERVENE:

   (A) arrange

   (B) suspend

   (C) come between

   (D) permit

   (E) decline

49. EMIT:

    (A) escape

    (B) enclose

    (C) inhale

    (D) expel

    (E) mumble

50. JEER:

    (A) heckle

    (B) whimper

    (C) revere

    (D) incite

    (E) celebrate

51. TOIL:

    (A) enjoy oneself

    (B) contrast

    (C) act like

    (D) pressure

    (E) exert oneself

52. EXCAVATE:

    (A) withstand

    (B) unearth

    (C) distract

    (D) occupy

    (E) surrender

53. ECLECTIC:

    (A) soothing

    (B) confined

    (C) assorted

    (D) rhythmic

    (E) perpetual

54. MAR:

    (A) despise

    (B) taint

    (C) furbish

    (D) contemplate

    (E) denounce

55. ADVERSE:

    (A) unstable

    (B) fortunate

    (C) unfavorable

    (D) compelling

    (E) invalid

56. LACKLUSTER:

    (A) excited

    (B) authoritarian

    (C) dull

    (D) dissatisfied

    (E) ferocious

CHALLENGE QUESTIONS

Use these questions to practice the most challenging questions you might see in both the Middle Level and Upper Level synonym sections. Challenge questions are much more frequent on the Upper Level exam than on the Middle Level exam.

1. ALOOF:
   (A) advantageous
   (B) lofty
   (C) abiding
   (D) distant
   (E) supercilious

2. BREVITY:
   (A) ardency
   (B) shortness
   (C) triviality
   (D) respiration
   (E) immutability

3. SUPERFLUOUS:
   (A) cursory
   (B) resplendent
   (C) tempestuous
   (D) extra
   (E) mellifluous

4. ANIMOSITY:
   (A) sympathy
   (B) hostility
   (C) disposition
   (D) altruism
   (E) vitality

5. REMINISCE:
   (A) repress
   (B) depreciate
   (C) begrudge
   (D) yearn for
   (E) recollect

6. DIGRESS:
   (A) dawdle
   (B) implicate
   (C) adjourn
   (D) deviate
   (E) extricate

7. PLAUSIBLE:
   (A) arbitrary
   (B) dubious
   (C) credible
   (D) laudable
   (E) malleable

8. CRITERION:
   (A) supposition
   (B) fulfillment
   (C) certainty
   (D) standard
   (E) member

9. ABYSMAL:

(A) faithful

(B) appalling

(C) explicable

(D) infallible

(E) ambivalent

10. POTENT:

(A) feckless

(B) powerful

(C) auspicious

(D) insidious

(E) exhilarating

11. ADVERSITY:

(A) inquisition

(B) misfortune

(C) grief

(D) intonation

(E) cadence

12. IMPAIR:

(A) criticize

(B) acquire

(C) harm

(D) conjoin

(E) deliberate

13. OBSCURE:

(A) indispensable

(B) tangible

(C) uncovered

(D) cryptic

(E) ameliorated

14. AMBIGUOUS:

(A) explicit

(B) unclear

(C) mystical

(D) grandiose

(E) dualistic

15. INCOMPETENT:

(A) inconsistent

(B) pacifist

(C) pertinent

(D) unskillful

(E) ingenious

16. PIOUS:

(A) radical

(B) articulate

(C) gelatinous

(D) secular

(E) devoted

17. SOMBER:

(A) deficient

(B) melancholy

(C) faulty

(D) drowsy

(E) temperate

18. DISSUADE:

(A) confront

(B) invalidate

(C) insult

(D) deter

(E) abandon

19. INNATE:

   (A) pointless
   (B) inherent
   (C) acquired
   (D) deprived of
   (E) miniscule

20. DELUSION:

   (A) opinion
   (B) misconception
   (C) extravagance
   (D) surveillance
   (E) propensity

21. BENIGN:

   (A) harmless
   (B) insufficient
   (C) vacant
   (D) injurious
   (E) misshapen

22. BEWILDER:

   (A) commence
   (B) deceive
   (C) orient
   (D) confuse
   (E) banish

23. ASSIMILATE:

   (A) recognize
   (B) interpret
   (C) understand
   (D) negotiate
   (E) incorporate

24. EFFUSIVE:

   (A) obese
   (B) harmonious
   (C) overflowing
   (D) integrative
   (E) parsimonious

25. REMORSE:

   (A) compunction
   (B) aversion
   (C) sentiment
   (D) misfortune
   (E) representation

26. ANALOGOUS:

   (A) uncompromising
   (B) corresponding
   (C) disparate
   (D) synthetic
   (E) transcribed

27. APPEASE:

   (A) commemorate
   (B) censure
   (C) erode
   (D) impede
   (E) satisfy

28. SLANDER:

   (A) admonish
   (B) debate
   (C) defamation
   (D) approval
   (E) attend to

29. CONTINGENT:

  (A) worldly

  (B) tentative

  (C) dependent

  (D) imperceptible

  (E) exotic

30. PERUSE:

  (A) browse

  (B) recover

  (C) bypass

  (D) overlook

  (E) reprocess

31. DAUNT:

  (A) instigate

  (B) broadcast

  (C) percuss

  (D) revoke

  (E) alarm

32. DEXTERITY:

  (A) assurance

  (B) aptitude

  (C) adroitness

  (D) slyness

  (E) affliction

33. CONVICTION:

  (A) belief

  (B) confusion

  (C) facility

  (D) concept

  (E) imprisonment

34. ALIENATE:

  (A) abduct

  (B) baffle

  (C) relinquish

  (D) estrange

  (E) contradict

35. ERADICATE:

  (A) neglect

  (B) repurpose

  (C) dismay

  (D) radiate

  (E) remove

36. PARODY:

  (A) spoof

  (B) tact

  (C) illustration

  (D) perplex

  (E) competition

37. EXACERBATE:

  (A) abolish

  (B) ostracize

  (C) worsen

  (D) flaunt

  (E) augment

38. PROLIFIC:

  (A) irrational

  (B) uncouth

  (C) zealous

  (D) foreshadowing

  (E) fruitful

39. DORMANT:

 (A) anxious

 (B) inactive

 (C) domestic

 (D) dependable

 (E) fatigued

40. SPORADIC:

 (A) crowded

 (B) calculating

 (C) fitful

 (D) linear

 (E) bountiful

41. ADHERE:

 (A) overlook

 (B) elude

 (C) cling

 (D) deteriorate

 (E) disown

42. ELOQUENT:

 (A) tranquil

 (B) ready

 (C) expert

 (D) verbose

 (E) articulate

43. ABYSS:

 (A) chasm

 (B) ignorance

 (C) accumulation

 (D) imitation

 (E) vehemence

44. AMIABLE:

 (A) appropriate

 (B) adroit

 (C) opposed to

 (D) agreeable

 (E) lustful

45. HEINOUS:

 (A) horrifying

 (B) empathetic

 (C) suspended

 (D) unyielding

 (E) primitive

46. WANE:

 (A) misguide

 (B) embolden

 (C) decrease

 (D) disconcert

 (E) glimmer

47. AFFINITY:

 (A) poise

 (B) candor

 (C) attraction

 (D) subversion

 (E) rendition

48. AVERSE:

 (A) righteous

 (B) accommodating

 (C) opposing

 (D) disproportionate

 (E) variable

49. CURTAIL:

    (A) astonish

    (B) implore

    (C) persevere

    (D) ridicule

    (E) abbreviate

50. EMULATE:

    (A) assuage

    (B) astound

    (C) imitate

    (D) reinforce

    (E) misrepresent

UPPER-LEVEL CHALLENGE QUESTIONS

Use these questions to practice the most challenging questions that you might see in an Upper Level synonym section. These questions would very rarely appear in a Middle Level section.

1. CHOLERIC:

   (A) benevolent
   (B) irritable
   (C) sickly
   (D) restricted
   (E) vociferous

2. GARRULOUS:

   (A) talkative
   (B) combative
   (C) derogatory
   (D) taciturn
   (E) limiting

3. JOCUND:

   (A) fortuitous
   (B) masculine
   (C) cheerful
   (D) large
   (E) ascetic

4. AMBIVALENT:

   (A) lavish
   (B) cranky
   (C) certain
   (D) irresolute
   (E) strolling

5. ABHOR:

   (A) support
   (B) request
   (C) irritate
   (D) hate
   (E) corrupt

6. FURTIVE:

   (A) changing
   (B) secretive
   (C) malignant
   (D) wise
   (E) defiant

7. AUDACIOUS:

   (A) puzzling
   (B) distressed
   (C) daring
   (D) fake
   (E) unnecessary

8. GREGARIOUS:

   (A) sociable
   (B) volatile
   (C) antique
   (D) reckless
   (E) agrarian

9. DOGMATIC:

    (A) superficial
    (B) opinionated
    (C) liberal
    (D) canine
    (E) rooted

10. BELLIGERENT:

    (A) noble
    (B) exuberant
    (C) argumentative
    (D) stubborn
    (E) brave

11. PRETENTIOUS:

    (A) priceless
    (B) nonchalant
    (C) sneaky
    (D) careful
    (E) pompous

12. RECALCITRANT:

    (A) incongruous
    (B) reluctant
    (C) noisy
    (D) disobedient
    (E) shy

13. AFFABLE:

    (A) disrespectful
    (B) weak
    (C) insignificant
    (D) lying
    (E) friendly

14. LAMENT:

    (A) subdue
    (B) scrutinize
    (C) bemoan
    (D) sever
    (E) laud

15. FRUGAL:

    (A) economical
    (B) negligible
    (C) atrocious
    (D) blundering
    (E) amphibious

16. FICKLE:

    (A) headstrong
    (B) vacillating
    (C) preserved
    (D) outrageous
    (E) fabricated

17. INSINUATION:

    (A) division
    (B) suggestion
    (C) junction
    (D) fiber
    (E) transgression

18. COMPLACENT:

    (A) stagnant
    (B) servile
    (C) redundant
    (D) hostile
    (E) contented

19. GLUTTONOUS:

    (A) guilty

    (B) greedy

    (C) fasten

    (D) cynical

    (E) murderous

20. INSOLENT:

    (A) educational

    (B) fervent

    (C) rude

    (D) narcissistic

    (E) tasteless

21. LETHARGIC:

    (A) sluggish

    (B) thorough

    (C) soothing

    (D) varied

    (E) authoritative

22. RAMPANT:

    (A) illogical

    (B) plentiful

    (C) kinetic

    (D) obedient

    (E) uncontrolled

23. MITIGATE:

    (A) save

    (B) forfeit

    (C) prove

    (D) relieve

    (E) merge

24. INADVERTENT:

    (A) detailed

    (B) nomadic

    (C) flamboyant

    (D) accidental

    (E) truthful

25. DESPONDENT:

    (A) obsessive

    (B) abominable

    (C) hopeless

    (D) regretful

    (E) bold

26. OSTENTATIOUS:

    (A) affectionate

    (B) generous

    (C) showy

    (D) poor

    (E) avian

27. ABATE:

    (A) obliterate

    (B) coalesce

    (C) placate

    (D) dwindle

    (E) apprehend

28. BANAL:

    (A) livid

    (B) commonplace

    (C) whimsical

    (D) prosperous

    (E) obligatory

29. CONDONE:

    (A) spread

    (B) nourish

    (C) accept

    (D) confirm

    (E) hoard

30. LISTLESS:

    (A) quiet

    (B) hidden

    (C) frank

    (D) unruly

    (E) lethargic

31. PRECOCIOUS:

    (A) incoherent

    (B) magnificent

    (C) advanced

    (D) childlike

    (E) idolized

32. GERMANE:

    (A) poignant

    (B) applicable

    (C) heroic

    (D) familiar

    (E) contaminated

33. CORPULENT:

    (A) squalid

    (B) stout

    (C) mortal

    (D) wealthy

    (E) energized

34. ARCANE:

    (A) secret

    (B) overused

    (C) royal

    (D) concave

    (E) obsolete

35. INANE:

    (A) fond of

    (B) dingy

    (C) silly

    (D) crazed

    (E) barren

36. HAPHAZARD:

    (A) wily

    (B) emotional

    (C) fractional

    (D) disorganized

    (E) argumentative

37. DISTENDED:

    (A) offensive

    (B) splendid

    (C) unsettled

    (D) swollen

    (E) calm

38. BALEFUL:

    (A) helpful

    (B) menacing

    (C) contemptuous

    (D) friendly

    (E) compliant

ANALOGIES

PART 2

ANALOGY STRATEGIES

The second 30 questions of the SSAT Verbal Section take the form of analogies. In this section, read about the best strategies for approaching the SSAT's analogy questions.

WHAT ARE ANALOGIES?

An **analogy** is a statement that shows a relationship between two words. Analogy questions give you two related words and then ask you to find two more words that share the same relationship. Here is an example:

Cow is to calf as

   (A) turtle is to mother
   (B) baby is to infant
   (C) wolf is to dog
   (D) hen is to chick
   (E) father is to child

This question is asking you to find the relationship between the words "cow" and "calf," and then pick an answer choice that demonstrates the same relationship.

What is the relationship between the words "cow" and "calf"? A cow is the mother of a calf.

A turtle isn't always the mother of a mother, so (A) is incorrect. A baby is not the mother of an infant, so (B) is incorrect. A wolf is not the mother of a dog, so (C) is incorrect. A father is not the mother of a child, so (E) is incorrect.

A hen is the mother of a chick, so therefore the only correct answer to this question is (D).

Just like the synonym questions, you can rest assured that every analogy question will have only **one correct answer**. Before moving onto the next question, be sure to look through all 5 answer choices to make sure you have really selected the correct answer. If multiple answers seem possible, it is your job to test out each answer choice to find which one best shows the same relationship as the words in the prompt. Be careful—the test will try to trick you by including many words that sound possible, but do not have exactly the same relationship! Continue reading for some strategies to help you avoid these misleading answer choices.

APPROACHING ANALOGIES

CREATE A CONNECTOR

Start by creating a **connector**, a sentence that joins together the two words in the question and shows their relationship clearly. Take a look at the words in the question and cross out the phrase "is to." Then, replace "is to" with a more specific connecting phrase that shows the words' relationship.

In the example below, cross out the words "is to" and write a new connector to join the words "cow" and "calf":

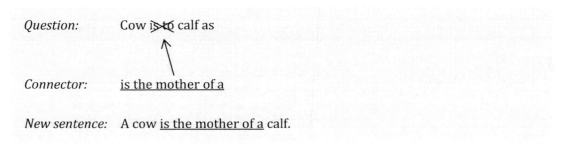

Once you have created your connector, plug your connector into all of your answer options to see which one makes sense. For example:

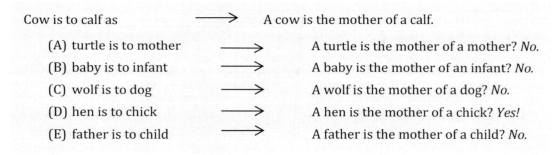

As we have seen before, the only sentence that makes sense using this connector is "a hen is the mother of a chick." Therefore, (D) is the correct answer.

BE SPECIFIC

Your connector needs to be as specific as possible. A connector that is too broad won't help you narrow down your answers. Consider the following example:

Knee is to leg as   *Your connector:*

    (A) neck is to chest

    (B) toe is to foot

    (C) elbow is to arm

    (D) hair is to head

    (E) lung is to rib

If you created a connector like "a knee is on a leg," then you are in trouble—a toe is on a foot, an elbow is on an arm, and hair is on a head! Which is correct?

Make your connector more specific: "a knee is the joint in the middle of a leg." The only answer that makes sense is "an elbow is the joint in the middle of an arm," so (C) is correct.

ORDER MATTERS

Order matters in analogies. Make sure you are always reading your connector in the same order for both the question and the answers. Look at the following example:

Flock is to sheep as   *Your connector:*

    (A) lion is to pride

    (B) kennel is to dog

    (C) goose is to gander

    (D) pack is to wolf

    (E) elephant is to herd

Your connector should read "a flock is a group of sheep." Answers (A) and (E) are in the wrong order—a lion isn't a group of prides, and an elephant isn't a group of herds! The correct answer is (D) because a pack is a group of wolves.

COMMON TYPES OF ANALOGIES

There are several common types of analogies on the SSAT that you should learn to recognize.

SYNONYM AND ANTONYM ANALOGIES

Some of the most basic word relationships are **synonyms** (words that mean the same thing) and **antonyms** (words that have opposite or contrasting meanings). Look at the following example:

Hope is to despair as   *Your connector:*

    (A) sadness is to apathy
    (B) happiness is to bliss
    (C) direction is to follow
    (D) giggle is to laugh
    (E) empty is to full

Hope and despair are antonyms, so your connector should read "hope is the opposite of despair." The first four answer choices may have something to do with emotions, but they do not have opposite meanings. In fact, "happiness" and "bliss" have similar meanings, as do "giggle" and "laugh." Answer (E) is the best choice because empty is the opposite of full.

Exercise #1: Look at the following pairs of words and decide whether they are synonyms or antonyms. Then, check your answers with the answer key. If you don't know any of the following words, look them up in a dictionary. The first question has been filled out for you.

1.   Certainty is to confusion: *antonyms*

2.   Worker is to laborer:

3. Adoring is to loving:

4. Praise is to criticism:

5. Helpful is to harmful:

6. Amazement is to awe:

Have you mastered the questions above? Try your hand at these more challenging words:

7. Diverting is to entertaining:

8. Bereavement is to loss:

9. Bliss is to sorrow:

10. Assess is to evaluate:

INTENSITY AND DEGREE ANALOGIES

Sometimes words can be synonyms, but differ in **intensity** or **degree**. For example, "rage" is similar to "anger," but "rage" is more intense. Here is an example:

Hungry is to starving as   *Your connector:*

    (A) dark is to light
    (B) unkind is to vicious
    (C) clean is to filthy
    (D) angry is to sad
    (E) rude is to disobedient

Your connector should read "hungry is less intense than starving" because hungry is a less intense version of starving. The correct answer is (B), because unkind is a less intense version of vicious. Dark and light are opposites, so (A) is incorrect. Clean and filthy are opposites, so (C) is incorrect. Angry and sad have different meanings, so (D) is incorrect. Rude and disobedient are related, but do not necessarily differ in degree, so (E) is incorrect.

Exercise #2: Decide whether the following pairs of words mean the same thing, or if they differ in intensity. If so, which word is more intense? Then, check your answers with the answer key. If you don't know any of the following words, look them up in a dictionary. The first question has been filled out for you.

1. Sprinkle is to thunderstorm: *Different, thunderstorm is more intense*

2. Tornado is to breeze:

3. Damp is to moist:

4. Dislike is to hatred:

5. Comical is to humorous:

Have you mastered the questions above? Try your hand at these more challenging words:

6. Jovial is to good-natured:

7. Jubilant is to pleased:

8. Vacant is to empty:

9. Trouble is to cataclysm:

10. Livid is to annoyed:

PART AND WHOLE ANALOGIES

Another common relationship involves **parts** and **wholes**. You may have to decide whether both words are part of the same whole, or whether one word is a part and the other word is a whole. Look at the following example:

Player is to team as   *Your connector:*

    (A) manager is to employee
    (B) actor is to cast
    (C) singer is to performer
    (D) baker is to bread
    (E) quarterback is to punter

Your connector should read "a player is a part of a team." This is a part-whole relationship. Be careful of answer (E)—both a quarterback and a punter are parts of a team, but a quarterback is not a part of a punter! The correct answer is (B) because an actor is part of a cast.

Exercise #3: Study the list of classifications in section 4, and see if you can match the following parts with their wholes. Then, check your answers with the answer key.

Parts	Wholes
1. Wolf	A. Constellation
2. Page	B. Tree
3. Soldier	C. Car
4. Ingredient	D. Class
5. Flower	E. Bouquet
6. Branch	F. Chain
7. Wheel	G. Book
8. Link	H. Army
9. Star	I. Recipe
10. Student	J. Pack

Too easy? Try your hand at these more challenging words:

Parts	Wholes
11. Stanza	K. Bed
12. Island	L. Symphony
13. Movement	M. Archipelago
14. Brig	N. Opera
15. Story	O. Jury
16. Fuselage	P. Poem
17. Sentence	Q. Ship
18. Oyster	R. Airplane
19. Aria	S. Anthology
20. Juror	T. Paragraph

EXAMPLES AND TYPES

Sometimes a word is not necessarily a part of a group, but an **example** or **type** of a larger category. Look at this example:

Hound is to dog as   *Your connector:*

    (A) feline is to lion

    (B) whale is to fish

    (C) influenza is to virus

    (D) beagle is to Dalmatian

    (E) hammer is to screwdriver

Your connector should read "a hound is a type of dog" or "a hound is an example of a dog." Answer (D) lists other types of dogs, but a beagle is not a type of Dalmatian. Answer (A) has the analogy backwards. Be careful of answer (B)—a whale is a mammal, not a type of fish! The correct answer is (C) because influenza is a type of virus.

Exercise #4: Study the list of classifications in section 4, and see if you can match the following examples or types with their groups. Then, check your answers with the answer key.

Example/Type	*Group*
1. Ant	A. Bird
2. Clarinet	B. Fish
3. Eagle	C. Insect
4. Soprano	D. Whale
5. French	E. Furniture
6. Cat	F. Singer
7. Sofa	G. Color
8. Shark	H. Woodwind
9. Yellow	I. Language
10. Humpback	J. Feline

Too easy? Try your hand at these more challenging words:

Example/Type	*Group*
11. Pine	K. Arachnid
12. Kangaroo	L. Rodent
13. Igneous	M. Conifer
14. Squirrel	N. Reptile
15. Lobster	O. Mollusk
16. Tortoise	P. Marsupial
17. Spider	Q. Crustacean
18. Clam	R. Rock

USE AND FUNCTION ANALOGIES

Use and **function** analogies name two objects connected by their function, or one object and another word describing how or by whom it is used. For example:

Pencil is to write as   *Your connector:*

    (A) fork is to knife

    (B) brush is to paint

    (C) hammer is to wood

    (D) pen is to story

    (E) cut is to scissors

Your connector should read "a pencil is used to write." The correct answer is (B) because a brush is used to paint. A fork and knife are both used together, but both are used to eat, so (A) is incorrect. A hammer is used with wood, but "wood" is not its function, so (C) is incorrect. A pen helps write a story, but "story" is not the pen's function, so (D) is incorrect. Scissors are used to cut, but the words are in the wrong order in (E), so this answer is also incorrect.

Another common use and function analogy relates to **professions** and tools they use. For example:

Carpenter is to hammer as   *Your connector:*

    (A) paint is to canvas

    (B) doctor is to stethoscope

    (C) handcuff is to policeman

    (D) tailor is to dress

    (E) lawyer is to law

Your connector should read "a carpenter uses a hammer." The correct answer is (B), because a doctor uses a stethoscope. Paint is applied by a brush, but the paint itself doesn't use the brush, so (A) is incorrect. A policeman uses handcuffs, but these words are in the wrong order, so (C) is incorrect. A tailor might make or alter a dress, but does not use the dress, so (D) is incorrect. A lawyer's profession is law, but law is not his or her tool, so (E) is incorrect.

Exercise #5: Fill in the blanks in the following sentences. Some of the questions may have many possible answers, and some of these possibilities are listed in the answer key. The first word has been filled out for you.

    1.   A spade is used by a *gardener* to *dig up soil*.

2. A stethoscope is used by a _____ to _____ .

3. A cleaver is used by a _____ to _____ .

4. A chisel is used by a _____ to _____ .

5. A plow is used by a _____ to _____ .

6. A scalpel is used by a _____ to _____ .

A third common use or function analogy relates to **measurement**, providing one word that describes how another word is measured. For example:

Barometer is to pressure as   *Your connector:*

   (A) heavy is to weight
   (B) thermometer is to heat
   (C) ladder is to climb
   (D) ruler is to long
   (E) narrow is to wide

Your connector should read "a barometer measures pressure." The correct answer is (B) because a thermometer measures heat. (A) is incorrect because heavy describes weight, but does not measure it. A ladder does not measure a climb, so (C) is incorrect. A ruler measures length, but not the concept of "long," so (D) is incorrect. Narrow and wide are opposites, so (E) is incorrect.

Exercise #6: Match the following devices with the quantities they measure. Then, check your answers with the answer key.

Device	*Quantity*
1. Ruler	A. Wind direction
2. Measuring cup	B. Time
3. Weather vane	C. Speed
4. Thermometer	D. Volume
5. Speedometer	E. Mileage
6. Barometer	F. Pressure
7. Odometer	G. Length
8. Chronometer	H. Temperature

LESS COMMON TYPES OF ANALOGIES

Here are some less frequent analogy types you may come across.

LOCATION ANALOGIES

Location analogies name places or nationalities that are connected by location. For example:

Germany is to Europe as   *Your connector:*

   (A) Mexican is to Spanish

   (B) Canada is to country

   (C) China is to Hong Kong

   (D) Argentina is to Brazil

   (E) Kenya is to Africa

Your connector should read "Germany is a country in the continent of Europe." The correct answer is (E) because Kenya is a country in the continent of Africa. Mexican and Spanish are the nationalities of two different countries, so (A) is incorrect. Canada is a country, but this relationship does not mention the continent where it is located, so (B) is incorrect. China is a country, but Hong Kong is not its continent—it is a region within China. Therefore, (C) is incorrect. Brazil and Argentina are both countries within South America, so (D) is incorrect.

SPELLING OR RHYMING ANALOGIES

Spelling or **rhyming** analogies are not very frequent, but occasionally show up as tricks! The words are not connected by meaning, but by the order of their letters. For example:

Tar is to rat as   *Your connector:*

   (A) mold is to cold

   (B) bur is to rub

   (C) light is to night

   (D) see is to saw

   (E) hair is to hare

Your connector should read "tar spelled backward is rat." Answer (B) is correct because "bur" spelled backwards is "rub." The words in answers (A) and (C) both rhyme, but neither shows a pair of words with letters reversed, so they are both incorrect. The words in answers (D) and (E) both sound similar, but their spelling is not related, so they are both incorrect.

VERTICAL ANALOGIES

Vertical analogies ask you to create a relationship between one question word and one answer word, rather than between the two words in the question. For example:

Dog is to cat as

(A) canine is to feline

(B) mouse is to chicken

(C) stallion is to mare

(D) iguana is to reptile

(E) bird is to sparrow

It's hard to write a strong connector for the two question words because they don't have a strong relationship. If you try the connectors "dogs and cats are two types of mammals," or even "dogs and cats are two types of pets," you'll soon realize that these connectors aren't specific enough to find one correct answer. In answer (B), mice and chickens are two animals, but a mouse is a mammal and a chicken is a bird. Answer (C) lists the names for male and female horses rather than two different animals. Answers (D) and (E) both list a specific animal that falls under a broader category, but not two animals belonging to the same category.

If you don't see a clear relationship between the two words in the question, look for a different type of relationship with the answer choices. If the first word in the question relates to the first word in one of the answer options, you might be dealing with a vertical analogy. "Dog" relates to "canine" in answer (A) because "canine" is an adjective relating to dogs. Check if the second word in the question and the second word in the answer choice have the same relationship. Does "cat" relate to "feline"? "Feline" is an adjective relating to cats, so (A) is the correct answer.

IF YOU GET STUCK

If you get stuck while solving an analogy, try some of these strategies to get back on track and avoid losing points.

WHAT IF YOU DON'T KNOW A WORD?

If you don't know a word in an analogy question, try using your knowledge of **context** to guess at a relationship. For example, let's pretend the question is "Barometer is to pressure," and you don't know what "barometer" means. Even if you don't know the exact meaning of "barometer," you may notice that it ends in "meter." Do you know any other words that end in meter? You probably know the word "thermometer," which measures temperature, so you might be able to guess that a barometer measures something. From here, you can let the other word "pressure" guide you. It would make sense to guess that barometer measures pressure. Now you can test your answer choices to see if this connector makes sense—if there is an answer choice where one device measures some type of quantity, you're probably on the right track!

If the answer choices contain words you don't know, don't assume that these answer choices are automatically wrong. First, use the **Process of Elimination** to narrow down your answer options based on your connector and the words you do know. Remember that you are looking for the **best fit**—if none of the other answer options seem exactly right, perhaps the answer with the unfamiliar word is the right one after all!

Keep in mind that the best way to prepare for unfamiliar words in the analogy section (and the entire Verbal Section) is to learn as much vocabulary as possible beforehand. Learn the words in the Analogy Reference charts that come after this section, and spend time working through the Vocabulary Building chapter that comes later. The more words you know, the more questions you will be able to answer!

WHAT IF YOU CAN'T WRITE A CONNECTOR?

If the relationship between the two words in the question is unclear and you're having trouble writing a connector, first check whether the question is a **vertical** analogy or a

THE VERBAL SECTION | 87

spelling/rhyming analogy. These two uncommon analogy types don't always make sense with a typical connector.

If this doesn't work, look at the **types of words** being used in the question. On the next page is a chart of the most common word types:

TYPES OF WORDS			
Word Type	**Definition**	**Examples**	**Sample Sentence**
Noun	a person, place, or thing: "things" can also include qualities or categories that you might not be able to touch or see	teacher, lawyer, city, Italy, animal, car, water, tool, hunger, comfort, curiosity, trust, emotion, science, art, biology	The young puppy ran quickly.
Verb	an action word: what the subject of the sentence (the main noun) is "doing"	run, hit, dig, carve, learn, hear, enjoy, understand, become, be	The young puppy ran quickly.
Adjective	a word that describes, identifies, or defines a noun	soft, sharp, green, full, loud, wet, happy, thoughtful, diligent, humorous, good	The young puppy ran quickly.
Adverb	a word that describes a verb, adjective, or another adverb: often ends in "-ly"	quickly, desperately, sadly, suddenly, freely, quietly, strangely, well	The young puppy ran quickly.

If you're able to identify the types of words in an analogy question, you can rest assured that the correct answer choice will most likely have the same types of words. For example, for the question "Axe is to chop," the first word is a noun and the second word is a related verb. The correct answer choice should also have a noun and a related verb, and you can eliminate any answer choices that don't follow this pattern.

WHEN SHOULD YOU GUESS?

You lose a quarter of a point for every wrong answer, so it is not always a good idea to guess. If you're not able to use the Process of Elimination to narrow down any of your answer options—you really have no idea!—then leave the question blank and move on. If you can eliminate at least one answer option that you know is incorrect, then you should guess. Your chances of getting the question right are still pretty good.

WORD CLASSIFICATIONS

SECTION 4

Here are some charts to help you remember some common word relationships. If you don't know some of these words, put them on your vocabulary flashcards!

GROUPS OF PEOPLE		
Whole	**Parts**	**Leader**
city	citizens	mayor
army	soldiers	general
jury	jurors	judge
choir	singers (sopranos, altos, tenors, basses)	conductor, director
cast	actors	director
orchestra	musicians, instruments	conductor

WRITTEN AND ARTISTIC CREATIONS			
Written and Artistic Creations	**Parts**	**Leader**	**Creator**
play	acts, scenes, lines	director	playwright
symphony	movements	conductor	composer
opera	acts, scenes, arias, songs	conductor	composer
newspaper	articles	editor	writers, editors, journalists
book	chapters, paragraphs	editor, publisher	writer
anthology	stories	editor, publisher	writers

INSTRUMENTS	
Group	**Examples**
winds	flutes, clarinets, oboes, bassoons, saxophones
percussion	drums, bells, chimes, cymbals, xylophones, pianos
brass	trumpets, trombones, tubas, horns
strings	violins, violas, cellos, double basses

PROFESSIONS		
Profession	**Duties**	**Possible Tools**
architect	designs buildings	sketchpad, drafting table, computer
tailor	makes and customizes clothing	scissors, needle, thread, thimble
cobbler	makes and fixes shoes and boots	needle, thread, awl, glue, shoe polish
blacksmith	forges metal, makes metal objects	forge, anvil, hammer, tongs
mason	builds things using stones or bricks	cement, mortar, chisel, bricks, stone, tiles
vendor	sells things	store, cart, wares
accountant	inspects/examines financial accounts	calculator, computer
apothecary (pharmacist)	prescribes, prepares, and sells medications	weights, scale, mortar, pestle, jars

SCIENTISTS	
Scientist	**Field of Study**
biologist	living organisms
botanist	plants
zoologist	animals
anthropologist	human beings and societies
archeologist	human artifacts and physical remains
paleontologist	fossils
astronomer	space, stars, planets, and the universe
geologist	physical structures of the earth (rocks, mountains, continents, etc.)
meteorologist	weather
optometrist	branch of medicine relating to eyesight
cardiologist	branch of medicine relating to the heart
podiatrist	branch of medicine relating to the feet
neurologist	branch of medicine relating to the brain
pediatrician	branch of medicine specializing in children's health

Ivy Global

MODES OF TRANSPORTATION		
Whole	**Parts**	**Operator**
ship	bow, stern, keel, cabins	captain
automobile	wheel, engine	driver, chauffeur
airplane	wings, fuselage, cabin	pilot
train	freight, cars, cargo, cabins, wheels	captain
helicopter	rotor, tail, cabin	pilot
submarine	hull, cabin, propeller, tower	helmsman

METRIC AND IMPERIAL UNITS OF MEASURE		
	Imperial	**Metric**
units of volume	cup, pint, quart, gallon	milliliter, liter
units of distance	inch, foot, yard, mile	centimeter, meter, kilometer
units of weight and mass	ounce, pound	gram, kilogram
units of temperature	Fahrenheit	Celsius

GEOLOGICAL FEATURES

Feature	Description
archipelago	group of islands
peninsula	a piece of land surrounded by water on three sides and connected to a larger landmass on the fourth side
channel	narrow body of water
bay	body of water bordered by land on three sides
strait	channel that connects two larger bodies of water
glacier	large mass of ice
mountain range	group of mountains
foothill	base of a mountain
peak	top of a mountain
dune	mound of sand
canyon	deep valley
plateau	raised area of flat land

CLIMATES

Climate	Description
tundra	cold, dry and windy
desert	arid (very dry), sandy
tropical	hot and humid, heavy rainfall in all months
temperate	moderate temperatures, all four seasons

Ivy Global

TYPES OF ROCKS	
Group	**Examples**
igneous	made from lava: pumice, basalt, obsidian
sedimentary	made from sand or pebbles: chalk, sandstone, flint, shale
metamorphic	changed by heat or pressure: diamond, quartz, marble

TYPES OF TREES	
Group	**Examples**
deciduous	trees that lose their leaves: maples, oaks, poplars
coniferous	trees with needles and cones: pines, spruces, firs
evergreen	trees that stay green: conifers, holly, eucalyptus, rainforest trees

GROUPS OF ANIMALS	
Whole	**Parts**
herd	antelopes, bison, buffalo, cattle, cows, deer, elephants, moose
colony	ants, bats, beavers, bacteria
swarm	ants, bees, flies
flock	birds, chickens, ducks, sheep
pack	wolves, dogs, coyotes, mules
school	fish, dolphins, whales
pod	dolphins, whales
pride	lions
bed	oysters, clams

TYPES OF ANIMALS

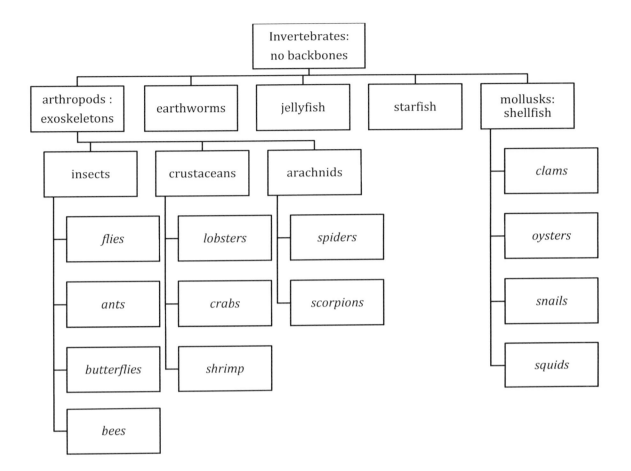

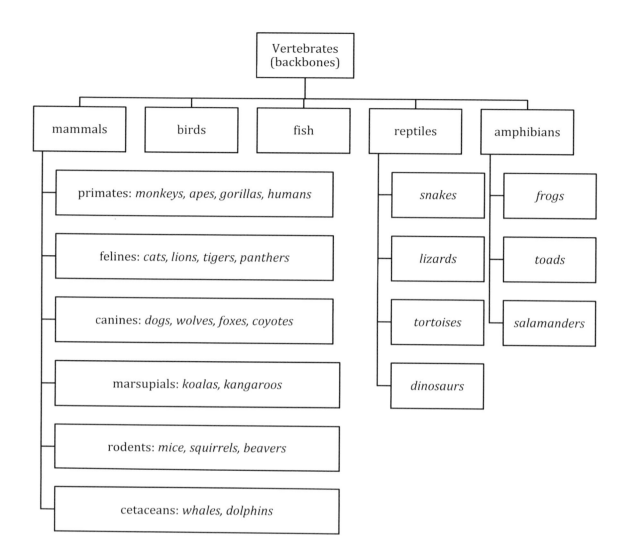

MALE, FEMALE, AND YOUNG ANIMALS		
Male	**Female**	**Offspring**
ram	ewe	lamb
rooster, cock	hen	chick
stag, buck	doe	fawn
gander	goose	gosling
bull	cow	calf
stallion	mare	colt, foal
boar, hog	sow	piglet
swan	swan	cygnet
lion	lioness	cub

ANALOGY PRACTICE QUESTIONS

In this section, you will find 185 practice questions to prepare you for the types of analogy questions you might find on the SSAT. There are 6 sets of questions, grouped by difficulty. Pay attention to the difficulty of each set to determine which questions are appropriate for the Middle and Upper Levels.

WARM-UP QUESTIONS

Use these questions to test your familiarity with basic analogy strategies for both the Middle and Upper Levels.

1. Soda is to can as banana is to

    (A) seed

    (B) eat

    (C) peel

    (D) fruit

    (E) split

2. President is to country as mayor is to

    (A) school

    (B) stadium

    (C) house

    (D) city

    (E) author

3. Desk is to office as

    (A) window is to attic

    (B) table is to kitchen

    (C) lamp is to ceiling

    (D) study is to library

    (E) ottoman is to sofa

4. Painter is to painting as architect is to

    (A) building

    (B) song

    (C) sculpture

    (D) wood

    (E) wall

5. Lamp is to lampshade as

(A) bird is to fly
(B) dog is to leash
(C) window is to curtain
(D) fire is to chimney
(E) snow is to ground

6. Bluebird is to fly as

(A) human is to stand
(B) mute is to talk
(C) lion is to attack
(D) otter is to swim
(E) frog is to amphibian

7. Ski is to mountain as swim is to

(A) valley
(B) rainforest
(C) park
(D) lake
(E) sunshine

8. Happy is to sad as

(A) messy is to sloppy
(B) smiling is to laughing
(C) nice is to mean
(D) angry is to tired
(E) confused is to puzzle

9. Butterfly is to caterpillar as

(A) puppy is to kitten
(B) frog is to tadpole
(C) crab is to lobster
(D) joey is to elephant
(E) cat is to sphinx

10. Hide-and-seek is to game as

(A) play is to win
(B) basketball is to baseball
(C) coat is to shirt
(D) follow is to lead
(E) fairy tale is to story

Ivy Global

BASIC QUESTIONS

Use these questions to practice the most basic difficulty level you might see in both the Middle and Upper Level analogy sections. The Middle Level exam will include more basic questions than the Upper Level exam.

1. Trim is to hair as prune is to

   (A) plum
   (B) grass
   (C) fruit
   (D) hedge
   (E) shear

2. Salmon is to fish as grizzly is to

   (A) burly
   (B) polar
   (C) hunt
   (D) bear
   (E) prey

3. Europe is to continent as Atlantic is to

   (A) Pacific
   (B) America
   (C) channel
   (D) glacier
   (E) ocean

4. Hunger is to food as

   (A) sadness is to fighting
   (B) thirst is to beverage
   (C) clown is to sick
   (D) tired is to bedtime
   (E) dirty is to clean

5. Laugh is to comedy as

   (A) film is to watch
   (B) scream is to horror
   (C) drama is to suspense
   (D) fantasy is to imagine
   (E) argue is to agree

6. Palm is to hand as

   (A) shoulder is to arm
   (B) ankle is to leg
   (C) neck is to spine
   (D) sole is to foot
   (E) bone is to tendon

7. Hinge is to door as

   (A) knee is to leg
   (B) spoke is to wheel
   (C) notebook is to spine
   (D) lead is to pencil
   (E) motion is to stillness

8. Musician is to band as

   (A) club is to member
   (B) performance is to an actor
   (C) playwright is to play
   (D) opera is to aria
   (E) singer is to chorus

9. Foot is to sock as hand is to

(A) bracelet

(B) glove

(C) ring

(D) palm

(E) sole

10. Car is to garage as

(A) bicycle is to vehicle

(B) boat is to dock

(C) train is to locomotive

(D) shed is to tractor

(E) pedestrian is to foot

11. Field is to wheat as

(A) plant is to carrot

(B) garden is to cultivate

(C) soil is to potato

(D) pasture is to cow

(E) vine is to trellis

12. Chef is to apron as

(A) ballerina is to tiara

(B) painter is to smock

(C) lawyer is to suit

(D) gardener is to glove

(E) fireman is to protect

13. Couch is to chair as

(A) expensive is to leather

(B) soft is to flexible

(C) pool is to lake

(D) bus is to car

(E) horse is to camel

14. Look is to cook as

(A) cool is to boot

(B) soot is to foot

(C) aroma is to drama

(D) manage is to carnage

(E) rough is to plough

15. Kite is to wind as

(A) candle is to wax

(B) chair is to wood

(C) lantern is to flame

(D) helium is to balloon

(E) surfboard is to wave

16. Mitten is to glove as

(A) spoon is to fork

(B) scarf is to hat

(C) snowball is to tennis ball

(D) boot is to ankle

(E) soup is to bread

17. Lion is to zebra as

(A) whale is to frog

(B) dog is to pet

(C) owl is to mouse

(D) squirrel is to hawk

(E) wolf is to predator

18. Mechanic is to wrench as

(A) spatula is to cook

(B) nurse is to health

(C) spinster is to wheel

(D) tailor is to needle

(E) carpenter is to wood

19. Painter is to writer as

(A) original is to novel

(B) brush is to pen

(C) literature is to art

(D) studio is to book

(E) creative is to famous

20. Tape measure is to inches as scale is to

(A) stand

(B) weight

(C) pounds

(D) fish

(E) metal

21. Author is to write as

(A) doctor is to surgery

(B) musician is to listen

(C) artist is to canvas

(D) architect is to design

(E) athlete is to motivate

22. Hive is to bee as

(A) bird is to nest

(B) forest is to dog

(C) den is to fox

(D) animal is to wild

(E) whale is to ocean

23. Mattress is to bed as cushion is to

(A) car

(B) rug

(C) couch

(D) pillow

(E) floor

24. General is to specific as broad is to

(A) certain

(B) unlikely

(C) tactless

(D) narrow

(E) thorough

25. Smell is to aroma as

(A) enjoy is to sound

(B) listen is to music

(C) kick is to feel

(D) film is to watch

(E) event is to observe

26. Captain is to ship as

(A) singer is to guitar

(B) pilot is to airplane

(C) band is to drummer

(D) school is to teacher

(E) student is to notebook

27. Ally is to enemy as

(A) courier is to message

(B) discovery is to victory

(C) teammate is to opponent

(D) monarch is to kingdom

(E) elephantine is to gargantuan

28. Dancer is to ballet as violinist is to

(A) trombone

(B) pitch

(C) symphony

(D) cellist

(E) auditorium

29. Grass is to lawn as

   (A) pavement is to sidewalk
   (B) tennis court is to clay
   (C) path is to gravel
   (D) wood is to meadow
   (E) gasoline is to car

30. Gaze is to eyes as

   (A) knee is to joint
   (B) grip is to hands
   (C) idea is to thought
   (D) tongue is to taste
   (E) smell is to aroma

31. Chef is to kitchen as

   (A) library is to librarian
   (B) astronaut is to planet
   (C) fireman is to hose
   (D) author is to bookstore
   (E) veterinarian is to clinic

32. Charcoal is to drawing as

   (A) clay is to sculpture
   (B) mirror is to glass
   (C) book is to paper
   (D) exhibit is to artist
   (E) oil is to acrylic

33. Neighborhood is to city as country is to

   (A) town
   (B) municipality
   (C) region
   (D) state
   (E) continent

MEDIUM QUESTIONS

Use these questions to practice the medium difficulty level you might see in both the Middle and Upper Level analogy sections. Questions like these will make up a majority of the Middle Level analogy section, and a smaller portion of the Upper Level section.

1. Rooster is to hen as

   (A) bull is to cow
   (B) trout is to bass
   (C) doe is to deer
   (D) ewe is to lamb
   (E) swan is to cygnet

2. Kick is to legs as

   (A) peddle is to feet
   (B) embrace is to arms
   (C) procure is to hands
   (D) ulcer is to stomach
   (E) satisfy is to mouth

3. Philosopher is to theory as

   (A) dancer is to ballet
   (B) doctor is to patient
   (C) inventor is to innovation
   (D) map is to explorer
   (E) writer is to paper

4. Latin is to language as

   (A) Greek is to Roman
   (B) poem is to novel
   (C) necklace is to diamond
   (D) English is to dialect
   (E) tango is to dance

5. Umbrella is to rain as

   (A) brush is to lint
   (B) shovel is to driveway
   (C) soap is to dirt
   (D) comb is to hair
   (E) parasol is to sun

6. Trainee is to apprentice as

   (A) workshop is to office
   (B) leader is to follower
   (C) expert is to master
   (D) craftsman is to inexperienced
   (E) teacher is to student

7. Sculptor is to statue as

   (A) playwright is to script
   (B) author is to newspaper
   (C) director is to review
   (D) masonry is to architecture
   (E) museum is to exhibit

8. Obstacle is to barrier as catastrophe is to

   (A) difficult
   (B) obscene
   (C) disaster
   (D) mourn
   (E) earthquake

9. Milliliter is to liter as

   (A) centimeter is to meter
   (B) pound is to weight
   (C) gram is to kilogram
   (D) inch is to foot
   (E) mile is to kilometer

10. Library is to book as museum is to

    (A) artifact
    (B) observation
    (C) idea
    (D) inspiration
    (E) antiquated

11. Optometrist is to dentist as

    (A) surgeon is to doctor
    (B) healthy is to sick
    (C) hands are to tongue
    (D) vision is to sight
    (E) eyes are to teeth

12. Wildebeest is to savannah as

    (A) reindeer is to tundra
    (B) wolf is to pack
    (C) dolphin is to lake
    (D) rainforest is to jungle
    (E) buffalo is to domestic

13. Cobbler is to shoe as

    (A) blacksmith is to anvil
    (B) engineer is to locomotive
    (C) tailor is to suit
    (D) sailor is to boat
    (E) scribe is to sandal

14. Magma is to fluid as

    (A) ice is to water
    (B) helium is to gas
    (C) opaque is to solid
    (D) molten is to frozen
    (E) nitrogen is to oxygen

15. Introduction is to conclusion as

    (A) prologue is to story
    (B) essay is to epilogue
    (C) period is to sentence
    (D) initiate is to terminate
    (E) narrate is to fiction

16. Walk is to run as

    (A) converse is to shout
    (B) cry is to sad
    (C) ponder is to think
    (D) look is to observe
    (E) quarrel is to whisper

17. Dance is to choreograph as

    (A) art is to explore
    (B) choir is to solo
    (C) author is to plan
    (D) poem is to ponder
    (E) music is to compose

18. Pastor is to congregation as teacher is to

    (A) student
    (B) district
    (C) class
    (D) city
    (E) education

19. Lieutenant is to officer as

    (A) politician is to businessman

    (B) judge is to juror

    (C) soldier is to army

    (D) physicist is to scientist

    (E) bureaucrat is to technician

20. Axe is to chop as scalpel is to

    (A) write

    (B) peel

    (C) incise

    (D) surgery

    (E) draw

21. Letter is to word as paragraph is to

    (A) phrase

    (B) essay

    (C) anthology

    (D) sentence

    (E) indent

22. Applaud is to appreciation as

    (A) heckle is to disapproval

    (B) thank is to favor

    (C) accept is to apology

    (D) promote is to diligence

    (E) cheer is to performance

23. Surgeon is to doctor as

    (A) heart is to vein

    (B) phenomenon is to science

    (C) oxygen is to gas

    (D) neurologist is to nurse

    (E) teacher is to principal

24. Celebrate is to grieve as

    (A) invention is to convention

    (B) carnival is to funeral

    (C) worship is to deity

    (D) party is to gala

    (E) relax is to spa

25. Penny is to dime as

    (A) quarter is to nickel

    (B) cent is to Euro

    (C) ten is to thousand

    (D) dime is to dollar

    (E) coin is to currency

26. Reading is to knowledge as

    (A) exercise is to lifestyle

    (B) walking is to efficiency

    (C) networking is to relationships

    (D) traveling is to geography

    (E) starving is to food

27. France is to Germany as

    (A) Egypt is to Italy

    (B) Cuba is to Argentina

    (C) Australia is to China

    (D) Canada is to England

    (E) Iraq is to Iran

28. Ram is to rum as

    (A) solid is to needy

    (B) hat is to hut

    (C) lug is to lag

    (D) port is to part

    (E) cow is to sow

29. Lazy is to action as accurate is to

    (A) mistake

    (B) exam

    (C) forthright

    (D) novel

    (E) complete

30. Biologist is to life as anthropologist is to

    (A) society

    (B) species

    (C) archaic

    (D) fossil

    (E) science

31. Ponder is to decide as

    (A) exercise is to stretch

    (B) meditate is to hesitate

    (C) browse is to select

    (D) decipher is to research

    (E) imitate is to flatter

32. Kangaroo is to joey as

    (A) goat is to kid

    (B) kitten is to cat

    (C) goose is to gander

    (D) bird is to nest

    (E) puppy is to mature

33. Pound is to kilogram as

    (A) centimeter is to millimeter

    (B) weight is to ton

    (C) meter is to distance

    (D) mile is to kilometer

    (E) gram is to volume

34. Iguana is to lizard as

    (A) bear is to wolf

    (B) goose is to swan

    (C) elk is to hyena

    (D) vole is to rodent

    (E) cat is to panther

35. Volume is to space as

    (A) circle is to circumference

    (B) altitude is to height

    (C) distance is to width

    (D) hypotenuse is to triangle

    (E) pressure is to barometer

36. Plant is to botanist as

    (A) animal is to handler

    (B) body is to anatomist

    (C) zoo is to zoologist

    (D) blood is to cardiologist

    (E) study is to scientist

37. Drain is to vacuum as

    (A) sink is to water

    (B) fatigue is to solitude

    (C) leak is to empty

    (D) gravity is to suction

    (E) faucet is to dirt

38. Husband is to spouse as sister is to

    (A) family

    (B) brother

    (C) avuncular

    (D) sibling

    (E) mother

39. Lime is to mile as

   (A) tile is to guile
   (B) lump is to mump
   (C) leek is to meek
   (D) fruit is to distance
   (E) time is to mime

40. Plumage is to feather as

   (A) tail is to mammal
   (B) coat is to fur
   (C) scale is to skin
   (D) coat is to shed
   (E) whisker is to nose

41. Blacksmith is to metal as

   (A) lawyer is to law
   (B) potter is to clay
   (C) designer is to blueprint
   (D) sculpture is to stone
   (E) yarn is to knitter

42. Reveal is to secretive as

   (A) unravel is to coil
   (B) support is to buttress
   (C) rethink is to diligent
   (D) annoy is to pacifist
   (E) share is to greedy

43. Gallery is to stage as

   (A) deep end is to pool
   (B) bleachers are to field
   (C) entrance is to ballroom
   (D) vestibule is to brownstone
   (E) lectern is to auditorium

44. Paralyzed is to move as

   (A) obtuse is to unclear
   (B) view is to blind
   (C) recall is to memory
   (D) mute is to speak
   (E) deaf is to ear

45. India is to Asia as

   (A) France is to Paris
   (B) Chicago is to America
   (C) Belgium is to Europe
   (D) Vietnam is to Cambodia
   (E) Swiss is to Switzerland

46. Meteorologist is to weather as

   (A) cardiologist is to bones
   (B) dermatologist is to lotion
   (C) writer is to treatise
   (D) geologist is to earth
   (E) zoologist is to study

47. Marriage is to relationship as anger is to

   (A) divorce
   (B) emotion
   (C) bond
   (D) animosity
   (E) irate

48. Muscle is to tissue as

   (A) heart is to blood
   (B) skin is to freckle
   (C) kidney is to organ
   (D) brain is to neuron
   (E) lung is to gland

49. Friend is to acquaintance as

    (A) colleague is to stranger

    (B) manager is to employee

    (C) mentor is to instructor

    (D) coach is to team

    (E) relative is to comrade

50. Cufflink is to wrist as

    (A) boot is to foot

    (B) buckle is to belt

    (C) ring is to jewelry

    (D) vest is to body

    (E) chain is to bracelet

51. Reservoir is to lake as

    (A) canal is to river

    (B) ocean is to sea

    (C) island is to peninsula

    (D) house is to apartment

    (E) tree is to forest

52. Coffee is to brew as

    (A) water is to boil

    (B) beer is to hop

    (C) soup is to stir

    (D) tea is to steep

    (E) milk is to curdle

DIFFICULT QUESTIONS

Use these questions to practice the more advanced questions you might see in both the Middle and Upper Level analogy sections. The Upper Level exam will include more difficult questions than the Middle Level exam.

1. Unicycle is to bicycle as

   (A) tricycle is to vehicle
   (B) united is to divided
   (C) solo is to duet
   (D) amorphous is to polymorphous
   (E) bilateral is to quadrilateral

2. Robust is to fragile as

   (A) resilient is to fragrant
   (B) integral is to unified
   (C) strong is to vulnerable
   (D) radiant is to uninformed
   (E) attractive is to lugubrious

3. Contemporary is to present as

   (A) traditional is to future
   (B) antiquated is to past
   (C) rustic is to foreign
   (D) electricity is to current
   (E) transpire is to history

4. Persevere is to quit as

   (A) subdue is to control
   (B) unite is to sever
   (C) solicit is to request
   (D) surmise is to tamper
   (E) tenacious is to persistent

5. Smile is to blissful as cry is to

   (A) sinister
   (B) irate
   (C) livid
   (D) morose
   (E) pompous

6. Obscure is to clarify as

   (A) nominate is to elect
   (B) damage is to repair
   (C) crystal is to glass
   (D) laugh is to ridicule
   (E) walk is to glide

7. Hypothesize is to verify as

   (A) proof is to evidence
   (B) experiment is to science
   (C) estimate is to presume
   (D) predict is to ascertain
   (E) guess is to fear

8. Reciprocal is to both as

   (A) generous is to gift
   (B) favorable is to luck
   (C) amenable is to cooperation
   (D) unilateral is to one
   (E) fanatical is to belief

9. Contagious is to spread as

   (A) tenuous is to break
   (B) continuous is to chase
   (C) repulsive is to stink
   (D) pernicious is to envy
   (E) moronic is to fail

10. Scrutinize is to examine as

   (A) analyze is to consider
   (B) detain is to demote
   (C) frequent is to attend
   (D) melody is to harmony
   (E) squint is to perceive

11. Accountant is to finances as

   (A) scientist is to methodology
   (B) podiatrist is to feet
   (C) professor is to university
   (D) musician is to clarinet
   (E) horticulture is to plants

12. Vigor is to energy as exuberance is to

   (A) stature
   (B) wisdom
   (C) enthusiasm
   (D) robust
   (E) austerity

13. Banish is to welcome as disperse is to

   (A) convene
   (B) exit
   (C) captivate
   (D) evacuate
   (E) neglect

14. Frank is to honest as

   (A) productive is to careless
   (B) wily is to sly
   (C) fierce is to ferocity
   (D) vain is to charitable
   (E) kinetic is to still

15. Universal is to all as

   (A) hedonist is to many
   (B) ubiquitous is to some
   (C) present is to absent
   (D) triad is to two
   (E) individual is to one

16. Feeble is to strength as

   (A) meager is to amount
   (B) fortunate is to chance
   (C) staunch is to opinion
   (D) weak is to hardy
   (E) lustrous is to light

17. Mankind is to philanthropist as nature is to

   (A) pollution
   (B) conservation
   (C) misanthropy
   (D) environmentalist
   (E) lush

18. Nocturnal is to bat as

   (A) sleepy is to student
   (B) gelatinous is to slug
   (C) diurnal is to animal
   (D) hairless is to rodent
   (E) evening is to creature

19. Messenger is to courier as

    (A) wanderer is to nomad
    (B) monarch is to kingdom
    (C) vendor is to market
    (D) orchid is to flower
    (E) pedestrian is to walk

20. Legible is to read as

    (A) audible is to sound
    (B) laudable is to praise
    (C) blatant is to obvious
    (D) edible is to food
    (E) comprehensible is to clear

21. Down is to condescend as up is to

    (A) admire
    (B) disparage
    (C) invigorate
    (D) suppress
    (E) wane

22. Hurt is to debilitated as

    (A) hungry is to satiated
    (B) frail is to solemn
    (C) happy is to ecstatic
    (D) exuberant is to despondent
    (E) fatigued is to tired

23. Odometer is to radiometer as

    (A) speedometer is to car
    (B) forecast is to weather
    (C) acceleration is to time
    (D) barometer is to pressure
    (E) distance is to radiation

24. Oblivious is to awareness as

    (A) insecure is to confidence
    (B) knowledge is to naïve
    (C) eloquent is to speech
    (D) fruitful is to productive
    (E) scarce is to detail

25. Superficial is to deep as

    (A) overt is to concealed
    (B) internal is to private
    (C) conspicuous is to notice
    (D) vivid is to bright
    (E) taut is to tension

26. Omnipotent is to frail as

    (A) potency is to mastery
    (B) ardor is to excitement
    (C) manacle is to chain
    (D) rogue is to bandit
    (E) reckless is to prudent

27. Phenomenon is to event as

    (A) lessen is to emphasis
    (B) conviction is to belief
    (C) orate is to speaker
    (D) excerpt is to book
    (E) occurrence is to rare

28. Nickname is to familiar as

    (A) tuxedo is to uptight
    (B) hug is to greeting
    (C) nomenclature is to scientific
    (D) pseudonym is to false
    (E) first name is to usual

29. Malnutrition is to nourishment as

(A) asphyxiation is to oxygen
(B) starvation is to hunger
(C) exhaustion is to insomnia
(D) appetite is to satisfy
(E) illness is to hospitalize

30. Exclusive is to restricted as

(A) manifold is to singular
(B) articulated is to explained
(C) satisfy is to desire
(D) homily is to silence
(E) liberated is to limited

31. Rent is to mortgage as

(A) house is to home
(B) city is to state
(C) license is to purchase
(D) continual is to immediate
(E) requirement is to request

32. Religion is to pious as

(A) education is to studious
(B) nationality is to proud
(C) society is to secular
(D) ambition is to successful
(E) kinship is to empathetic

33. Catastrophic is to unfortunate as

(A) tattered is to shambles
(B) destitute is to underprivileged
(C) recondite is to complex
(D) meager is to buoyant
(E) amused is to happy

34. Query is to response as

(A) call is to hang up
(B) problem is to clarity
(C) mistake is to correction
(D) confusion is to decision
(E) ask is to answer

35. Blue is to cyan as pink is to

(A) color
(B) dark
(C) painted
(D) tint
(E) magenta

36. Abduct is to kidnap as expedite is to

(A) lag
(B) diminish
(C) amplify
(D) transmit
(E) accelerate

37. Microscope is to magnify as

(A) gyroscope is to spin
(B) stethoscope is to doctor
(C) phenomenon is to observe
(D) telescope is to extend
(E) periscope is to reflect

38. Romantic is to rational as

(A) fanciful is to analytical
(B) beloved is to liked
(C) reasonable is to stern
(D) controversial is to logical
(E) musical is to artistic

39. Roster is to directory as

(A) list is to guide
(B) employees are to employer
(C) names are to dates
(D) dial is to telephone
(E) audition is to callback

40. Fruitless is to futile as essential is to

(A) frivolous
(B) necessary
(C) erudite
(D) ultimate
(E) surmise

CHALLENGE QUESTIONS

Use these questions to practice the most challenging questions you might see in both the Middle Level and Upper Level analogy sections. Challenge questions are much more frequent on the Upper Level exam than on the Middle Level exam.

1. Vendor is to ware as apothecary is to

   (A) goods
   (B) clothing
   (C) service
   (D) medicine
   (E) supply

2. Nomadic is to stationary as

   (A) stiff is to limber
   (B) impeccable is to flawless
   (C) miniscule is to tiny
   (D) contagious is to infectious
   (E) innate is to natural

3. Apology is to redress as

   (A) injury is to insult
   (B) speech is to action
   (C) mistake is to reparation
   (D) sorrow is to lamentation
   (E) subsidy is to nationalization

4. Allegiance is to animosity as

   (A) fidelity is to respect
   (B) loyalty is to hatred
   (C) admiration is to adoration
   (D) oath is to pledge
   (E) trust is to denial

5. Chasm is to gulf as

   (A) grotto is to cave
   (B) devour is to nourish
   (C) mesa is to plain
   (D) anomaly is to order
   (E) mountain is to valley

6. Dilute is to strengthen as

   (A) belligerent is to aggressive
   (B) recede is to decrease
   (C) question is to query
   (D) satiate is to saturate
   (E) abbreviate is to lengthen

7. Disgusting is to repulsive as charming is to

   (A) irritating
   (B) loquacious
   (C) patronizing
   (D) endearing
   (E) jubilant

8. Fallow is to uncultivated as

   (A) build is to homestead
   (B) farm is to irrigation
   (C) mild is to temperate
   (D) innate is to acquired
   (E) flora is to fauna

9. Pale is to wan as

(A) temperate is to extreme

(B) taut is to tight

(C) first is to final

(D) superb is to terrible

(E) fail is to thrive

10. Celestial is to mundane as

(A) planet is to sun

(B) respectful is to awestruck

(C) delicious is to savory

(D) sky is to earth

(E) religious is to reverent

11. Spontaneous is to unplanned as

(A) cruel is to inhibited

(B) gregarious is to kindhearted

(C) laudable is to praiseworthy

(D) significant is to diminished

(E) necessity is to surfeit

12. Agree is to dissent as

(A) abort is to begin

(B) condone is to accept

(C) forthright is to honest

(D) wither is to slim

(E) reprimand is to scold

13. Voluntary is to unintentional as

(A) deliberate is to accidental

(B) misguided is to erroneous

(C) fair is to equitable

(D) quick is to hurried

(E) thorough is to wearied

14. Residual is to vestige as

(A) omnipotent is to servant

(B) masterful is to novice

(C) unwanted is to gift

(D) lucrative is to career

(E) excessive is to surplus

15. Atypical is to customary as

(A) usual is to expected

(B) difficult is to rigmarole

(C) exceptional is to mediocre

(D) convention is to tradition

(E) amoral is to ordinary

16. Intricate is to basic as

(A) angry is to enraged

(B) aggressive is to pacific

(C) complicated is to dull

(D) master is to student

(E) adorned is to embellished

17. Sympathetic is to feeling as

(A) observing is to following

(B) voracious is to eating

(C) choleric is to ranting

(D) melancholic is to weeping

(E) symbiotic is to living

18. Bad is to abject as

(A) ordinary is to regular

(B) tired is to exhausted

(C) direct is to abstract

(D) correct is to mistaken

(E) whim is to fancy

19. Unbridled is to control as

(A) corroded is to morality

(B) neglected is to attention

(C) guilty is to conscience

(D) mistaken is to certainty

(E) plausible is to reason

20. Epitaph is to inscription as

(A) writing is to reading

(B) cursive is to chisel

(C) tomb is to monument

(D) stone is to papyrus

(E) eternal is to temporary

21. Verdant is to desert as

(A) vast is to ocean

(B) arid is to jungle

(C) shady is to forest

(D) frozen is to tundra

(E) flat is to prairie

22. Enduring is to ephemeral as

(A) sculpture is to masterpiece

(B) sumptuous is to scanty

(C) momentary is to transitory

(D) frigid is to aesthetic

(E) prosaic is to ordinary

23. Evident is to surface as

(A) prevalent is to many

(B) important is to question

(C) ancient is to time

(D) obscure is to depths

(E) fictional is to book

24. Surmise is to guess as taint is to

(A) fascinate

(B) supposition

(C) blemish

(D) trip

(E) ignore

25. Avid is to ardent as customary is to

(A) unusual

(B) malice

(C) habitual

(D) digressive

(E) languish

26. Cryptic is to understand as

(A) difficult is to concern

(B) resolve is to enigma

(C) controversy is to challenge

(D) obscure is to perceive

(E) rejoice is to conundrum

27. Valid is to legitimate as redundant is to

(A) affirmed

(B) unnecessary

(C) misguided

(D) sanctioned

(E) superb

UPPER-LEVEL CHALLENGE QUESTIONS

Use these questions to practice the most challenging questions that you might see in an Upper Level analogy section. These questions would very rarely appear in a Middle Level section.

1. Quotidian is to annual as

   (A) common is to random
   (B) month is to week
   (C) infrequent is to constant
   (D) official is to unannounced
   (E) day is to year

2. Miserly is to magnanimous as

   (A) avarice is to greed
   (B) drab is to resplendent
   (C) brave is to heroic
   (D) sunlight is to winter
   (E) generous is to praiseworthy

3. Pantheist is to monotheist as

   (A) polyglot is to monolingual
   (B) religious is to secular
   (C) polygon is to triangle
   (D) lens is to monocle
   (E) idol is to deity

4. Affable is to gregarious as

   (A) amicable is to moody
   (B) morose is to somber
   (C) logic is to sentiment
   (D) negligent is to responsible
   (E) admiration is to emotion

5. Frame is to canvas as

   (A) lens is to camera
   (B) television is to screen
   (C) proscenium is to stage
   (D) rectangle is to square
   (E) full is to empty

6. Permission is to approbation as

   (A) omen is to noise
   (B) failure is to attempt
   (C) lie is to oration
   (D) reproof is to admonishment
   (E) ridicule is to praise

7. Epistolary is to letter-writing as

   (A) horse is to equestrian
   (B) pedestrian is to dull
   (C) ambulatory is to walking
   (D) revisionist is to editing
   (E) careerist is to employment

8. Stoic is to passion as

   (A) serene is to turmoil
   (B) gratitude is to appreciation
   (C) limp is to movement
   (D) ornery is to annoyance
   (E) sullen is to mood

9. Moribund is to sprightly as

   (A) morbid is to ghastly
   (B) blighted is to blessed
   (C) namesake is to benediction
   (D) happy is to ecstatic
   (E) burdened is to wealthy

10. Severance pay is to dismissal

    (A) retirement is to pension
    (B) bail is to imprisonment
    (C) fee is to contract
    (D) alimony is to divorce
    (E) donation is to gift

11. Signature is to generic as

    (A) specialized is to unique
    (B) luxurious is to necessary
    (C) eccentric is to conventional
    (D) spectacular is to foundational
    (E) mediocre is to passable

12. Sepulchral is to crypt as

    (A) shadowy is to landscape
    (B) menial is to boredom
    (C) chromatic is to rainbow
    (D) lament is to funeral
    (E) exuberant is to elder

13. Rotund is to corpulent as

    (A) sweet is to sour
    (B) master is to acolyte
    (C) tall is to dwarfish
    (D) magnificent is to mediocre
    (E) slender is to slim

14. Derivative is to original as

    (A) replica is to inferior
    (B) forgery is to genuine
    (C) excellent is to average
    (D) calculate is to solution
    (E) random is to coincidence

15. Temerity is to meekness as

    (A) ruin is to destruction
    (B) sophistication is to elegance
    (C) meander is to wander
    (D) naïve is to infuriated
    (E) excitement is to calmness

16. Aphorism is to brief as

    (A) bereft is to plenty
    (B) catastrophe is to devastating
    (C) affluent is to attain
    (D) euphemism is to lengthy
    (E) phrase is to subject

17. Conjunction is clause as

    (A) yoke is to ox
    (B) sentence is to paragraph
    (C) relation is to family
    (D) knot is to commitment
    (E) rope is to chain

18. Mischievous is to innocent as

    (A) miscreant is to vandal
    (B) naïve is to blissful
    (C) slovenly is to patriotic
    (D) brave is to craven
    (E) cranky is to inconsolable

19. Preclude is to stimulate as

    (A) accede is to comply

    (B) prohibit is to promote

    (C) malign is to inhibit

    (D) condemn is to tolerate

    (E) rebuke is to endorse

20. Gratuitous is to immoderate as

    (A) frivolous is to inane

    (B) modest is to arrogant

    (C) ruckus is to rigmarole

    (D) mezzanine is to byzantine

    (E) aesthetic is to utility

21. Renegade is to adherent as

    (A) frenzy is to equanimity

    (B) pulverize is to deconstruct

    (C) rebel is to traitor

    (D) abscond is to runaway

    (E) frugal is to economical

22. Parallel is to intersect as

    (A) continuous is to waver

    (B) celibate is to wed

    (C) inanimate is to die

    (D) allegorical is to story

    (E) wise is to regret

23. Exile is to separation as

    (A) clear is to obvious

    (B) vacation is to sojourn

    (C) militant is to army

    (D) remit is to removal

    (E) libel is to insult

THE READING SECTION

CHAPTER 4

INTRODUCTION

The SSAT Reading Section (40 minutes) tests your ability to understand short passages from a variety of different sources. The section has 40 questions based on approximately seven or eight passages. Genres may include informative passages, persuasive passages, short stories, and poetry. You will be asked to locate information about the author's main idea, specific details, and style. You may also be asked to expand logically on the information presented in the passage and infer what may come next. However, you will never need to rely on any of your own prior knowledge about the material; all of the information needed to answer these questions will be given directly in the passage.

APPROACHING THE READING SECTION

TIME MANAGEMENT

Pace yourself carefully. You are only given points for answering the questions, not reading the passages, so don't spend too long reading any one passage. Focus on the shorter passages first and save the long passages for last.

Read quickly, trying to understand the main points of the passage rather than the small details. Don't waste time trying to understand every piece of information in the passage. If something doesn't make sense to you, try to get an overall sense of what the author is saying and move on.

ANSWER QUESTIONS OUT OF ORDER

Answer questions about the main idea or the main purpose first, and then turn to questions that ask about specific details in the passage. If a question looks like it will take a long time to answer, circle it and save it for last. If a question makes reference to a particular line number, reread those lines before answering the question.

PROCESS OF ELIMINATION

Use the **Process of Elimination** to narrow down your answer choices, eliminating answers that are obviously wrong or have nothing to do with what is being asked. Then decide among the remaining answer choices which one best answers the question. Remember that you are being asked to find the best answer, not the one that immediately seems correct. Check all of the possible answer choices before making your selection.

VOCABULARY BUILDING

Use your practice reading passages to help develop your vocabulary. Circle words you don't understand, look them up, and add them to your vocabulary flashcards or journal.

CRITICAL READING STRATEGIES

The Reading Section on the SSAT doesn't only test whether you are able to understand a passage. The section also tests whether you are able to read **critically**, which means examining and interpreting what the passage means as a whole. This means that you should look not only for the facts of the passage, but also what the author is saying about those facts and how the author is saying it.

For every passage you read, ask yourself:

1. What are the author's **topics**, or the key details being discussed in this passage?
2. What is the author saying about these topics, or what is the **main point** of the passage?
3. What is the author's **purpose** in this passage?

In this section, we'll discuss how to go about answering these questions. We'll take a look at several strategies that will build your critical reading skills and help you become a more active reader for the SSAT. Because you have a unique learning style, some of these strategies might work better for you than others. Identify the strategies that help you the most, and practice using these for each new passage you read.

UNDERSTANDING THE PASSAGE

Your first step to understand the passage is to identify the basic facts that the author is discussing. As you read, stop yourself after each paragraph and take the time to mentally **summarize** the basic facts that you have read. Summarizing these basic facts **in your own words** is important because it allows you to prove to yourself that you have really understood what the passage is saying. The questions on the SSAT might also ask you to recognize concepts from the passage in slightly different words, so you can't be tied down to the exact words that the author uses.

THE 5 W'S

What is the best way to quickly summarize the passage? You may have heard about the **5 w's:** "who," "what," "where," "when," and "why." As you read, ask yourself these five questions:

1. **Who** is involved in this passage? If the passage is fiction, look for the characters and the person telling the story. If the passage is nonfiction, look for any people being discussed and think about who might be writing this passage.

2. **What** is being discussed in this passage? Look for the major concepts in each section of the passage.

3. **Where** are the events in this passage taking place? If the passage is fiction, where is the story taking place? If it is nonfiction, look for any important places that are being discussed.

4. **When** are the events in the passage taking place? If this passage is fiction, can you guess when the story might be taking place? If the passage is nonfiction, look for any clues that might tell you the dates of the events taking place. Also see if you can guess when the author might have written the passage.

5. **Why** is the information in this passage important? In other words, how are the ideas in the passage connected, and what purpose or main point is the author illustrating with all of these details? We'll discuss this in greater detail in the next section.

KEY WORDS

As you read, underline the **key words** that answer these questions in the passage. Be an **active reader** and read with your pencil! Underlining as you read will improve your concentration and keep you focused on the most important information in the passage. Identify whether the words you underline answer the questions "who," "what," "where," "when," or "why."

As you read, also pay close attention to how the author connects information within the passage. Underline any **transitional words** or phrases that the author uses to move from one idea to another. The author might use words like "additionally," "furthermore," or "consequently" to show how one idea follows from or supports another. She might use words like "but," "yet," or "however" to show how one idea contrasts with another.

Take a look at the example passage below. What key words would you underline to answer the questions "who," "what," "where," "when," and "why"? What other transitional words would you underline? You might try something like this:

The <u>duck-billed platypus</u> is a small animal, native to <u>Australia</u>, with many <u>unusual characteristics</u>. It is a very <u>odd-looking</u> animal; in fact, when Europeans first heard about the platypus, many thought such an odd-looking animal must be a fraud. Its head and feet are like a duck's, its body is like a

Line 5   weasel's, and its tail is like a beaver's. Its <u>webbed feet</u> help it swim, its <u>odd-shaped tail</u> helps it to store fat, and its <u>duck-like beak</u> helps it find food in rivers.

A platypus is a mammal, <u>but</u> is remarkably <u>unlike almost every other mammal</u>. The platypus <u>lays eggs</u>; it doesn't give birth like other mammals.

10   Also, although all mammals give their young milk, the platypus has an unusual way of doing this: it actually <u>sweats milk</u> all over its body. But <u>despite</u> these differences, the platypus <u>has fur</u>, like other mammals.

<u>Finally</u>, the platypus has some <u>amazing abilities</u>. The platypus can <u>see electricity</u>: it senses electricity coming from other animals in the water and

15   uses this ability to catch food and avoid predators. The platypus also has <u>venomous spurs</u> on its feet that allow it to defend itself. An animal that gets too close to the platypus's feet will be stung with a poison.

Let's see how these key words helped us answer the 5 w's for this passage:

1. **Who** is being discussed in this passage? This passage is about the duck-billed platypus, which is the first word we underlined.

2. **What** is being discussed in this passage? This passage focuses on several unusual characteristics of the duck-billed platypus: its odd looks, difference from other mammals, and amazing abilities. We underlined these characteristics in the passage.

3. **Where** are the events in this passage taking place? The passage says that the duck-billed platypus lives in Australia, so we underlined that place in the passage.

4. **When** are the events in this passage taking place? This passage doesn't specifically tell us this information. But because the passage is written in the present tense, we can assume that it is talking about a type of animal that is alive today.

5. **Why** is the information in this passage important? We underlined the transitional words "but," "despite," and "finally" in order to keep track of how the ideas in this passage support or contrast with each other. We'll talk about the author's main idea and purpose in the next section, but all of the information included in this passage seems to be describing *why* the platypus is unusual.

You might have decided that other concepts are also important, and might have underlined some additional words. However, don't underline too many words in any paragraph! Only focus on the *key* words, those that are the most important and those that answer the 5 w's for the passage.

Exercise #1: Read the following passages and underline the key words that answer the questions "who," "what," "where," "when", and "why," as well as any transitional words or phrases. Then, use these key words to answer the 5 w's in your own words. Have a trusted reader check your work.

A banana split is an ice cream-based dessert. In its classic form, it is served in a long dish called a boat. A banana is cut in half lengthwise and laid in the dish. There are many variations, but the classic banana split is made with scoops of vanilla, chocolate and strawberry ice cream served in a row
Line 5   between the split banana. Pineapple topping is spooned over the strawberry ice cream, chocolate syrup over the vanilla, and strawberry topping over the chocolate. It is garnished with crushed nuts, whipped cream, and maraschino cherries.

David Evans Strickler, a 23-year-old apprentice pharmacist at Tassel
10   Pharmacy in Latrobe, Pennsylvania, invented the banana-based triple ice cream sundae in 1904. The sundae originally cost 10 cents, twice the price of other sundaes. It quickly caught on with students of nearby Saint Vincent College, who spread news of the sundae by word-of-mouth.

Walgreens is credited with spreading the popularity of the banana split.
15   The early drug stores operated by Charles Rudolph Walgreen in the Chicago area adopted the banana split as a signature dessert. Fountains in the stores attracted customers who might otherwise have been just as satisfied having their prescriptions filled at some other drug store in the neighborhood. But Walgreens offered them something special – the banana split.

1. **Who** is being discussed in this passage?

2. **What** is being discussed in this passage?

3. **Where** are the events in this passage taking place?

4. **When** are the events in this passage taking place?

5. **Why** is the information in this passage important?

Sunscreen is a lotion, spray, or gel applied to the skin to help protect against sunburn. The chemicals in sunscreen absorb or reflect some of the sun's ultraviolet radiation. The effectiveness of sunscreen is called its Sun Protection Factor, or SPF. Sunscreens with a higher SPF provide more

Line 5   protection against UV-B rays, the ultraviolet radiation that causes sunburn.

Medical organizations such as the American Cancer Society recommend the use of sunscreen because it can help prevent certain skin cancers associated with sun exposure. However, many sunscreens do not offer the full protection needed to reduce the risk of skin cancer. This is because many

10   sunscreens do not block UV-A rays, another form of ultraviolet radiation that does not cause sunburn but can still increase the risk of skin cancer. Broad-spectrum sunscreens have been designed to address this concern by protecting against both UV-A and UV-B radiation.

6. **Who** is being discussed in this passage?

7. **What** is being discussed in this passage?

8. **Where** are the events in this passage taking place?

9. **When** are the events in this passage taking place?

10. **Why** is the information in this passage important?

ANALYZING THE PASSAGE

Understanding the 5 w's of the passage will help you with your basic comprehension. The next step to becoming a critical reader is to understand how these basic facts are organized.

PARAGRAPH TOPICS

Within each paragraph of a passage, some facts will be more important than others. The **topic** of a paragraph is its main focus. As you read, think about how the key words you underlined might support the main topic of each paragraph.

Let's walk through the duck-billed platypus passage again. Here, we'll use the key words we underlined to identify the topic of each paragraph:

- The topic of the first paragraph is the unusual way the duck-billed platypus looks. We can tell this by the first couple of sentences, where we underlined the key words "unusual characteristics" and "odd-looking." The rest of the paragraph gives us more details about this idea. The platypus's odd looks include its beak, its tail, its feet, and its body. As the paragraph goes on, we are told that some of its odd-looking features have purposes, which we also underlined.

- The second paragraph is about why the platypus is different from other mammals, which was one of our key words. The paragraph goes on to tell some key ways that the platypus is different: it lays eggs and sweats milk. It also tells us one way that the platypus is like other mammals: it has fur.

- The third paragraph is about some special abilities of the platypus: its ability to see electricity and to inject poison from its feet. Our key words included the phrases "see electricity" and "venomous spurs."

If you have time, you might want to write in the margin of your passage a few words that describe each paragraph's topic. For the duck-billed platypus passage, you might write:

Unusual way the platypus looks

The <u>duck-billed platypus</u> is a small animal, native to Australia, with many <u>unusual characteristics</u>. It is a very <u>odd-looking</u> animal; in fact, when Europeans first heard about the platypus, many thought such an odd-looking animal must be a fraud. Its head and feet are like a duck's, its body is like a weasel's, and its tail is like a beaver's. Its <u>webbed feet</u> help it swim, its <u>odd-shaped tail</u> helps it to store fat, and its <u>duck-like beak</u> helps it find food in rivers.

Different from other mammals

A platypus is a mammal, but is <u>remarkably unlike almost every other mammal</u>. The platypus <u>lays eggs</u>; it doesn't give birth like other mammals. Also, although all mammals give their young milk, the platypus has an unusual way of doing this: it actually <u>sweats milk</u> all over its body. But despite these differences, the platypus has fur, like other mammals.

Special abilities

Finally, the platypus has some <u>amazing abilities</u>. The platypus can see <u>electricity</u>: it senses electricity coming from other animals in the water and uses this ability to catch food and avoid predators. The platypus also has <u>venomous spurs</u> on its feet that allow it to defend itself. An animal that gets too close to the platypus's feet will be stung with a poison.

MAIN POINT

After you have discovered the author's topics in a passage, your next step is to identify the author's **main point,** or what the author is saying *about* these topics. The main point helps answer one of the "why" questions of your 5 w's: why is the information in this passage important? All of the information in the passage serves to prove or illustrate one central idea, and this idea is the author's main point. The main point connects all of the paragraphs in the passage and shows how they are working together.

For example, in the duck-billed platypus passage above, we identified the topics of each of the three paragraphs. How would you write a sentence that describes what the author is saying *about* these topics, connecting all three paragraphs? Each paragraph discusses some way that the platypus is an unusual animal. Therefore, you might write:

The duck-billed platypus is an unusual animal because it looks strange, is different from other mammals, and has some special abilities.

Notice how this main point includes the topics of all three paragraphs: they all work together to show how the platypus is unusual!

PURPOSE

Connected to the main point is the passage's **purpose**. This is answers another one of the "why" questions of your 5 w's: why might the author have written this passage? What is he or she trying to do? In order to answer this question, think about what type of passage you are reading. Would this passage most likely occur in an encyclopedia? If so, the author's purpose might be to explain or describe something. Would the passage occur in a newspaper? If so, the author might be trying to report an event, or to convince you of something. Would the passage occur in a book of short stories? If so, the author is probably telling you a story.

Here are the main purposes of most passages you will encounter:

- to explain or describe
- to convince or persuade
- to narrate or tell a story

The duck-billed platypus passage would most likely fall under the first category: you could say that the author's purpose is to *describe* some features of the platypus.

Exercise #2: Re-read the following passages and answer the questions that follow, referring back to your 5 w's in Exercise #1. Have a trusted reader check your work.

> A banana split is an ice cream-based dessert. In its classic form, it is served in a long dish called a boat. A banana is cut in half lengthwise and laid in the dish. There are many variations, but the classic banana split is made with scoops of vanilla, chocolate and strawberry ice cream served in a row
>
> Line 5 between the split banana. Pineapple topping is spooned over the strawberry ice cream, chocolate syrup over the vanilla, and strawberry topping over the chocolate. It is garnished with crushed nuts, whipped cream, and maraschino cherries.
>
> David Evans Strickler, a 23-year-old apprentice pharmacist at Tassel
> 10 Pharmacy in Latrobe, Pennsylvania, invented the banana-based triple ice cream sundae in 1904. The sundae originally cost 10 cents, twice the price of other sundaes. It quickly caught on with students of nearby Saint Vincent College, who spread news of the sundae by word-of-mouth.
>
> Walgreens is credited with spreading the popularity of the banana split.
> 15 The early drug stores operated by Charles Rudolph Walgreen in the Chicago area adopted the banana split as a signature dessert. Fountains in the stores attracted customers who might otherwise have been just as satisfied having their prescriptions filled at some other drug store in the neighborhood. But Walgreens offered them something special – the banana split.

1. What are the topics of each paragraph?

   Paragraph 1:

   Paragraph 2:

2. How would you state the main point of this entire passage? Write your answer as a full sentence.

3. How would you describe the purpose of this passage?

Line 5

10

> Sunscreen is a lotion, spray, or gel applied to the skin to help protect against sunburn. The chemicals in sunscreen absorb or reflect some of the sun's ultraviolet radiation. The effectiveness of sunscreen is called its Sun Protection Factor, or SPF. Sunscreens with a higher SPF provide more protection against UV-B rays, the ultraviolet radiation that causes sunburn.
>
> Medical organizations such as the American Cancer Society recommend the use of sunscreen because it can help prevent certain skin cancers associated with sun exposure. However, many sunscreens do not offer the full protection needed to reduce the risk of skin cancer. This is because many sunscreens do not block UV-A rays, another form of ultraviolet radiation that does not cause sunburn but can still increase the risk of skin cancer. Broad-spectrum sunscreens have been designed to address this concern by protecting against both UV-A and UV-B radiation.

4. What are the topics of each paragraph?

   Paragraph 1:

   Paragraph 2:

5. How would you state the main point of this entire passage? Write your answer as a full sentence.

6. How would you describe the purpose of this passage?

TRICKY VOCABULARY

As you read, you might find words that you don't recognize. Don't panic! Keep reading, and try to guess the meaning of these words **in context**, by looking for clues nearby in the sentence.

Take a look at the sample sentence below:

> A _cacophony_ of squealing brakes, clanking metal, and a blaring horn announced the train's entrance into the station.

If you don't know the meaning of the word "cacophony," try to guess based on the context of the sentence itself. The words "squealing," "clanking," and "blaring" are all types of unpleasant noise. Based on these clues, you might conclude that "cacophony" is a word to describe a loud, unpleasant noise—and you would be correct!

Here's another example:

> The unexpected result was an _anomaly_, and additional experiments produced more typical results.

If you don't know what the word "anomaly" means, look at the clues nearby in the sentence. The word is being used to describe an "unexpected result," which is in contrast with "more typical results" later on. Based on this information, you might conclude that an "anomaly" is something unexpected and not typical. Indeed, an "anomaly" is defined as an unusual or unexpected event.

Exercise #4: Read the new passages below, using the critical reading strategies you have practiced. Then, guess a definition for each underlined word based on context. When you are done, look up each word in a dictionary to check whether you guessed correctly. If you don't know any of the other words in the passage, look those up as well!

The Mississippi is well worth reading about. It is not a commonplace river, but on the contrary is in all ways remarkable. Considering the Missouri its main branch, it is one of the longest rivers in the world—four thousand three hundred miles. It seems safe to say that it is also the crookedest river in the world, since in one part of its journey it uses up one thousand three hundred miles to cover the same ground that the crow would fly over in six hundred and seventy-five.

Line 5

The difference in rise and fall is also remarkable—not in the upper, but in the lower river. The rise is tolerably underline uniform down to Natchez (three hundred and sixty miles above the mouth)—about fifty feet. But at Bayou La Fourche the river rises only twenty-four feet; at New Orleans only fifteen, and just above the mouth only two and one half.

10

The Mississippi is remarkable in still another way—its disposition to make prodigious jumps by cutting through narrow necks of land, and thus straightening and shortening itself. More than once it has shortened itself thirty miles at a single jump! These cut-offs have had curious effects: they have thrown several river towns out into the rural districts, and built up sand bars and forests in front of them. The town of Delta used to be three miles below Vicksburg: a recent cutoff has radically changed the position, and Delta is now two miles above Vicksburg.

15

What meaning might you guess for the underlined words, based on how they are used in the passage?

1. commonplace:

2. uniform:

3. prodigious:

4. rural:

Once a master said to a child, "If you will study diligently, learn, and do good unto others, your face shall be filled with light."

So the child studied busily, learned, and <u>sought</u> how she could do good unto others. And every little while she ran to the glass to see if the light was coming. But at each time she was disappointed. No light was there. Try as faithfully as she would, and look as often as she would, it was always the same.

I do not know if she doubted the master or not; but it is certain she did not know what to make of it. She <u>grieved</u>, and day after day her disappointment grew. At length she could bear it no longer, so she went to the master and said:

"Dear master, I have been so <u>diligent</u>! I have tried to learn and to do good unto others. Yet every time I have sought in my face the light which you promised, it has not been there. No, not a single time."

Now the master listened <u>intently</u>, and watching her face as she spoke, he said, "You poor little one, in this moment, as you have spoken to me, your face has been so filled with light that you would not believe. And do you know why? It is because every word you have spoken in this moment has come from your heart."

What meaning might you guess for the underlined words, based on how they are used in the passage?

5. sought:

6. grieved:

7. diligent:

8. intently:

TYPES OF PASSAGES

The SSAT Reading Section includes approximately seven or eight short passages that you will need to read and analyze under a time limit. In this section, we'll discuss the four main types of passages you will see on the exam: informative passages, persuasive passages, short stories, and poems. Continue reading for specific strategies to help you analyze each type of passage.

INFORMATIVE PASSAGES

Informative passages explain or describe a main topic. You might find an informative passage in an encyclopedia, textbook, or even a newspaper story that informs readers about a recent event. On the SSAT, you might see a wide range of topics, from science to art to history.

MAJOR COMPONENTS

A common structure for informative passages includes the following components:

- **Introduction**: The opening sentences of a passage normally introduce the reader to the main topic of the passage. However, sometimes the introduction for an SSAT passage will be very brief, and sometimes it might be missing altogether! In that case, it will be up to you to figure out how the ideas in the passage are connected.

- **Body**: In an informative passage, each paragraph will give information about a particular idea related to the main topic. For example, in a passage about ice cream, one paragraph might be about how ice cream is made, and another might detail the history of ice cream. In the previous section, we looked at strategies for identifying the key ideas in each body paragraph.

- **Conclusion**: The final sentences of a passage might summarize the main idea of the passage. However, in an SSAT passage, the conclusion might be very brief or missing altogether.

To illustrate these components, let's take another look at the platypus passage from the last section, which is an informative passage:

> The duck-billed platypus is a small animal, native to Australia, with many unusual characteristics. It is a very odd-looking animal; in fact, when Europeans first heard about the platypus, many thought such an odd-looking animal must be a fraud. Its head and feet are like a duck's, its body is like a weasel's, and its tail is like a beaver's. Its webbed feet help it swim, its odd-shaped tail helps it to store fat, and its duck-like beak helps it find food in rivers.
>
> A platypus is a mammal, but is remarkably unlike almost every other mammal. The platypus lays eggs; it doesn't give birth like other mammals. Also, although all mammals give their young milk, the platypus has an unusual way of doing this: it actually sweats milk all over its body. But despite these differences, the platypus has fur, like other mammals.
>
> Finally, the platypus has some amazing abilities. The platypus can see electricity: it senses electricity coming from other animals in the water and uses this ability to catch food and avoid predators. The platypus also has venomous spurs on its feet that allow it to defend itself. An animal that gets too close to the platypus's feet will be stung with a poison.

(Line markers: Line 5, 10, 15)

Does this passage have an introduction? We might call the first sentence of the passage its (very brief) introduction, because it states the main topic of the entire passage: "The duck-billed platypus is a small animal, native to Australia, with many unusual characteristics."

The body of this passage includes the rest of the first paragraph and the next two paragraphs. As we have already seen, each of these paragraphs describes a specific topic related to the main idea: the way the platypus looks, the way it is unlike other mammals, and some of its special abilities.

Does this passage have a conclusion? No—there is no sentence or paragraph at the end that summarizes the main idea of the passage again. This is an example of a passage that ends before its conclusion. It might be incomplete—the author might go on to talk about some more unusual traits of the platypus!

PARAGRAPH STRUCTURE

Many informative passages also have special internal structures within their paragraphs. Just like the passage as a whole, each paragraph has a topic sentence that serves as its introduction. The topic sentence introduces readers to the main idea of the paragraph. The next few sentences can be thought of as the body of the paragraph; they present **supporting details** related to the topic sentence. Finally, a paragraph might end with a concluding sentence that summarizes the main topic of the paragraph. The **concluding sentence** can also provide a transition to the next paragraph.

For example, let's take a look at the second paragraph of the platypus passage again:

> A platypus is a mammal, but is remarkably unlike almost every other mammal. The platypus lays eggs; it doesn't give birth like other mammals.
> 10 Also, although all mammals give their young milk, the platypus has an unusual way of doing this: it actually sweats milk all over its body. But despite these differences, the platypus has fur, like other mammals.

The topic sentence of this paragraph is its first sentence: "The platypus is a mammal, but is remarkably unlike almost every other mammal." This sentence tells us that the topic of the paragraph is how the platypus is different from other mammals.

The body of this paragraph includes the second and third sentences, which provide supporting detail about how the platypus is different from other mammals. These details include its egg-laying and milk-sweating habits.

The final sentence of this paragraph might be called its conclusion because it explains why the platypus is still a mammal, despite these differences.

STRATEGIES

When you read an informative passage, ask yourself the same three questions we discussed in the Critical Reading section:

1. What are the author's **topics**, or the key details being discussed in this passage?
2. What is the author saying about these topics, or what is the **main point** of the passage?
3. What is the author's **purpose** in this passage?

The third question should be easy to answer: the purpose of an informative passage is to inform, explain, or describe. To answer the first two questions, review the strategies from the Critical Reading section. Looking for the main structure of the passage and the internal structure of each paragraph will help you locate this information.

Be careful: even if the topic of the passage is familiar to you, don't allow your reading to be swayed by your own opinion or prior knowledge! The SSAT will only test you about what the author is saying. Ignore any information you might already know about the topic and look only at the information on the page in front of you.

Exercise #1: Read the sample informative passage below, and then answer the questions that follow. Ask a trusted reader to check your work.

> One of the Seven Wonders of the Ancient World, the Hanging Gardens of Babylon is the only one of the Wonders that may have been a legend.
>
> The gardens were attributed to King Nebuchadnezzar II, who ruled the ancient city-state of Babylon between 605 and 562 BC. He is said to have *Line 5* constructed the gardens to please his homesick wife, Amytis of Media, who longed for the plants of her homeland. The gardens were so massive that they required a minimum of 8,200 gallons of water per day to remain lush and green. To prevent flooding and erosion from the daily watering, Nebuchadnezzar is reported to have used massive slabs of stone beneath and *10* around the gardens.
>
> Unfortunately, several earthquakes after the Second Century BC are said to have destroyed the gardens. While ancient Greek and Roman writers documented the Hanging Gardens of Babylon, there is no definitive archaeological evidence confirming their existence.

1. Identify each of the following structural components of the passage as a whole:

    Introduction:

    Body:

    Conclusion:

2. For the second paragraph (lines 3-9), identify the following components:

    Topic sentence:

    Supporting details:

3. What are the author's topics, or the key details being discussed in this passage?

4. What is the author saying about these topics, or what is the main point of the passage?

5. What is the author's purpose in this passage?

PERSUASIVE PASSAGES

In a persuasive passage, the author tries to convince the reader of a specific position or argument. A persuasive passage might come from a political speech, an opinion essay, or a newspaper op-ed or letter to the editor.

MAJOR COMPONENTS

A persuasive passage differs from an informative passage because the author is presenting an opinion about a situation, rather than simply explaining or describing a topic. This opinion is called the author's **thesis**, and an author normally uses specific supporting points or **evidence** to prove his or her opinion. Authors can use **objective evidence**, or facts and statistics from outside sources. Authors can also use **subjective evidence**, or examples from their own experiences. While a persuasive passage written with objective evidence will sound more detached and analytical, a persuasive essay written with subjective evidence will sound more personal.

Persuasive passages follow the same basic structure as informative passages, with a few differences:

- **Introduction**: The opening sentences of a passage normally introduce the reader to the author's main argument and thesis. Just like informative passages, however, the introduction for a persuasive passage on the SSAT might be very brief or missing altogether. In that case, it will be up to you to find the author's main argument and thesis by reading the rest of the passage.

- **Body**: In a persuasive passage, each paragraph will provide a specific reason or example that proves why the author's thesis is true. These paragraphs contain the author's evidence, either from outside sources (objective) or personal experience (subjective).

- **Conclusion**: The final sentences of a passage might summarize the main argument of the passage. However, in an SSAT passage, the conclusion might be very brief or missing altogether.

To illustrate these components, let's take a look at this example persuasive passage:

Cell phones have become a staple of modern life. While they have many benefits, such as improved communication, they can also be dangerous and counterproductive.

For one, cell phone use while driving is becoming increasingly

Line 5   controversial. Being distracted while operating a motor vehicle has resulted in an alarming increase in the number of car accidents. Because of this, many jurisdictions prohibit the use of mobile phones while driving. Egypt, Israel, Japan, Portugal, and Singapore banned both handheld and hands-free use of a mobile phone; others—including the UK, France, and many U.S. states—

10   banned handheld phone use only, allowing hands-free use.

In addition, cell phone use is being closely watched in schools. Because so many students have been using them to cheat on tests and bully others, cell phone use is usually restricted in schools. The benefits of cell phone use in schools have yet to be found because students' use of cell phones has, for the

15   most part, threatened the school's security, distracted other students, and encouraged gossip and other social activities that harm learning.

Besides being monitored in cars and schools, many cell phones are banned in school locker room facilities, public restrooms, and swimming pools due to the built-in cameras that most phones now feature.

Does this passage have an introduction? Yes, the first paragraph of the passage states both the main topic of the passage (cell phone usage) as well as the author's position about this topic. The author's thesis is stated in the second sentence: "While they have many benefits, such as improved communication, they can also be dangerous and counterproductive." Based on this thesis statement, we expect that the rest of the passage will prove why and how cell phones can be dangerous and counterproductive.

The body of this passage includes the second, third, and fourth paragraphs. Each of these paragraphs explains a specific situation where cell phones may be dangerous:

- Paragraph 2: Cell phones can be dangerous to use while driving.
- Paragraph 3: Cell phones can be dangerous to use in schools.
- Paragraph 4: Cell phones can be dangerous to use in locker rooms, restrooms, and swimming pools.

In each paragraph, the author provides specific details about why cell phones can be dangerous in each of these situations. All of these details work together as the author's evidence to support her thesis.

Does this passage have a conclusion? No—there is no sentence or paragraph at the end that summarizes the author's thesis and argument again. This is another example of a passage that ends before its conclusion. If the author were to continue the passage, what do you think she would discuss next?

STRATEGIES

When you read a persuasive passage, start by asking yourself the same three questions we discussed in the Critical Reading section:

1. What are the author's **topics**, or the key details being discussed in this passage?
2. What is the author saying about these topics, or what is the **main point** of the passage?
3. What is the author's **purpose** in this passage?

The third question should be easy to answer: the purpose of a persuasive passage is to persuade or convince you of the author's opinion. To answer the first two questions, review the strategies from the Critical Reading section. In addition, help yourself by looking for the main components of the passage: the author's thesis and supporting evidence.

If you're having difficulty understanding the passage, try to imagine who is speaking and whom he or she might be speaking to. Is this the type of passage that would be delivered as a speech or a letter to a group of people, or as a speech or a letter to one specific person? If so, who do you think those people are? What type of situation might have led the author to propose this argument?

If you're having difficulty locating the author's main point or thesis, pay close attention to the author's **tone**. Because a persuasive passage presents an opinion, the author will frequently have a **positive** or **negative** feeling about the topic he or she is discussing. In the cell phone passage above, the author uses words like "dangerous," "counterproductive," "controversial," "alarming," and "threatened" to describe cell phone usage. These words indicate that the author feels negatively about using cell phones in the situations she is describing.

Be careful: even if you disagree with the author's position, don't allow your reading to be swayed by your own opinion! The SSAT will only test you about what the author is saying, so only look at the argument on the page in front of you.

Exercise #2: Read the following sample persuasive passage, and then answer the questions that follow. Ask a trusted reader to check your work.

The purpose of Black History Month is to draw attention and pay tribute to people, organizations, and events that have shaped the history of African Americans and their contributions to American society. In this spirit, we should honor Delta Sigma Theta, a black women's organization that fought for

Line 5   civil rights and made a difference in the lives of many for over a century.

Delta Sigma Theta was founded in 1913 by 22 women at Howard University in Washington. The sorority of college-educated women pledged to perform public service in the black community. Nearly six weeks after its founding, Delta Sigma Theta members took part in the historic Women's

10   Suffrage March in Washington, and were the only African-Americans present. The Deltas have participated in every major civil rights march since.

In addition to its political involvement, Delta Sigma Theta has a strong tradition of community involvement. For years, the sorority's local chapters have funded programs providing assistance to persons in need and promoting

15   academic excellence. The groups work as mentors to young people and provide scholarships to help them pursue their education.

Today, Delta Sigma Theta has 260,000 members. For the next century, these sorority sisters say they will continue to leave their mark on black history while helping transform the lives of young people.

1. Identify each of the following structural components in the passage as a whole:

    Introduction:

    Body:

    Conclusion:

2. What are the author's topics, or the key details being discussed in this passage?

3. What is the author saying about these topics, or what is the main point of the passage?

4. Who might the author be addressing in this passage?

5. What specific evidence does the author use to support his or her thesis?

6. What is the author's tone in this passage?

SHORT STORIES

Unlike informative and persuasive passages, a short story is an example of fiction. Informative and persuasive passages discuss real-life people, places, and events. By contrast, works of fiction discuss people, places, and events that are made up by the author's imagination. Novels are examples of fiction, and many short story passages on the SSAT might be taken from sections of a larger book. Other short story passages might stand alone by themselves, designed by the author to tell a brief story about made-up characters and events.

MAJOR COMPONENTS

Short stories have five main components. We can think of these components in terms of the "5 w's": the who, what, where, when, and why of the story.

- **Characters** are the *who* of the story: the people (and sometimes animals) that exist in the world of the story.
- The **narrator** is another *who* of the story: the person telling the story. The narrator can be a character in the story, or somebody outside of the story.
- The **setting** is *when* and *where* the story takes place.
- The **plot** is *what* happens in the story, or the major events that take place.
- The **conflict** is *why* and *how* the plot moves forward. Often the characters need to achieve something, but there is some sort of obstacle in their way. The plot of the story centers on why and how they choose to overcome this obstacle.

To illustrate these components, let's take a look at this example short story:

> A Wolf had got a bone stuck in his throat. He was in the greatest agony, and he ran up and down, beseeching every animal he met to help him. He promised that the animal who could successfully remove the bone would receive a very handsome reward. A Crane heard his entreaties and promises,
> Line 5 and she decided to help. She ventured her long neck down the Wolf's throat and drew out the bone. She then modestly asked for the promised reward. The Wolf grinned and showed his teeth. He replied, "Ungrateful creature, why would you need any other reward? You have put your head into a Wolf's jaws, and brought it safely out again!"
> 10 Those who provide help only in the hope of a reward must not be surprised if, in their dealings with evil men, they meet with more jeers than thanks.

Who are the characters in this story? In other words, who is this story about? The Wolf and the Crane are the two animals who interact in this story, so they are the story's characters.

Who is the story's narrator? In other words, who might be telling the story? The narrator does not seem to be another character in the story because he or she does not interact with the characters or take place in the events. We can conclude that the narrator is someone outside of the story.

What is the story's setting? In other words, when and where does the story take place? We can tell that this story took place in the past, but the exact time isn't specified—it might have taken place long ago, or just yesterday. Similarly, the place for this story is unclear, but we might guess that it takes place somewhere that wolves and cranes live.

What is the plot of the story, and what is the conflict that moves the plot forward? The Wolf has a bone stuck in his throat, and he needs another animal's help in order to remove this bone. The plot centers on how he gets another animal (the Crane) to help him: by promising a reward that isn't what the Crane expects!

STRATEGIES

To find the major components of a short story, simply go back to your "5 w's" and ask yourself the following questions:

- Who are the characters in the story, and who is the narrator telling the story?
- When and where is the story set?
- What happens in the story?
- Why and how does this happen? What conflict do the characters need to overcome?

For some short stories, you might not be able to answer all of these questions. For example, the story of the Wolf and the Crane did not have a clear setting. Make sure you only use the information in the story to answer these questions—don't use your own opinion or speculate too much. The SSAT will only ask you about information that can be answered on the basis of the story alone.

Be careful: don't confuse the story's narrator with its author! Every story has its **own point of view**, which is the perspective of the person telling the story. This may or may not be the same as the author's point of view, because the author can invent a completely made-up narrator! If you're not sure who might be the narrator of the story, focus on the words the narrator uses to show his or her point of view:

- If the narrator uses the word "I" to tell the story ("I talked to Sarah yesterday"), we call this a **first-person point of view**. The narrator is most likely a character in the story who is interacting with the other characters and taking part in the events.

- If the narrator uses the words "he" or "she" to tell the story ("She talked to Sarah yesterday"), we call this a **third-person point of view**. There are some exceptions, but the narrator is frequently not a character in the story. Instead, the narrator is outside of the story, telling about events that he or she did not take part in.

Finally, in addition to the main components of a story, you might be asked to analyze a major **theme** of a story. A story's theme can be described as its "main idea," or the message it conveys about life and behavior.

For example, the last sentence of the Wolf and Crane story summarizes a specific lesson to be learned: "Those who provide help only in the hope of a reward must not be surprised if, in their dealings with evil men, they meet with more jeers than thanks." What does this mean? You might interpret this as saying that people should not volunteer to do nice things only on the basis of a reward, because evil men won't appreciate their efforts.

Not every story will have a clear-cut lesson for the reader, so it will be up to you to decide if there is any theme you can take away from the story. Do the characters find success or disappointment, and why might this be? Do the characters end up with a greater understanding of themselves and others? How might the events in the story relate to other events you have experienced in real life? Relating a story to your own life is a great way to better understand the characters, events, and major themes in a story.

Exercise #3: Read the sample short story below, and then answer the questions that follow. Ask a trusted reader to check your work.

> The next time that Ginger and I were together in the paddock, she told me about her first place.
>
> "After my breaking in," she said, "I was bought by a dealer to match another horse. For some weeks he drove us together before selling us to a
>
> *Line 5* fashionable gentleman in London. I had been driven hard by the dealer, and I hated it worse than anything else. But now, my new owner drove us even harder because he thought we looked more stylish. We were often driven about in the Park and other fashionable places. It was dreadful."
>
> She continued, "I like to toss my head about, and hold it as high as any
>
> *10* horse. But know that if you tossed your head up high and had to hold it there for hours, your neck would ache until you did not. The worst was when we had to stand by the hour waiting for our mistress at some grand party or entertainment. If I stamped with impatience, the whip was laid on. It was enough to drive one mad."
>
> *15* "Did not your master take any thought for you?" I asked.
>
> "No," said she.

1. Who are the characters in this story?

2. Who is the narrator telling the story? Is the narrator one of the characters, or is the narrator someone outside of the story?

3. When and where is the story set?

4. What happens in the story?

5. Why and how does this happen? What conflict do the characters need to overcome?

6. Is there any lesson or theme from this story that you can relate to your own life?

POETRY

Poetry is a form of writing that expresses an idea through highly imaginative language, often in short lines rather than sentences and paragraphs. Nursery rhymes and song lyrics are both examples of very basic poetry. Poems on the SSAT tend to be more complex, and reading this type of poetry can be challenging if you haven't encountered it much before. Don't panic—this section will equip you will all of the tools you need to start understanding poetry!

MAJOR COMPONENTS

Instead of sentences and paragraphs, poems use different organizations of words in order to convey ideas in a more imaginative way. Here are the basic components of a poem:

- A **line** of a poem is a group of words that take up one line of text on the page. After each line, there is a break and the next line starts below. A line can express a thought, a part of a thought, or focus on one specific image. The lines of a poem can all be the same length, or they can have different lengths.

- A **stanza** is a group of lines in a poem, like a "paragraph" within a poem. Stanzas are set apart from each other by spaces. They are used to group together lines that are somehow related.

- The **meter** of a poem is the rhythm made by the pattern of stressed and unstressed syllables in the words in each of its lines. Not every poem has a meter, and the SSAT does not frequently ask about meter.

- The **rhyme** of a poem is the way that words at the ends of its lines sound similar. For example, "bat" and "pat" both rhyme, as do "show" and "glow," and "time" and "mime." Not every poem rhymes, however, and the SSAT does not frequently ask about rhyme.

Let's take a look at the major structural components of the following sample poem:

> Both gentlemen, and yeomen bold,
> Or whatever you are,
> To have a stately story told
> Attention now prepare:
>
> *Line 5* It is a tale of Robin Hood
> Which I to you will tell;
> Which, being rightly understood,
> I know will please you well.
>
> This Robin (so much talked on)
> *10* Was once a man of fame,
> Knighted earl of Huntington,
> Lord Robin Hood by name.

This poem has three stanzas, or three main groupings of lines. Each stanza has four lines of text. The poem has a regular meter: if you were to read it out loud, you could tap your foot to the rhythm of the words. The poem also has rhyme: in general, the first and third lines of each stanza rhyme, as do the second and fourth lines. For example, in the second stanza, "Hood" rhymes with "understood," and "tell" rhymes with "well."

The SSAT doesn't frequently ask about the technical elements of a poem's structure, but it is helpful to understand these ideas when you are first reading a poem so you can get a sense of its organization.

FIGURATIVE LANGUAGE

Within a poem, the poet often uses **figurative language** to add a heightened meaning. Figurative language uses a word's connotation, or the feelings and symbols associated with a word, rather than just its literal meaning. Let's now look at some of the most common types of figurative language.

Imagery uses descriptive words from the five senses to create a vivid image in the reader's mind. For example, the poet might describe the sun as "a fiery blaze of gold." This evokes a vivid image of the sun's color, brightness, and heat.

A **symbol** is a word that represents another concept or idea within a poem. For example, a poet might talk about the spring in order to symbolize rebirth or renewal. Here are some other very common symbols used in poetry:

SYMBOL	MEANING
sleep	death
dreams	fate, the future
light (sun, stars, moon)	good, hope, freedom
dark	evil, magic, the unknown
spring	youth, birth, life
winter	death, dying, old age
owl	wisdom
dove	peace
rose	love, beauty
crown	wealth, royalty
ring	love, commitment

A **simile** is a device that compares two things using the words "like" or "as." For example, a poet might say that a man's laugh is "like a thunderclap." From this comparison, we can conclude that the man's laugh is loud, booming, and startling.

A **metaphor** is also a device that compares to things, but does not use the words "like" or "as." Using the example above, the poet might say that the man's laugh "is a thunderclap." The poet is not saying that the man's laugh is literally caused by a thunderstorm, but that it resembles a thunderclap in its loudness and startling qualities.

Finally, **personification** is a technique that gives human characteristics to animals, objects, or ideas. For example, a poet might say that "winter jealously steals the world's warmth." This statement personifies the season of winter by describing it as a thief and giving it the human characteristic of jealousy.

Let's look at the use of figurative language in a sample poem:

Slowly, silently, now the moon
Walks the night in her silver shoon;
This way, and that, she peers, and sees
Silver fruit upon silver trees;
Line 5   One by one the casements catch
Her beams beneath the silvery thatch;
Couched in his kennel, like a log,
With paws of silver sleeps the dog;
From their shadowy cote the white breasts peep
10   Of doves in a silver-feathered sleep;
A harvest mouse goes scampering by,
With silver claws and a silver eye;
And moveless fish in the water gleam,
By silver reeds in a silver stream.

In this poem, the author uses imagery to paint a vivid picture of the world turned "silver" by moonlight. The fruit and the trees are silver, the dog's paws are silver, the doves' feathers are silver … even the mouse's eye is silver! This is a highly visual image. Can you find any images in the poem related to other senses, such as sound, taste, smell, or touch?

Can you find the one simile in this poem? It is located in line 7: "Couched in his kennel, like a log / With paws of silver sleeps the dog." What does it mean to say that the dog is "like a log"? This suggests that he is sleeping soundly.

The third major device in this poem is personification. In this case, the moon is being given human qualities: "she" is walking around, wearing silver "shoon" (shoes), and looking "this way, and that." We don't normally think of the moon as something that can walk, wear shoes, and look around, but this poem very playfully makes us imagine all of these characteristics!

STRATEGIES

When you first encounter a poem, it can be difficult to understand what is going on. Help yourself by re-writing the poem in straightforward language, stating each thought in your own words as best you can. As an example, let's break down the Robin Hood poem stanza by stanza, and re-write each thought as a single sentence:

	Both gentlemen, and yeomen bold,	*Gentlemen and bold people, or*
	Or whatever you are,	*whoever, pay attention because*
	To have a stately story told	*you're going to be told an*
	Attention now prepare:	*important story:*
Line 5	It is a tale of Robin Hood	*I will tell you a story about Robin*
	Which I to you will tell;	*Hood, which you should enjoy if you*
	Which, being rightly understood,	*understand it properly.*
	I know will please you well.	
10	This Robin (so much talked on)	*Robin, whom everyone talks about,*
	Was once a man of fame,	*was once a very famous man. He*
	Knighted earl of Huntington,	*was the Earl of Huntington and was*
	Lord Robin Hood by name.	*named Lord Robin Hood.*

As you try to re-write the poem in your own words, you might come across unusual or old-fashioned vocabulary words. For instance, "yeomen" is not a word we use very frequently these days; it used to mean someone who owned a small property or farm. Don't let these kinds of words throw you off! See what you can guess of their meaning by looking at the rest of the sentence. For example, "yeoman" and "gentlemen" are both in the same line, so we can guess that they are two different types of people.

Exercise #4: How would you re-write the poem about the moon in more straightforward language? Give this a try by rewriting the poem below as full sentences in your own words. Guess the meaning of any words you don't know, and then look up these words in a dictionary. Have a trusted reader check your work.

Slowly, silently, now the moon
Walks the night in her silver shoon;
This way, and that, she peers, and sees
Silver fruit upon silver trees;
Line 5   One by one the casements catch
Her beams beneath the silvery thatch;
Couched in his kennel, like a log,
With paws of silver sleeps the dog;
From their shadowy cote the white breasts peep
10   Of doves in a silver-feathered sleep;
A harvest mouse goes scampering by,
With silver claws and a silver eye;
And moveless fish in the water gleam,
By silver reeds in a silver stream.

Once you have a better understanding of the poem's basic meaning, look for any figurative language the author is using. Ask yourself:

- What **images** does the poet use? What kinds of sensations do these evoke?
- Does it seem like the author is using any **symbols**? If so, what might these represent?
- Does the author compare any two things using **simile** or **metaphor**? If so, what do these comparisons suggest?
- Does the author use **personification**? If so, what animal, object, or concept is being given human characteristics, and which characteristics?

The answers to all of these questions will help you understand the overall **theme** of the poem, or the main idea the poet is trying to convey. The theme of the Robin Hood poem is fairly straightforward: the poet is simply introducing a story about a famous person, and we might guess that the poem will continue to tell us why this person is famous. For the poem about the moon, the theme is a little more subtle: the poet is describing what the moon "sees" when she casts her moonlight over a sleeping house. While this poem doesn't have a straightforward message, it evokes very peaceful and calm feelings about the moonlit night.

Exercise #5: Read the following sample poem, and then answer the questions that follow. Ask a trusted reader to check your work.

If there were dreams to sell,
　　　What would you buy?
Some cost a passing bell;
　　　Some a light sigh,
Line 5　That shakes from Life's fresh crown
Only a rose-leaf down.
If there were dreams to sell,
Merry and sad to tell,
　　　And the crier rang the bell,
10　　　What would you buy?

A cottage lone and still,
　　　With bowers nigh,
Shadowy, my woes to still,
　　　Until I die.
15　Such pearl from Life's fresh crown
Fain would I shake me down.
Were dreams to have at will,
This best would heal my ill,
　　　This would I buy.

1. How many stanzas are in this poem? How many lines are in each stanza?

2. Next to each stanza in the poem, re-write each thought as a full sentence in your own words. Guess the meaning of any words you don't know, and then look up these words in a dictionary.

3. What images does the poet use? What kind of sensations do these evoke?

4. Below are some of the symbols in this poem. What might each of these represent?

    "a light sigh" (line 4):

    "Life's fresh crown" (line 5 and 15):

    "a cottage lone and still" (line 12):

    a "pearl" (line 15):

5. How would you summarize the main idea or theme of this poem?

TYPES OF QUESTIONS

Now that you have learned about the types of passages that will appear on the SSAT, let's look at the types of questions that you will be asked about each passage. Questions on the Reading section fall into four main categories:

1. Main Idea
2. Specific Detail
3. Genre or Tone
4. Inference

Identifying the type of question will help you pick the best strategy to use. Continue reading to learn specific strategies for each question type.

MAIN IDEA QUESTIONS

Main Idea questions ask about the author's main topic, point, theme, or thesis. Some examples of Main Idea questions include:

- What is the main idea, main point, or central idea of this passage?
- What is this passage primarily about?
- What is the purpose of this passage?
- What is a likely title for this passage?

STRATEGIES

The best preparation for a Main Idea question is to be a **critical reader**! Review the reading strategies outlined in the Critical Reading section. Remember to summarize in your own words what the author is saying in each paragraph, and take note of any key words or main topics. Then ask yourself, "What are the author's topics, and what is the author saying about these topics?" Look for the answer option that matches your answer to this question.

Remember that the main idea of a passage is the common thread that connects the entire passage, tying all of the paragraphs together. If you have trouble finding the main idea, think about how all of the paragraphs might work together to describe a broader topic. Pay close attention to the first and last sentences of the passage, because they frequently give you information about its main idea.

PROCESS OF ELIMINATION

If you are stuck, use the Process of Elimination to narrow down your answer options by crossing out answers that are wrong. First, eliminate any answer choices that are **unrelated**. If you see an answer option that has little to do with the concepts in the passage, cross it out and move on!

Then, eliminate answer options that are **too broad** or **too specific**. If the passage is describing what the types of food that turtles eat, the main topic is not simply "turtles" – this is too broad! The passage isn't talking about every aspect of turtles, just about their diet. By contrast, if the passage is describing the history of cars, the main topic is not "Henry Ford" – this is too specific! Henry Ford may be an important person in the passage, but he doesn't summarize the passage as a whole.

EXAMPLE

As an example, let's look at the duck-billed platypus passage again. Now we'll go on to answer a Main Idea question about this passage:

The duck-billed platypus is a small animal, native to Australia, with many unusual characteristics. It is a very odd-looking animal; in fact, when Europeans first heard about the platypus, many thought such an odd-looking animal must be a fraud. Its head and feet are like a duck's, its body is like a

Line 5 weasel's, and its tail is like a beaver's. Its webbed feet help it swim, its odd-shaped tail helps it to store fat, and its duck-like beak helps it find food in rivers.

A platypus is a mammal, but is remarkably unlike almost every other mammal. The platypus lays eggs; it doesn't give birth like other mammals.

10 Also, although all mammals give their young milk, the platypus has an unusual way of doing this: it actually sweats milk all over its body. But despite these differences, the platypus has fur, like other mammals.

Finally, the platypus has some amazing abilities. The platypus can see electricity: it senses electricity coming from other animals in the water and

15 uses this ability to catch food and avoid predators. The platypus also has venomous spurs on its feet that allow it to defend itself. An animal that gets too close to the platypus's feet will be stung with a poison.

What is the main topic of this passage?

(A) wildlife of Australia

(B) mammals

(C) the unusual qualities of the platypus

(D) why the platypus lays eggs

(E) odd-looking animals

This question is asking us to find the central concept that is the focus of the entire passage. We can eliminate answer choices (A) and (B), because they are too general. The platypus is both a mammal and lives in Australia, but the passage does not mention any other mammals or wildlife of Australia. We can eliminate (E) for the same reason. Answer choice (D) can be eliminated because the passage never mentions why the platypus lays eggs, and egg-laying is just one of the behaviors of the platypus discussed in this passage. Answer (C) is the best choice because the entire passage is about how the platypus is unusual.

SPECIFIC DETAIL QUESTIONS

Specific Detail questions ask you to summarize or interpret specific information mentioned in the passage. Some examples of Specific Detail questions include:

- What does the author mean by the phrase "____" in lines 4-6?
- The word "____" as it is used in line 10 most likely means ...
- Which of the following questions is/are answered in the passage?
- Which of the following does NOT appear as evidence in the passage?
- The author gives all of the following reasons EXCEPT ...

STRATEGIES

All of the information you need to answer a Specific Detail question can be found in the passage. Always **go back to the passage** to see where you might find the information you need. If a specific line number is given in the question, re-read that line as well as the lines above and below it. If there is no line number given, look at the main words in the question and scan for these words or their synonyms in the passage.

Sometimes a question won't give you a line number where you can find the answer. In this case, first underline the main points in the question. Then, quickly **skim** the passage to find this information. "Skimming" means only looking over the key words and phrases in the passage, without reading all of the details again. Review pages 128-131 in this book to practice finding key words in a passage. Instead of reading each sentence in full, look only at the most important words: words that answer the 5 w's or provide important transitions and connections between ideas. Pay close attention to special terms and proper nouns, and ignore small connecting words like "the" and "of." Once you have found the information the question is asking about, stop and circle it.

After you have located the information you need, pick the answer choice that best matches what is written in the passage. Be careful: don't rely on your memory, opinion, or background knowledge to answer these questions! Only base your answer off of what the author says in the passage. Circle or star the words or phrases in the passage that support the answer choice you think is correct.

SPECIAL TYPES OF QUESTIONS

Pay close attention to the words *NOT*, *LEAST*, and *EXCEPT* in the questions. When you see one of these words, circle it so you are sure you are answering the question correctly. For example, take a look at the following question:

> Which of the following do NOT appear as evidence in the passage?

This question asks you to sort through the answer options and find the only option that doesn't occur in the passage. These types of questions will often require you to look up multiple pieces of information, so they will take a long time to answer. You may want to save them for the end if you are running short on time.

Roman numeral questions (I, II, and III) also ask you to check multiple pieces of information in the passage.

For example, take a look at this question from the duck-billed platypus passage:

> Which of the following statements are true, according to the passage?
>
> I. The duck-billed platypus is originally from Australia.
> II. The duck-billed platypus is very rare.
> III. The duck-billed platypus can live in water.
>
>
> (A) I only
> (B) II only
> (C) I and II only
> (D) I and III only
> (E) I, II, and III

In this question, you first need to go through the passage and check to see whether each of the Roman numeral statements is true. Circle the statements that are true, and cross out the statements that are not true. Then, pick the answer (A) through (E) that matches the correct combination of statements. For example, the duck-billed platypus passage only tells us that the platypus is from Australia and can live in water. The passage doesn't say whether or not the platypus is rare, so you'd pick answer choice (D) I and III only. Because Roman numeral questions are also time-consuming, you may also want to save them for the end if you're running short on time.

Finally, **vocabulary in context** questions ask you to pick the correct definition of a word in the context of the passage. These questions are tricky—these words often have multiple possible definitions! For example, look at the following question from the duck-billed Platypus passage:

> As it is used in line 6, the word "store" most likely means...

There are many different meanings of the word 'store.' It can refer to a shop or a supply of something that might be needed later, or it can refer to the action of keeping something for later. To make sure you have picked the author's definition, plug the answer choices back into the original sentence and re-read each of them in context to make sure they make sense.

PROCESS OF ELIMINATION

If you are stuck, use the Process of Elimination to narrow down your answer options by crossing out answers that are wrong. First, cross out answers that refer to another **section of the passage**. If the question is asking about one paragraph or a specific line, look for the answer in only that section of the passage, reading a few lines above and a few lines below. Don't base your answer on information that you find somewhere else.

Then, cross out answers that are **not stated specifically in the passage**. The SSAT might tempt you to rely on your own knowledge or opinion of the topic—but don't make this mistake! In order to get the correct answer, you should only consider what the author says in the passage. Double-check that your answer choice is stated specifically in the passage.

EXAMPLE

As an example, let's look at the duck-billed platypus passage again. This time we'll go on to answer a Specific Detail question about this passage:

The duck-billed platypus is a small animal, native to Australia, with many unusual characteristics. It is a very odd-looking animal; in fact, when Europeans first heard about the platypus, many thought such an odd-looking animal must be a fraud. Its head and feet are like a duck's, its body is like a
Line 5 weasel's, and its tail is like a beaver's. Its webbed feet help it swim, its odd-shaped tail helps it to store fat, and its duck-like beak helps it find food in rivers.

A platypus is a mammal, but is remarkably unlike almost every other mammal. The platypus lays eggs; it doesn't give birth like other mammals.
10 Also, although all mammals give their young milk, the platypus has an unusual way of doing this: it actually sweats milk all over its body. But despite these differences, the platypus has fur, like other mammals.

Finally, the platypus has some amazing abilities. The platypus can see electricity: it senses electricity coming from other animals in the water and
15 uses this ability to catch food and avoid predators. The platypus also has venomous spurs on its feet that allow it to defend itself. An animal that gets too close to the platypus's feet will be stung with a poison.

Which of the following is NOT mentioned in the passage as an unusual feature of the platypus?

(A) its beak

(B) its tail

(C) its feet

(D) its fur

(E) its milk

Did you notice the word NOT in the question? This question is asking us to find the one feature that the author does not say is unusual about the platypus. We need to go through each of the answer options and find where they are mentioned in the passage. We can then eliminate the features that the author says are unusual.

In the first paragraph, the author tells us that duck-like beak of the platypus is quite strange, so we can eliminate answer choice (A). Its tail, too, is singled out, so we can eliminate (B). Its feet are both webbed and have poison in them, so we can be very certain of eliminating (C). Although other mammals produce milk, it's strange that the platypus sweats milk, so we can eliminate (E). We are left with answer choice (D). Although the passage talks about the fur of the platypus, it also mentions that other mammals have fur, so we can safely say that its fur is NOT unusual.

GENRE AND TONE QUESTIONS

Genre and Tone questions ask you to analyze how the author is writing. The author's genre is the type of passage—is this an informative passage, a persuasive passage, a short story, or a poem? The author's tone is his or her attitude toward the topic— is the author presenting the facts in a neutral manner, or getting emotionally involved? Some examples of Genre and Tone questions include:

- *This passage would most likely be found in …*
- *What type of passage is this?*
- *The author's tone could best be described as …*

STRATEGIES

Review the section on Passage Types. As you are reading, ask yourself what **type of passage** you are reading and where this passage would most likely be found. Would the passage most likely occur in a history or science textbook? In a diary? In a newspaper? As part of a short story or poem? These questions will help you identify the genre of the passage.

Often, the author's tone will match the genre of the passage. An informative passage, like you might find in a history or science textbook, will most likely be presenting facts. We would describe this tone as neutral, objective, or analytical. A persuasive passage, such as a diary entry or letter to the editor, might be more emotionally involved. The author's attitude toward the subject might be positive or negative.

If you are having trouble finding the tone of the passage, look for any **positive or negative words** that might indicate the author's opinion about the topic. In a short story or poem, look for images and other figurative language. These may give you information about the mood the author is trying to create.

Once you have identified the tone of the passage, you'll need to match it to an answer choice on the SSAT. The SSAT likes to use very challenging vocabulary words to define tone! Prepare yourself by learning all of the words in following chart. If these are unfamiliar, look them up and add them to your vocabulary flashcards or journal.

TONE WORDS			
Positive	**Negative**	**Humorous**	**Neutral**
admiring	bitter	amused	ambivalent
appreciative	critical	comical	analytical
assertive	condescending	flippant	apathetic
authoritative	concerned	ironic	detached
celebratory	contemptuous	mocking	disinterested
enthusiastic	cynical	sarcastic	indifferent
empathetic	disparaging	satiric	informative
exuberant	dubious		matter-of-fact
jubilant	harsh		objective
impassioned	hostile		unbiased
lighthearted	indignant		unconcerned
passionate	outraged		unemotional
reverent	skeptical		
	somber		

EXAMPLE

As an example, let's look at the duck-billed platypus passage again. This time we'll go on to answer a Tone question about this passage:

The duck-billed platypus is a small animal, native to Australia, with many unusual characteristics. It is a very odd-looking animal; in fact, when Europeans first heard about the platypus, many thought such an odd-looking animal must be a fraud. Its head and feet are like a duck's, its body is like a

Line 5 weasel's, and its tail is like a beaver's. Its webbed feet help it swim, its odd-shaped tail helps it to store fat, and its duck-like beak helps it find food in rivers.

A platypus is a mammal, but is remarkably unlike almost every other mammal. The platypus lays eggs; it doesn't give birth like other mammals.

10 Also, although all mammals give their young milk, the platypus has an unusual way of doing this: it actually sweats milk all over its body. But despite these differences, the platypus has fur, like other mammals.

Finally, the platypus has some amazing abilities. The platypus can see electricity: it senses electricity coming from other animals in the water and

15 uses this ability to catch food and avoid predators. The platypus also has venomous spurs on its feet that allow it to defend itself. An animal that gets too close to the platypus's feet will be stung with a poison.

The author's tone in this passage could best be described as

(A) informative

(B) argumentative

(C) humorous

(D) mournful

(E) ecstatic

We could approach this question in several ways. We could re-read the passage with each of the tones in mind, and then eliminate the answers which don't work. However, we could also look at the passage and realize that its main purpose is just to give us information about the platypus. It is not trying to convince us of anything, so we can eliminate answer choice (B). The passage is not humorous, even though there are interesting parts, so we can eliminate (C). The passage is also not mournful or ecstatic, so we can eliminate (D) and (E). We are left with (A), which works well, as the passage is just giving us information.

INFERENCE QUESTIONS

Inference questions ask you to make a logical guess or assumption based on the information in the passage. You may need to interpret the meaning of a phrase or image, or "read between the lines" to discover what the author implies but does not state directly. You may need to make a logical prediction about what would come next in the passage. Some examples of Inference questions include:

- The author would most likely agree with which following statement?
- The image in line ___ of the passage most likely represents ...
- It can be inferred from the passage that ...
- It is suggested in the passage that ...
- What would the author most likely discuss next?

STRATEGIES

If the question asks you to interpret a certain image or phrase, go back to that section of the passage and **re-read it carefully**. Think about why the author would include that image or phrase in the passage. What is the **author's purpose** in including this information? Is the author trying to evoke a positive, negative, humorous, or sarcastic tone? Pick an answer choice that best matches the author's primary purpose in the passage.

Keep in mind that your guess or inference should always logically expand the author's argument. Remember the author's main point in the passage and look for an answer choice that is connected to this main point. Don't be swayed by your own opinion or prior knowledge of the topic, and make sure you can back up any guess with information in the passage.

If the question is asking you to guess **what might happen next** in the passage, think about the author's purpose in the passage and its main point. Then, think about what other information could be included in the passage to continue expanding upon this main point. Pick the answer option that best connects with the main point, without going off track or starting a new topic.

Pay particular attention to images and metaphors in poetry. These often have many levels of meaning beyond the literal surface reading. For instance, a young plant may represent growth or new life, whereas a dead plant or falling leaves may represent death or old age. Review the Passage Types section for more examples of common imagery in poetry.

PROCESS OF ELIMINATION

If you are stuck, use the Process of Elimination to narrow down your answer options by crossing out answers that are wrong. First, eliminate any answers that are **unrelated** to the main idea of the passage. If you see an answer choice that is irrelevant or off-topic, cross it out and move on!

Then, eliminate any answers that aren't supported by the **author's own words** in the passage. If you can't find some words, phrases, or sentences in the passage to support an answer choice, cross it out! Don't rely on interpretations based on your own prior knowledge or personal opinion of the passage. Remember that all answers should be based on what the author thinks and says.

EXAMPLE

Let's look at the duck-billed platypus passage one more time. This time we'll go on to answer two Inference questions about this passage:

> The duck-billed platypus is a small animal, native to Australia, with many unusual characteristics. It is a very odd-looking animal; in fact, when Europeans first heard about the platypus, many thought such an odd-looking animal must be a fraud. Its head and feet are like a duck's, its body is like a
>
> Line 5 weasel's, and its tail is like a beaver's. Its webbed feet help it swim, its odd-shaped tail helps it to store fat, and its duck-like beak helps it find food in rivers.
>
> A platypus is a mammal, but is remarkably unlike almost every other mammal. The platypus lays eggs; it doesn't give birth like other mammals.
>
> 10 Also, although all mammals give their young milk, the platypus has an unusual way of doing this: it actually sweats milk all over its body. But despite these differences, the platypus has fur, like other mammals.
>
> Finally, the platypus has some amazing abilities. The platypus can see electricity: it senses electricity coming from other animals in the water and
>
> 15 uses this ability to catch food and avoid predators. The platypus also has venomous spurs on its feet that allow it to defend itself. An animal that gets too close to the platypus's feet will be stung with a poison.

In lines 2-3, the Europeans most likely thought the platypus was a fraud for which of the following reasons?

(A) The people who brought it back were not trustworthy.

(B) The platypus was so strange, they could not believe it was real.

(C) They had been tricked before.

(D) They did not trust Australians.

(E) Europeans did not like new ideas.

This question is asking us to guess an explanation for a statement that isn't specifically explained in the passage. To answer this question well, we should read the rest of the paragraph. The paragraph is about how strange the appearance of the platypus was. This should make us suspicious that (B) is the right answer right away. Indeed, there is no evidence at all for any of the other answers, so (B) is the best answer.

According to the passage, it would be easier for the platypus to be considered a mammal if

(A) it didn't lay eggs

(B) it didn't swim in the water

(C) it didn't have fur

(D) it lived outside Australia

(E) it ate plants

The wording makes this is a bit of a tricky question, so we have to be careful. First, we need to spot what is distinctive about the platypus that makes it unusual as a mammal. In lines 7-11, the passage mentions two distinctive traits that are unusual about the platypus in this regard: its method of giving its young milk, and the fact that it lays eggs. In order to decide what would make the platypus less unusual as a mammal, we should look for an answer that contradicts or downplays one of these unusual traits.

We can safely eliminate (D) and (E) quickly, as the passage mentions nothing about where mammals live or what they can eat. We may be tempted to say (B) because most mammals live on land, but the passage doesn't say anything about this. Remember that it's very important to base our answer only on what is stated in the passage. In fact, some mammals, like whales and dolphins, live their whole lives in water. Answer choice (C) may be another tempting answer, as all mammals have fur or hair. But in this case, taking the platypus's fur away would only make it less likely to be classified as a mammal, not more. Answer choice (A) is the correct answer, as the platypus's egg-laying was one factor that made it difficult to be classified as a mammal.

READING PRACTICE QUESTIONS

In this section, you will find 161 questions to prepare you for the types of reading passages you might find on the SSAT. There are 5 sets of questions, grouped by difficulty. Pay attention to the difficulty of each set to determine which questions are appropriate for the Middle and Upper Levels.

Read each passage carefully and then answer the questions about it. For each question, decide on the basis of the passage which of the choices best answers the question.

BASIC PASSAGES

Use these questions to practice the most basic difficulty level you might see in both the Middle and Upper Level Reading sections. The Middle Level exam will include more basic passages than the Upper Level exam.

	Long ago in Japan lived a brave warrior known to all as Tawara Toda, or "My Lord Bag-of-Rice." His real name was Fujiwara Hidesato, and this is the story of why he changed his name.
	One day Fujiwara was in search of adventures when he came to the
Line 5	bridge of Seta-no-Karashi. No sooner had he set foot on the bridge than he saw lying right across his path a huge serpent-dragon. Its body was so big that it looked like the trunk of a large pine tree and it took up the whole width of the bridge. One of its huge claws rested on the railing of one side of the bridge, while its tail lay right against the other. The monster seemed to be asleep, and
10	as it breathed, fire and smoke came out of its nostrils.
	At first Fujiwara could not help feeling alarmed at the sight of this horrible reptile lying in his path, for he must either turn back or walk right over its body. He was a brave man, however, and putting aside all fear went forward dauntlessly. Crunch, crunch! he climbed over the dragon's body and
15	without even one glance backward he went on his way.

1. A good title for this passage would be

   (A) The Bridge of Seta-no-Karashi
   (B) Horrible Reptiles
   (C) Fujiwara and the Giant Dragon
   (D) Japanese Magic Tales
   (E) Living Dangerously in Japan

2. The dragon could be described as

   (A) angry and violent
   (B) small but dangerous
   (C) evil and hideous
   (D) powerful but kind
   (E) large and frightening

3. Based on the context, "dauntlessly" (line 14) probably means

   (A) without hope
   (B) without fear
   (C) without looking
   (D) without courage
   (E) without practicing

4. When Fujiwara encountered the dragon, its tail was

   (A) lying against the railing
   (B) scaly and brown
   (C) dangling over the side of the bridge
   (D) as big as the entire bridge
   (E) 50 feet long

5. What might the passage discuss next?

   (A) what Fujiwara did before getting to the bridge
   (B) the meeting between a different Japanese hero and a different dragon
   (C) an adventure Fujiwara had on another occasion
   (D) the person Fujiwara crossed the bridge to look for
   (E) how meeting the dragon led Fujiwara to change his name

Every time you turn on a light, you have Thomas Alva Edison to thank. Born in 1847, Thomas Edison was an American inventor and businessman.

In 1866, at the age of 19, Edison moved to Kentucky, where he worked the shift at the Associated Press news wire. Edison requested the night shift,
Line 5 which allowed him plenty of time to spend on his two favorite pastimes—reading and experimenting.

Edison was constantly experimenting. He developed many devices that greatly influenced life around the world, including the phonograph, the motion picture camera, and a long-lasting, practical light bulb. A local newspaper
10 reporter nicknamed him "The Wizard of Menlo Park" because he was one of the most prolific inventors in history. In fact, he holds over 1,093 United States patents in his name, as well as many patents in the United Kingdom, France, and Germany. Edison is credited with numerous inventions that contributed to mass communication, such as a stock ticker, a mechanical vote recorder, a
15 battery for an electric car, electrical power, recorded music, and motion pictures.

6. What is the main idea of this passage?

(A) Thomas Edison saved the world.
(B) Thomas Edison was the world's most important scientist.
(C) Thomas Edison was a highly influential inventor.
(D) Thomas Edison loved to read.
(E) Thomas Edison was a child prodigy.

7. Which of the following is true, according to the passage?

(A) All of Edison's patents are held in the United States.
(B) The electric car is one of Edison's inventions.
(C) Edison was born in Kentucky.
(D) Edison invented the light bulb when he was 19 years old.
(E) Edison's inventions improved communication.

8. Edison requested the night shift at the Associated Press news wire because

(A) he was too tired to work during the day
(B) he wanted to work on his reading and experiments during the day
(C) he wanted to work under the cover of darkness
(D) he wanted to work alone
(E) he wanted to publicize his experiments through the Associate Press

9. According to line 10, Edison was most likely called "The Wizard of Menlo Park" because

(A) he used magic
(B) he taught at an academy in Menlo Park
(C) he convinced the residents of Menlo Park that he had supernatural powers
(D) he produced an impressive number of inventions in Menlo Park
(E) he was a skilled newspaper writer

Bacteria are very small organisms made up of one cell. They are among the simplest single-celled organisms on Earth. There are more individual bacteria than any other sort of organism on the planet. Most bacteria live in the ground or in water, but many live inside or on the skin of other organisms, including humans. There are about ten times as many bacterial cells as human cells in each of our bodies. Some bacteria can cause diseases, but others help us in everyday activities like digesting food. Some even work for us in factories, producing cheese and yogurt.

Line 5

Pathogenic bacteria, the harmful kind, enter the human body from the air, water or food. Once inside, these bacteria attach themselves to or invade specific cells in our respiratory system, digestive tract or any open wound. There they begin to reproduce and spread while using the human body as a source of their own nutrients and energy.

10

10. This passage would likely be found in
   (A) a book about different types of organisms
   (B) a scientific treaty about treating and curing diseases
   (C) a newspaper article
   (D) a manual on food production
   (E) the diary of a biologist

11. What would be the best title for this passage?
   (A) How Germs Spread
   (B) How Cheese and Yogurt are Made
   (C) Characteristics of Bacteria
   (D) Single-Celled Organisms
   (E) Killer Bacteria: How to Protect Ourselves

12. According to the passage, all of the following statements are true EXCEPT
   (A) In the human body, bacterial cells vastly outnumber human cells.
   (B) Bacteria are the most numerous organisms on the planet.
   (C) Bacteria can live on land, water, or other organisms.
   (D) Harmful bacteria only attack the respiratory system.
   (E) Humans use bacteria to help digest food.

13. In line 9, the term "pathogenic" most likely refers to

    (A) single-celled bacteria
    (B) bacteria that cause disease
    (C) digestive bacteria
    (D) bacteria that live in the air, water, or food
    (E) bacteria that reproduce

14. With which of the following statements would the author most likely agree?

    (A) Bacteria do more harm than good.
    (B) The human body would function better without bacteria.
    (C) Bacteria are the only life forms made up of one cell.
    (D) Bacteria are highly complex organisms.
    (E) There are many different types of bacteria.

A certain king had a beautiful garden, and in the garden stood a tree which bore golden apples. These apples were always counted each morning due to their enormous value. About the time when they began to grow ripe, it was found that one of them was gone. The king became very angry at this, and
Line 5   ordered the gardener to keep watch all night under the tree.

The gardener set his eldest son to watch, but he fell asleep at midnight. In the morning, another apple was gone. Then the second son was ordered to watch, but he, too, fell asleep at midnight. Another apple was gone in the morning. The third son offered to keep watch, but the gardener refused. He
10   was afraid that some harm might come to him. However, as apples kept disappearing, the gardener at last agreed to let his youngest son keep watch for the night.

The boy, eager to solve the mystery, remained alert. As the clock struck twelve, he heard a rustling noise in the air, and a golden bird landed on the
15   tree. While the bird snapped at one of the apples with its beak, the gardener's son jumped up and shot an arrow at it. But the arrow did no harm, and the bird flew away with one less golden feather.

15. In line 2, the word "bore" most likely means

(A) dull
(B) tiresome
(C) produced
(D) bare
(E) contained

16. According to the passage, why did the gardener originally refuse to let his third son keep watch over the garden?

(A) The gardener did not like his third son as much as his first and second sons.
(B) The gardener loved his third son more than his first and second sons.
(C) The gardener had other tasks for his third son to do.
(D) The gardener was afraid that his third son might get hurt.
(E) The gardener did not trust his third son.

17. The gardener's third son could be described as

    (A) young and foolish
    (B) curious and resourceful
    (C) cautious and reserved
    (D) tall and athletic
    (E) stubborn and rude

18. According to the passage, when did the apples start disappearing?

    (A) when the king's first son was born
    (B) when a second tree was planted
    (C) when the king's castle was built
    (D) when the gardener was hired
    (E) when the apples became ripe

19. It is implied that the golden bird

    (A) was the gardener's pet
    (B) was responsible for all of the apples that had gone missing
    (C) was wounded by the boy's arrow
    (D) was exceptionally valuable to the king
    (E) was well-known as a thief around the kingdom

An object one hundredth of an inch in diameter is about the smallest thing that can be easily seen by the unassisted eye. Take a piece of card and punch a little hole through it with the point of a small needle, hold it towards a lamp or a window, and you will see the light through it.

Line 5
This hole will be about 1/100 of an inch, and you will find that you can see it best when you hold it at a certain distance from your eye; and this distance will not be far from ten inches, unless you are near-sighted. Now bring it towards your eye and you will find it becomes blurred and indistinct. You will see by this experiment that you cannot see things distinctly when you

10
hold them too close to your eye, or in other words, that you cannot bring your eye nearer to an object than eight or ten inches and see it well at the same time.

You could see things much smaller than one hundredth of an inch if you could get your eye close enough to them without them appearing blurry. How

15
can that be done? With a microscope.

20. The main purpose of this passage is

(A) to describe the anatomy and function of the human eye

(B) to instruct the reader how to perform a complex experiment

(C) to introduce the problem that the microscope helps to solve

(D) to tell how the microscope was invented

(E) to lament the limitations of sight

21. According to the passage, things that are 1/100 of an inch are

(A) easy to see from about four inches away

(B) the smallest things we can see without a microscope

(C) impossible to see without a microscope

(D) hard to see from more than eight inches away

(E) only hard to see if you are near-sighted

22. According to the passage, what happens when you bring something too close to your eye?

(A) You risk injuring yourself.

(B) You blink rapidly.

(C) You can see it much better.

(D) You become near-sighted.

(E) You can't see it clearly.

23. The final paragraph suggests that the microscope is

(A) a key to new discoveries

(B) an essential tool of daily life

(C) an imaginary machine

(D) not a useful object

(E) the most important invention of the modern era

24. The tone of the passage is

    (A) bossy

    (B) informative

    (C) critical

    (D) fanciful

    (E) argumentative

The 1910 Cuba hurricane was said to be one of the worst tropical cyclones that has ever hit Cuba. The storm formed in the southern Caribbean Sea on October 9, 1910. It grew stronger as it moved northwest. It then made landfall on the western end of Cuba. The storm made a loop over open water,

Line 5 and then began moving towards the United States. After crossing Florida, the storm moved near the rest of the southeastern United States and passed out to sea.

Because of the storm's loop, some reports said it was actually two hurricanes. In Cuba, the storm was one of the worst disasters in the island's

10 history. Strong winds and much rain caused flooding in streets, ruined crops (mostly tobacco), and damaged farms. Thousands of peasants, or workers, lost their homes. In Florida, the storm also caused damage and caused flooding in some areas. It is not known exactly how much damage the storm caused. However, losses in Havana, Cuba's capital city, were over $1 million. At least

15 100 people died in Cuba alone.

25. The primary purpose of the passage is

(A) to describe the climate of the Caribbean Sea

(B) to compare and contrast the economies of Cuba and Florida

(C) to give a complete history of hurricanes in the south-eastern United States

(D) to describe one tropical storm's effects on a particular region

(E) to describe how a hurricane is formed

26. All of the following questions can be answered by the passage EXCEPT

(A) What was the path of the hurricane?

(B) What was the total cost of damage from the hurricane?

(C) How many people died in Cuba as a result of the hurricane?

(D) Where did the hurricane first make landfall?

(E) What is Cuba's capital?

27. The author's tone in this passage can best be described as

(A) outraged

(B) informative

(C) pessimistic

(D) enthusiastic

(E) humorous

Ivy Global

28. Which of the following statements is true, according to the passage?

(A) The hurricane travelled primarily in a northeastern direction.

(B) The only crop damaged by the hurricane was tobacco.

(C) The hurricane's path led some to believe that there were actually two hurricanes.

(D) The hurricane caused more damage in Florida than in Cuba.

(E) The 1910 Cuba hurricane was the worst tropical storm in the history of the southeastern United States.

29. With which of the following statements would the author most likely agree?

(A) There will never be a hurricane as deadly as the 1910 Cuba hurricane.

(B) Governments should do more to protect their citizens from the effects of hurricanes.

(C) The Caribbean Sea has one of the most volatile climates in the world.

(D) Cuban farmers should diversify their crops.

(E) Hurricanes can be extremely destructive natural disasters.

MEDIUM PASSAGES

Use these questions to practice the medium difficulty level you might see in both the Middle and Upper Level reading sections. Passages like these will make up a majority of the Middle Level section, and a smaller portion of the Upper Level section.

> "Who-oo-ee!" The gleeful shout came from the lips of a little girl who stood, with her hands cupped about her lips, on the edge of a streamlet which divided the village of Domremy into two parts. She was a slight little maiden, of some twelve years, and as she gave the call she danced about in the warm
>
> Line 5 sunshine as though unable to keep still from the mere joy of being. Her hair was very dark and very abundant. Her eyes were wonderful for their blueness and the steadfastness of their gaze. Her face, though pretty, was remarkable not so much for its beauty as for the happiness of its expression. She stood still listening for a moment after sending forth her call, and then, as the morning
>
> 10 quiet remained unbroken, she sent forth the cry again in a clear, sweet voice that penetrated into the farthest reaches of the village:
>
> "Who-oo-ee!"
>
> This time the shout was caught up instantly, and answered by many voices. The village wakened suddenly into life, as there poured forth from the
>
> 15 cottages a goodly number of boys and girls who came running toward the little maid eagerly.

1. The mood of the girl in this passage could be described as

   (A) irritable
   (B) complacent
   (C) frightened
   (D) cheerful
   (E) imaginative

2. The girl is described as having all of the following EXCEPT:

   (A) a happy expression
   (B) lots of dark hair
   (C) a strong, pretty voice
   (D) very blue eyes
   (E) delicate, white hands

3. According to the passage, the girl most likely "danced about" (line 4) because

   (A) she was trying to keep warm in the chilly morning air
   (B) she was glad to be alive
   (C) she was singing a dancing tune
   (D) she was anxious to leave
   (E) she was performing a local ritual

4. It can be inferred from the passage
    that the girl was trying to

    (A) annoy the villagers

    (B) summon the village children

    (C) warn the villagers of an attack

    (D) show off her beautiful singing
        voice

    (E) wake up one specific person

The optical microscope, sometimes called the "light microscope," uses visible light and a system of lenses to magnify images of things that are too small to be seen with the naked eye. Optical microscopes are the oldest type of microscope and were designed in close to their present form in the 17th century. Basic optical microscopes can be very simple, although there are many complex designs which aim to improve the clarity and detail of the image produced.

Another optical invention of the 17th century was the telescope. Like the microscope, the telescope made it possible to study things that were previously hard or impossible to see—but in this case, because they were too far away, not because of their size. 17th century astronomers relied on telescopes to help them develop new theories about the movements of the distant stars and planets.

The first microscopes and telescopes used visible light to make very small or very distant things visible, but in the 20th century, telescopes were developed that use other forms of light, like infrared light and x-rays. Meanwhile, scientists in the 1930s developed an electron microscope that uses electrons instead of visible light to generate magnified images.

5. Which of the following best expresses the main idea of the passage?

(A) The microscope is a powerful tool that significantly advanced the field of medicine.

(B) The telescope was invented in the 17th century by Johannes Kepler.

(C) The 20th century saw many developments in optical technology.

(D) The microscope and the telescope were both invented in the 17th century, and were both developed further in the 20th century.

(E) The original forms of microscopes and telescopes were better than the ones we use today.

6. According to the passage, all of the following is true of optical microscopes EXCEPT

(A) they use visible light to produce magnified images

(B) they were invented in the 17th century

(C) they use electrons instead of visible light

(D) they can be fairly simple or more complex in design

(E) they haven't changed very much since they were invented

7. The telescope is similar to the microscope in that it

   (A) now uses infrared light
   (B) helped people see what they previously could not
   (C) was invented in the 1930s
   (D) helped scientists develop theories about the stars
   (E) did not use optical light

8. The passage suggests that "distant stars and planets" (line 13)

   (A) are hard to study without the use of a telescope
   (B) are very small as well as very distant
   (C) were first discovered by astronomers in the 1800s
   (D) orbit the sun
   (E) are easy to see with a microscope

9. Which of the following would most likely come next in this passage?

   (A) a discussion of the invention of television in the 20th century
   (B) an argument that the microscope is more valuable to society than the telescope
   (C) a biography of the inventor who developed the electron microscope
   (D) an explanation of which 16th century theories were overturned by the telescope
   (E) more detail about the development of 20th century microscopes and telescopes

Hanami ("flower viewing") is the Japanese traditional custom of enjoying the beauty of flowers, especially cherry blossoms, or sakura. The practice of Hanami is more than a thousand years old, and is still very popular in Japan today. It takes place in the spring. The blossoms only last for a week or two, usually from March to April, and they are followed by the media and waited for by most of the Japanese people. Full bloom usually comes about one week after the opening of the first blossoms. Another week later, the blooming peak is over and the blossoms are falling from the trees.

Line 5

The practice of Hanami is many centuries old. It is said to have started during the Nara Period (710-784) when the Chinese Tang Dynasty influenced Japan in many ways, one of which was the custom of enjoying flowers. The sakura were considered sacred by the Japanese, and they were so important that they still are a cultural symbol of Japan. People believed that gods inhabited the trees, and the Hanami party was used to divine that year's harvest and to announce the season of planting rice. The Japanese people today continue the tradition of Hanami, gathering in great numbers wherever the flowering trees are found. Thousands of people fill the parks to hold feasts under the flowering trees, and sometimes these parties go on until late at night.

10

15

10. Which of the following best expresses the central idea of the passage?

(A) The sakura, or cherry blossom, is a sacred Japanese flower.

(B) Hanami is an ancient Japanese tradition that is still popular today.

(C) Hanami takes place in March and April, when the sakura blossoms appear.

(D) Traditional Japanese religion worships the natural world.

(E) Flowers should be celebrated because their beauty is so short-lived.

11. What is the most likely meaning for the word "divine," as it is used in line 14?

(A) predict

(B) holy

(C) exquisite

(D) plead

(E) deity

12. According to the passage, what was the original purpose of the Hanami tradition?

(A) to admire the beauty of the sakura

(B) to pay tribute to the Tang Dynasty

(C) to honor the gods and the harvest season

(D) to build national spirit through communal celebrations

(E) to celebrate the coming of the spring

13. According to the passage, the sakura

I. bloom for a short time in March or April

II. are the blossoms of the cherry tree

III. were first planted in Japan in 710

(A) I only

(B) II only

(C) I and II only

(D) I and III only

(E) I, II, and III

"Peggy! Where are you? Aunt Helen wants you! Wherever are you hiding?"

Getting no response to her calls, the speaker, a girl of fifteen, ran out across the farmyard. She peeped into the cart-shed. She searched in the kitchen garden, but there was nothing to be seen except the daffodils under the gooseberry-bushes. Round through the orchard she sped, bringing down a shower of cherry-blossom as she brushed against the trees, but without any sign of the truant. Here and there Lilian ran—now peeping into the garage, now peering at the top of a ladder, now rummaging in the tool-shed, then back through the sand-quarry into the stack-yard, where there was a very good chance that the young lady might be hidden away; but Lilian's efforts were fruitless, and she was just turning away to give up the useless search, when the sound of a laugh attracted her to the barn. The door was slightly ajar, and she peeped in.

On the floor among the straw sat a little boy of eight or nine years old, gazing with delight into the rafters of the roof. Lilian glanced up, and beheld a sight which made her gasp with horror. The barn was spanned by a great cross-beam, which ran across the whole length from one end to another. Mounted on this, fully fifteen feet above the ground, a girl was slowly walking along, her gray eyes bright with excitement and her arms stretched out on either side to balance herself as she went on her perilous journey.

14. A good title for this passage could be

(A) The Daredevil Girl
(B) Angry Aunt Helen
(C) A Day in the Country
(D) A Game of Hide-and-Seek
(E) Lilian the Tattletale

15. In line 12, the word "fruitless" most likely means

(A) slow
(B) dangerous
(C) stunted
(D) unsuccessful
(E) breathless

16. It can be inferred from the passage that Peggy is

(A) older than Lilian
(B) rude and disrespectful
(C) a trained gymnast
(D) a girl who frequently likes to hide away in the stack-yard
(E) a girl who frequently gets injured

17. The narrator of this passage is

(A) Lilian
(B) Peggy
(C) Aunt Helen
(D) the little boy in the barn
(E) not a character in the story

18. This passage would likely be found in

   (A) a rule book for children
   (B) a history book on gymnastics
   (C) a novel
   (D) a newspaper
   (E) a play

We modern people love the sound of the word "big." We pride ourselves upon the fact that we belong to the "biggest" country in the world and possess the "biggest" navy and grow the "biggest" oranges and potatoes, and we love to live in cities of "millions" of inhabitants and when we are dead we are

Line 5   buried in the "biggest cemetery of the whole state."

A citizen of ancient Greece, could he have heard us talk, would not have known what we meant. "Moderation in all things" was the ideal of his life and mere bulk did not impress him at all. And this love of moderation was not merely a hollow phrase used upon special occasions: it influenced the life of

10   the Greeks from the day of their birth to the hour of their death. It was part of their literature and it made them build small but perfect temples. It found expression in the clothes which the men wore and in the rings and the bracelets of their wives. It followed the crowds that went to the theatre and made them hoot down any playwright who dared to sin against the iron law of

15   good taste or good sense.

19. According to the passage, the principle of moderation

   I.   influenced ancient Greeks for their entire lives
   II. had a direct impact on Greek fashion and theatre
   III. was worshipped in temple services

   (A) I only
   (B) II only
   (C) I and II only
   (D) I and III only
   (E) I, II and III

20. A good title for this passage might be

   (A) Ancient Greece and the Love of Small Things
   (B) Quality over Quantity in Ancient Greece
   (C) Architecture through the Ages
   (D) Art and Culture in Ancient Greece
   (E) What's Wrong with the Modern World

21. Why would a citizen of Ancient Greece be unable to understand our modern preoccupation with size?

(A) Ancient Greece was geographically smaller than modern countries.

(B) Ancient Greeks had no practical use for oversized objects.

(C) Ancient Greeks valued beauty and restraint and connected these qualities to good taste and good sense.

(D) In ancient Greece, immoderation and lack of restraint was a crime punishable in the court of law.

(E) Ancient Greece was a very old civilization and not developed enough to understand the importance of size.

22. In line 14, to "hoot down" most likely means

(A) to jeer at

(B) to applaud

(C) to throw stones at

(D) to perform onstage

(E) to prohibit a work from being performed

Once upon a time there lived in Verona two great families named Montagu and Capulet. They were both rich, and I suppose they were as sensible, in most things, as other rich people. But in one thing they were extremely silly. There was an ancient quarrel between the two families, an

Line 5   argument so old that no one could remember what it was about or whom exactly it had concerned. But this quarrel hovered over Verona like a black cloud, ready to erupt into a storm at any moment. Instead of making it up like reasonable folks, they made a sort of pet of their quarrel, and would not let it die out. A Montagu wouldn't speak to a Capulet if he met one in the street—

10   nor a Capulet to a Montagu—or if they did speak, it was to say rude and odious things, which often ended in a fight. And their relations and servants were just as foolish, so that street fights and duels and skirmishes of that kind were always growing out of the Montagu-and-Capulet quarrel.

23. An appropriate title for this passage would be

(A) How to Annoy Your Neighbor

(B) The Fight that Wouldn't End

(C) Famous People from Verona

(D) Lives of the Rich and Ridiculous

(E) A History of the Ruling Families of Verona

24. The "odious things" mentioned in lines 10-11 are probably

(A) empty invitations

(B) bad jokes

(C) horrible insults

(D) filthy vermin

(E) thoughtful critiques

25. To what does the author compare the quarrel between the Montagus and Capulets?

(A) the constant threat of bad weather

(B) a ghost that hovers over Verona

(C) an angry young man who always wants to start a fight

(D) an animal roaring through the streets

(E) a feud between two countries

26. By "they made a sort of pet of their quarrel" (line 8), the author means that

   (A) the families tried to end the quarrel, but it lived on like a cat with nine lives

   (B) the families were annoyed by the quarrel, the way people are annoyed by stray animals

   (C) the families kept the quarrel alive by feeding and nurturing it

   (D) the families felt they had an understanding of the quarrel's history

   (E) the families believed the quarrel would never end

27. The author would likely agree that

   (A) the mayor of Verona should intervene in the quarrel before things get worse

   (B) the heads of the two families are more responsible for the quarrel than their servants

   (C) it is immoral to fight with your neighbors

   (D) the Montagus and Capulets should have stopped fighting a long time ago

   (E) the quarrel between the Montagus and Capulets is a terrible tragedy

Bowling is an indoor game played upon an alley with wooden balls and nine or ten wooden pins, but up to the year 1840 it was played on a green, like cricket or baseball, one of the chief spots for bowling being the square just north of New York's Battery that is still called Bowling Green. The first covered alleys were made of hardened clay or of slate, but today's are built up of alternate strips of pine and maple wood, fastened together and to the bed of the alley.

Originally nine pins, set up in a diamond shape, were used, but during the first part of the 19th century the game of "nine-pins" was prohibited by law, on account of the excessive betting connected with it. This law, however, was soon evaded by the addition of a tenth pin, resulting in the game of "ten-pins," which is what we play today. The ten pins are set up at the end of the alley in the form of a triangle in four rows: four pins at the back, then three, then two, and one as head pin.

Several other varieties of bowling are popular in America, the most popular being "Cocked Hat," which is played with three pins, one in the head-pin position and the others on either corner of the back row. The pins are usually a little larger than those used in the regular game, and smaller balls are used. There is also "Candle Pin," which uses thin pins tapering towards the top and bottom, but is otherwise similar to the regular game. The old-fashioned game with nine pins is still played from time to time under the name "Head Pin."

28. The main subject of this passage is

(A) how to bowl
(B) various historical and contemporary forms of bowling
(C) the gamed of "Cocked Hat"
(D) popular American pastimes
(E) how bowling survived despite laws prohibiting it

29. Which of the games mentioned uses the least number of pins?

(A) Nine-pins
(B) Ten-pins
(C) Cocked Hat
(D) Candle Pin
(E) Head Pin

30. Which of the following puts the history of the bowling alley in the right order?

(A) Bowling started outdoors, then moved into wooden alleys, which were then replaced by stone alleys.

(B) Bowling started in wooden alleys, then moved outdoors, then returned indoors to stone alleys.

(C) Bowling started outdoors, then moved indoors to stone alleys, which were then replaced by wooden alleys.

(D) Bowling started in stone alleys, which were replaced by wooden alleys, then moved outdoors.

(E) Bowling started in wooden alleys, which were replaced by stone alleys, then moved outdoors.

31. According to the passage, Bowling Green

(A) was named for its resemblance to a bowling alley

(B) was once a very popular spot for outdoor bowling

(C) is still the main place to bowl in New York City

(D) is an indoor bowling alley near the Battery

(E) is the only place that New York City law allowed bowling to be played in the 19th century

32. When the author says that "this law was soon evaded by the addition of a tenth pin," (lines 10-11), she means that

(A) ten pin bowling was a good alternative for people who did not want to gamble

(B) when a tenth pin was added to the game, the law was rewritten to ban both nine- and ten-pin bowling

(C) legislators soon overturned the law against nine-pin bowling, citing the fact that ten-pin bowling, a nearly identical game, was still allowed

(D) an additional law was written stating that it was only legal to bowl with ten pins

(E) since the law was specifically against the game of nine-pin bowling, by adding a tenth pin players could continue to bowl legally

Richard Wagner was unlike most of the other great composers. He did not show any talent for music until he was almost a man. All that he thought of was writing plays. When he did study, he was so bright and worked so hard that he learned in less than a year more than many learn in a lifetime.

Line 5　　　When we read the stories of Charles Dickens we make many friends. And they are among the very best we ever have. There are Little Nell, Paul Dombey, Sam Weller, Oliver Twist, and a host of others. Writers like Dickens bring all sorts of people before us. But few composers can do such a thing. Yet there are some who do this, and one of the greatest is Richard Wagner. In his operas a

10　　　host of people live, people as real and as interesting as those in the stories of Charles Dickens. There is Walter, who sings the Prize Song in Die Meistersinger, and Eva, whom he loves. And in the same opera there is Beckmesser, the fussy old schoolmaster kind of a man. And Hans Sachs, the cobbler.

15　　　Nor was Wagner satisfied with making characters who were merely people just like ourselves. There are in the operas by Richard Wagner, gods and goddesses, giants and Rhine maidens, and Nibelungs. Wagner was able to evoke these characters through his operatic compositions.

33. A good title for this passage would be

(A) Richard Wagner and Charles Dickens: Two Great Composers
(B) Wagner: The Storytelling Composer
(C) Unforgettable Characters in Novels
(D) A History of Famous Composers
(E) It Takes All Sorts to Make a World

34. Which of the following is NOT stated or implied by the passage?

(A) Wagner was a talented playwright.
(B) Most composers show a talent for music at a young age.
(C) Charles Dickens has created many likeable characters.
(D) Wagner wrote an opera called Die Meistersinger.
(E) Wagner was not satisfied with making characters who were just ordinary people.

35. It can be inferred from this passage that a "Nibelung" (line 17) might be any of the following EXCEPT

    (A) a wizard with the power to raise the dead
    (B) a dragon
    (C) a magical sprite no bigger than an apple seed
    (D) a ghost warrior
    (E) an ordinary human being

36. This passage would likely appear in

    (A) a biography of Charles Dickens
    (B) a compendium of famous fictional characters
    (C) a book on eminent composers
    (D) the Arts & Entertainment Section of a newspaper
    (E) an autobiography by Richard Wagner

The mountain and the squirrel
Had a quarrel;
And the former called the latter "Little Prig."
Bun replied,
Line 5   "You are doubtless very big;
But all sorts of things and weather
Must be taken in together
To make up a year
And a sphere.
10   And I think it's no disgrace
To occupy my place.
If I'm not so large as you,
You are not so small as I,
And not half so spry.
15   I'll not deny you make
A very pretty squirrel track;
Talents differ: all is well and wisely put;
If I cannot carry forests on my back,
Neither can you crack a nut."

37. "Bun" (line 4) probably refers to

  (A) the poet
  (B) the squirrel
  (C) the mountain
  (D) a reader
  (E) a bystander

38. Which of the following best states the main idea of this poem?

  (A) Slow and steady wins the race.
  (B) An apple a day keeps the doctor away.
  (C) Squirrels are the rulers of the animal kingdom.
  (D) It takes all kinds to make a world.
  (E) Don't make a mountain out of a molehill.

39. The squirrel asserts that he is superior to the mountain in which of the following ways?

  I.   He is smaller and can move around.
  II.   He has hands, feet, and eyes.
  III.   His bushy tail is prettier than the mountain's forest.

  (A) I only
  (B) I and II
  (C) II and III
  (D) I and III
  (E) I, II, and III

40. The squirrel would probably agree
    that

    (A) it would be better to be a
        mountain than a squirrel
    (B) mountains have no place in the
        world
    (C) squirrels are better than bats in
        every way
    (D) mountains and squirrels are
        both good for different things
    (E) mountains are not good places
        to play

DIFFICULT PASSAGES

Use these questions to practice the more advanced passages you might see in both the Middle and Upper Level reading sections. The Upper Level exam will include more difficult passages than the Middle Level exam.

> Mme. Marie S. Curie arrived in New York on Wednesday on the Olympic. During her speaking tour in the United States, she will receive a gift of 1 gram of radium from a committee of American women who wish to honor the great French chemist for her discovery of that substance with her husband. Mme.
>
> *Line 5* Curie proposes to use this gift, which is valued at $100,000, in her attempts to discover new methods for making radium more useful in the treatment of cancer. Mme. Curie is convinced that radium is a cure for cancer, but she corrected statements published yesterday which made it appear that she believed the substance to be a cure for all types of cancer. "What Mme. Curie said," explained her secretary, "was that radium was a specific treatment for
>
> *10* many forms of the disease. She did not wish to be understood as asserting that it could effect a cure in every case."

1. This passage would most likely be found in

   (A) a mystery novel
   (B) a biography
   (C) a newspaper
   (D) a medical journal
   (E) a personal diary

2. Why was Mme. Curie in the United States?

   (A) She was visiting the United States to give lectures.
   (B) She had come to the United States to purchase radium.
   (C) She was born in the United States and was returning home after studying radium in France.
   (D) She was moving to the United States permanently to continue her work.
   (E) She was attending the Olympic Games.

3. The "substance" in line 4 is

   (A) an explosive
   (B) a type of cancer
   (C) a food product
   (D) a type of perfume
   (E) a chemical called radium

4. What is Mme. Curie's position on the use of radium to treat cancer?

   (A) It is dangerous and should not be attempted.
   (B) In the future, radium will be used to cure every kind of cancer.
   (C) Radium is probably not effective in treating cancer, but it is worth researching.
   (D) Radium can effectively treat many types of cancer, but not all.
   (E) The cost of radium is far too high for it to be a useful cancer treatment for most patients.

Ivy Global

Line 5

Books are as essentially a part of the home where boys and girls are growing into manhood and womanhood as any other part of the furnishings. Parents have no more right to starve a child's mind than they have his body. A child needs tools for his brain as much as for his hands. All these things are found, and found only, in books.

The child is helpless to provide himself with these necessaries for life. The majority of parents are eager that their children shall start early and right on that road which leads to honorable success. But it is impossible for any parent, by no matter how liberal an expenditure, to collect books that shall adequately cover all a child's needs and interests. This is the task of experts. We at The Bookshelf Company are experts. The Bookshelf is a collection of written material that creates a desire for knowledge, and then satisfies that desire. The Editors have selected all the most important subjects and have brought them to life with vivid illustrations. Order your copy of The Bookshelf today.

10

15

5. What is the primary purpose of this passage?

   (A) to sell the reader a copy of The Bookshelf
   (B) to inspire children to read
   (C) to teach the reader about different types of books
   (D) to question whether reading is important
   (E) to convince local governments to open more libraries

6. The author gives all of the following reasons to buy The Bookshelf EXCEPT

   (A) the tools a child needs for his/her brain can only be found in books
   (B) most parents are eager for their children to be successful
   (C) it is important that a child have all his or her learning materials assembled in a single publication
   (D) books should be as important in a home as furniture
   (E) children can't provide themselves with the necessities of life

7. The tone of this passage could be best described as

(A) objective
(B) optimistic
(C) bitter
(D) persuasive
(E) unbiased

8. In lines 8-10, the author implies that

(A) no matter how long a parent searches, he or she will never be able to find enough information to satisfy his or her child's curiosity

(B) no matter how much money a parent spends, he or she will never be able to collect enough books to address his or her child's interests and needs

(C) no matter how hard a parent tries, he or she will never be able to collect the books required by his or her child's school.

(D) no matter what the parents' politics, they will never be good at educating their own children

(E) even if a parent teaches his or her child the values of liberty, the parent must back up his or her argument with books

Alexander Graham Bell is commonly credited as the inventor of the first practical telephone. Bell was the first to obtain a patent, in 1876, for an "apparatus for transmitting vocal or other sounds telegraphically", after experimenting with many primitive sound transmitters and receivers. Bell was

Line 5 also an astute and articulate business man with influential and wealthy friends.

Bell did for the telephone what Henry Ford did for the automobile. Although not the first to experiment with telephonic devices, Bell and the companies founded in his name were the first to develop commercially practical telephones around which a successful business could be built and

10 grown. Bell adopted carbon transmitters similar to Edison's transmitters and adapted telephone exchanges and switching plug boards developed for sending telegraphs. Watson and other Bell engineers invented numerous other improvements to telephony. Bell succeeded where others failed to assemble a commercially viable telephone system; it can therefore be argued that Bell

15 invented the telephone industry.

9. According to the passage, Alexander Graham Bell

I.   was the first inventor to experiment with telephonic devices

II. along with other engineers, invented many improvements to telephony

III. was as important to the development of telephones as Henry Ford was to the development of automobiles

(A) I only
(B) II only
(C) III only
(D) I and II only
(E) II and III only

10. The tone of this passage can be best described as

(A) amused
(B) biased
(C) worshiping
(D) doubtful
(E) informative

11. Which of the following questions does the passage answer?

(A) Who is commonly credited as the inventor of the telephone?
(B) Who was the first scientist to experiment with telephonic devices?
(C) Why did Bell become interested in transmitting sound?
(D) Where was Bell's first telephone company?
(E) How many years did Bell spend developing a commercially viable telephone?

12. The author of the passage would
    most likely agree that

    (A) Watson deserves as much
        credit for the invention of the
        telephone as Bell

    (B) Bell was only able to invent the
        telephone because of his
        influential and wealthy friends

    (C) the telephone is equal in
        importance to the automobile

    (D) other inventors experimented
        with telephonic devices at the
        same time as Bell

    (E) Bell single-handedly invented
        the telephone industry

They were not railway children to begin with. I don't suppose they had ever thought about railways except as a means of getting around. They were just ordinary suburban children, and they lived with their Father and Mother in an ordinary red-brick-fronted villa and 'every modern convenience', as the house-agents say.

There were three of them. Roberta was the eldest. Of course, Mothers never have favorites, but if their Mother HAD had a favorite, it might have been Roberta. Next came Peter, who wished to be an Engineer when he grew up; and the youngest was Phyllis, who meant extremely well.

These three lucky children always had everything they needed: pretty clothes, good fires, and a lovely nursery with heaps of toys. They had a kind nursemaid, and a dog who was called James. They also had a Father who was just perfect—never cross, never unjust, and always ready for a game. You will think that they ought to have been very happy. And so they were, but they did not know HOW happy till the pretty life in the Red Villa was over and done with, and they had to live a very different life indeed.

The dreadful change came quite suddenly.

13. According to the passage, what kind of children were Roberta, Peter, and Phyllis?

(A) spoiled children who take all the luxuries in their lives for granted
(B) ordinary children who are comfortable and happy
(C) selfish children who don't care about the misfortunes of others
(D) children who were interested in railways from a very young age
(E) inquisitive children who thrive off adventure

14. Which of the following qualities does the author think is necessary for perfection in a father?

(A) giving lots of gifts
(B) owning a nice house
(C) enjoying games
(D) enjoying travel by railway
(E) not having favorites

15. When the narrator states "they were not railway children to begin with" (line 1), she most likely means that

    (A) the children had not, as yet, developed a life-long fascination with railways

    (B) the children had not yet inherited the railway that would make them famous

    (C) the children were not yet interested in the railway they were to destined to construct

    (D) the children spent little time repairing the bit of railway that passed near their home

    (E) It is impossible to know what the author means by the phrase at this point of the story, but it is implied that we will know soon.

16. In lines 6-7, why does the narrator tell us that "Mothers never have favorites?"

    (A) to playfully question the impartiality of the mother

    (B) to remind the reader of the qualities that every good mother should possess

    (C) to surprise a reader who may have thought that it was acceptable for mothers to have favorites

    (D) to instruct a reader who may also be a parent that it is unkind to have favorites

    (E) to imply that the children were all too aware that their mother had a favorite

17. The last line of the passage ends on a tone that could be best described as

    (A) neutral

    (B) resentful

    (C) suspenseful

    (D) amusing

    (E) pessimistic

Historically and in many parts of the world, women's participation in the profession of medicine has been significantly restricted, although women's practice of medicine, informally, in the role of caregivers, or in the allied health professions, has been widespread. Most countries of the world now guarantee

Line 5   equal access by women to medical education. While gender parity has yet to be achieved within the medical field worldwide, in some countries female doctors outnumber male doctors. This is the case in Canada and will be the case in England in the next six years.

While people often think of Americans like Ann Preston and Elizabeth Blackwell as the first important female physicians, the earliest cited woman

10   doctor dates all the way back to Ancient Egypt. Her name was Merit Ptah. She was born sometime around 2700 BCE and is possibly the first named woman in all of science as well. Her picture can be seen on a tomb in the necropolis near the step pyramid of Saqqara. Her son, who was a High Priest, described her as "the Chief Physician."

18. A good title for this passage would be

(A) The Life and Times of Merit Ptah
(B) Early Doctors Around the World
(C) Women In Medicine
(D) Elizabeth Blackwell: First Female Doctor?
(E) Medicine in Ancient Egypt

19. According to the passage, the number of female doctors worldwide

(A) is not known
(B) is declining compared to the number of male doctors
(C) is the same as the number of male doctors
(D) is much greater than the number of male doctors
(E) is not yet equal to the number of male doctors

20. According to the passage, which of the following statements is true?

(A) There are almost as many female doctors as male doctors in Canada.
(B) Elizabeth Blackwell was the first important female physician.
(C) Women have only become involved in medicine in the past hundred years.
(D) Most countries allow women to study medicine.
(E) It cannot be confirmed that Merit Ptah was the first female doctor.

21. The passage answers all of the following questions EXCEPT

    (A) What nationality were Ann Preston and Elizabeth Blackwell?

    (B) How many children did Merit Ptah have?

    (C) In what country do female doctors outnumber male doctors?

    (D) When was Merit Ptah born?

    (E) What was the profession of Merit Ptah's son?

London's Millennium Bridge reopened yesterday after an almost two-year closure due to the alarming wobble that gave it the nickname the "Wobbly Bridge." The bridge's engineers say that the wobble has been eliminated and the bridge is finally ready for use.

Line 5

The steel suspension bridge, which carries pedestrians across the Thames, was commissioned to celebrate the millennium. Construction began in 1998, with the grand opening on 10 June 2000. It was nicknamed the "Wobbly Bridge" after flocks of enthusiastic Londoners crossing the bridge on the day of its opening felt an unexpected (and, for some, uncomfortable)

10

swaying motion. The bridge was closed later that day. After two days of maintaining limited access to the bridge, City officials announced that the bridge would be closed for modifications.

The bridge's engineers have attributed the wobble to a phenomenon whereby pedestrians crossing a bridge that has a sideways sway have an

15

unconscious tendency to match their footsteps to the sway, thereby exacerbating it. The tendency of a suspension bridge to sway when troops march over it in step is well known, which is why troops are required to break step when crossing such a bridge.

22. What is the central idea of this passage?

(A) London's Millennium Bridge was poorly designed.

(B) London's Millennium Bridge suffered an initial setback but has been reopened to the public.

(C) It is important for large groups to break step when crossing a bridge.

(D) London's Millennium Bridge would not have had initial problems if the engineers had not rushed to complete it.

(E) Most suspension bridges are unsafe.

23. This passage would most likely be found in

(A) an engineer's log entry

(B) a newspaper

(C) an encyclopedia

(D) a manual on bridge-building

(E) a book of world records

24. Which of the following places the events of the passage into the order in which they occurred?

(A) Construction of the bridge began; the bridge was commissioned; the bridge was closed to the public.

(B) Construction of the bridge was finished; the bridge was opened with limited access; the bridge was opened to the entire public; the bridge was closed for two years.

(C) Construction of the bridge was finished; crowds of London residents crossed the bridge; the bridge was nicknamed the "Wobbly bridge."

(D) The bridge was closed to the public; the bridge was re-opened to the public; the bridge was first nicknamed the "Wobbly bridge."

(E) The bridge was nicknamed the "Wobbly bridge"; construction of the bridge was finished; crowds of London residents crossed the bridge.

25. The passage answers all of the following questions EXCEPT

(A) What body of water does the Millennium Bridge cross?

(B) Why did walkers experience a swaying sensation as they crossed the bridge?

(C) How long did the bridge remain closed to the public after its initial opening in 2000?

(D) Why did the engineers not take into account the tendency of a suspension bridge to sway?

(E) Had the tendency of a suspension bridge to sway ever been observed in a different context?

26. According to the passage, what must soldiers do when crossing certain bridges?

(A) march in a special, dance-like way

(B) cross one at a time, because the bridge may collapse under too much weight

(C) stop marching in unison, so that their footfalls do not make the bridge sway too much

(D) start and stop as they proceed along the bridge, to keep up the suspense

(E) match their footsteps to the sway of the bridge, so that they will not fall off

Alice was beginning to get very tired of sitting by her sister on the bank, and of having nothing to do. Once or twice she had peeped into the book her sister was reading, but it had no pictures or conversations in it, "and what is the use of a book," thought Alice, "without pictures or conversations?"

Line 5   So she was considering in her own mind (as well as she could, for the day made her feel very sleepy and stupid), whether the pleasure of making a daisy-chain would be worth the nuisance of getting up and picking the daisies, when suddenly a White Rabbit with pink eyes ran close by her.

There was nothing so very remarkable in that, nor did Alice think it so very much out of the way to hear the Rabbit say to itself, "Oh dear! Oh dear! I *10* shall be too late!" But when the Rabbit actually took a watch out of its waistcoat-pocket and looked at it and then hurried on, Alice started to her feet, for it flashed across her mind that she had never before seen a rabbit with either a waistcoat-pocket, or a watch to take out of it, and, burning with curiosity, she ran across the field after it and was just in time to see it pop *15* down a large rabbit-hole, under the hedge. In another moment, down went Alice after it!

27. According to the passage, Alice is surprised to encounter

(A) a rabbit capable of talking
(B) a rabbit who is able to tell the time
(C) a rabbit who owns a watch
(D) a rabbit with pink eyes
(E) a rabbit who wishes to be followed

28. Which of the following best describes Alice's situation in the in the first two paragraphs of the passage?

(A) She is bored to death, but can't think of a single thing to do with herself.
(B) She is bored of being bored, but still can't muster the energy to do anything.
(C) She wishes to read her sister's book, but her sister won't allow it.
(D) She is too tired to do all the things she longs to do.
(E) She is grumpy even though it's a beautiful day.

29. Which characters in the passage speak aloud?

   (A) Alice only
   (B) the White Rabbit only
   (C) Alice and the White Rabbit
   (D) Alice, the White Rabbit and the narrator
   (E) the narrator only

30. In line 7, why would it be a "nuisance" for Alice to get up and pick daisies?

   (A) It would require energy, and Alice has none at the moment.
   (B) Alice's sister might get worried about where she has gone.
   (C) Picking daisies is boring.
   (D) It might distract Alice's sister from her book, which would annoy her.
   (E) It would take a great deal of time to pick the daisies, and by the time she was ready to make her chain her sister might be ready to go home.

The Seville Fair, or Feria de Abril, is held in the Andalusian capital of Seville, Spain. The fair generally begins two weeks after the Semana Santa, or Easter Holy Week. Today, it is a cherished regional event, with people dressing in the vibrant colors of traditional flamenco garb, and celebrating until the wee
Line 5   hours of the morning.

The practice of holding festivities two weeks after Easter dates back to the middle ages, but the modern Fair began in 1847, when it was originally organized as a livestock fair. In the following year an air of festivity began to transform the fair, due mainly to the emergence of the first three casetas
10   (lavishly decorated marquee tents which are temporarily built on the fairground). During the 1920s, the fair reached its peak and became the spectacle that it is today.

The fair officially begins at midnight on Monday, and runs six days, ending on the following Sunday. Each day the fiesta begins with the parade of
15   carriages and riders, at midday, carrying Seville's most eminent citizens. They make their way to the bullring, La Real Maestranza, where the bullfighters and breeders meet. From around nine at night until six or seven the following morning, at first in the streets and later only within each caseta, you will find crowds partying and dancing flamenco, drinking sherry, and eating tapas.

31. According to the passage, the Seville Fair

    I.   is the most popular event in Andalusia
    II. runs for six days and six nights
    III. reached its current level of popularity in the 1920s

    (A) I only
    (B) II only
    (C) I and II only
    (D) I and III only
    (E) II and III only

32. A good title for this passage would be

    (A) Vibrant Festivals of Spain
    (B) A Cultural History of Seville
    (C) Feria de Abril: The Annual Festival of Seville
    (D) A Traveller's Guide to Andalucia
    (E) The Rise and Fall of the Seville Fair

33. According to the passage, what was responsible for transforming the Seville Fair from a livestock event to a full-blown festival?

   (A) The people of Seville celebrated until the wee hours of the morning.

   (B) The Casino of Seville remained open for the entire duration of the fair.

   (C) Seville's leading citizens began participating in the bullfights.

   (D) Three decorated marquee tents were set up on the fairground.

   (E) The fair officially began at midnight instead of in the morning.

34. It can be inferred from the passage that "flamenco garb" (line 4) is

   (A) a modern style of dress with sleek lines and bright colors

   (B) a pious style of dress popular in the 1920s

   (C) an old-fashioned style of dress worn by the upper-classes

   (D) an old-fashioned, bright style of dress, suitable for dancing

   (E) a vibrant fashion made famous in Spain in the 1840s

35. Which of these would the author most likely discuss next?

   (A) recipes for making tapas

   (B) the controversies surrounding bullfighting in Spain

   (C) Seville's eminent citizens from history

   (D) how Easter is celebrated in Seville

   (E) special events that happen during the week of the Seville Fair

Ivy Global

UP! up! my Friend, and quit your books;
Or surely you'll grow double:
Up! up! my Friend, and clear your looks;
Why all this toil and trouble?

Line 5   The sun, above the mountain's head,
A freshening luster mellow
Through all the long green fields has spread,
His first sweet evening yellow.

Books! 'tis a dull and endless strife:
10   Come, hear the woodland linnet,
How sweet his music! on my life,
There's more of wisdom in it.

And hark! how blithe the throstle sings!
He, too, is no mean preacher:
15   Come forth into the light of things,
Let Nature be your teacher.

36. What does the speaker want his friend to do?

   (A) study harder, as books are invariably the best teachers
   (B) take a break from studying and come outside
   (C) learn how to sing as sweetly as the birds in the woods
   (D) bring his books outdoors to read in the sunshine
   (E) quit school and join him on an adventure

37. It can be inferred from the poem that a "linnet" (line 10) is a type of

   (A) prophet
   (B) music
   (C) flower
   (D) bird
   (E) book

38. In lines 7-8, what has spread his "first sweet evening yellow" through the fields?

   (A) the woodland linnet
   (B) the singing throstle
   (C) nature
   (D) the mountain top
   (E) the sun

39. The tone of the poem can be best described as

   (A) angry
   (B) melancholy
   (C) blissful
   (D) imploring
   (E) somber

40. The speaker would most likely agree with which of the following statements?

(A) Nature can be as good a teacher as a book.

(B) It is important to spend several hours outdoors each day.

(C) Birds are the loveliest animals.

(D) Music is a more beautiful art form than literature.

(E) It's a shame that schools don't have outdoor classrooms.

CHALLENGE PASSAGES

Use these questions to practice the most challenging passages you might see in both the Middle Level and Upper Level reading sections. Challenge passages are much more frequent on the Upper Level exam than on the Middle Level exam.

The Bayeux Tapestry is an embroidered cloth nearly 230 feet long that depicts the events leading up to the Norman conquest of England in 1066, focusing on the relationship and struggle for power between William, Duke of Normandy, and Harold, Earl of Wessex and later King of England, which
Line 5 culminated in the Battle of Hastings. The tapestry consists of a series of scenes with Latin captions, embroidered on linen with colored woolen yarns. It is likely that it was commissioned by Bishop Odo, William's half-brother, and made in England in the 1070s. In 1729 the hanging was rediscovered by scholars at a time when it was being displayed annually in Bayeux Cathedral.
10 The tapestry is now exhibited at Musée de la Tapisserie de Bayeux in Bayeux, France, in the region of Normandy.

One of the reasons for the tapestry's importance is its depiction of Halley's Comet. A comet is a small icy Solar System body that, when close enough to the Sun, displays a visible coma (a thin, fuzzy, temporary
15 atmosphere) and sometimes also a tail. Halley is the only short-period comet (a comet that appears at least once every 200 years that is clearly visible to the naked eye from Earth, and thus the only naked-eye comet that might appear twice in a human lifetime. In 1066, the comet was seen in England and thought to be a bad omen. The comet is represented on the Bayeux Tapestry as a fiery
20 star with a streaming tail. Farther on, the tapestry depicts the bloody Battle of Hastings, where King Harold met his untimely death.

1. What is this passage primarily about?

    (A) the depiction of Halley's Comet in European art
    (B) an important European artifact
    (C) the details of the Battle of Hastings
    (D) the importance of depicting history through art
    (E) the myth that comets are bad omens

2. Halley's Comet is remarkable because it

    (A) was seen only once in Normandy, just before the Norman Conquest
    (B) appears in many novels and paintings
    (C) might be seen twice in a lifetime without a telescope
    (D) crashed in England during the Battle of Hastings
    (E) can only be seen from Bayeaux

3. According to the passage, the Bayeux Tapestry

(A) vanished for several hundreds of years until it was rediscovered by scholars in 1729

(B) was displayed annually at the Bayeux Cathedral for an unknown number of years before it was put on exhibit

(C) was taken by scholars from the Bayeux Cathedral because they objected to the tapestry being associated with religion

(D) was commissioned by William several years before the Battle of Hastings

(E) was made in the Bayeux Cathedral in the 1070s

4. It can be inferred from the passage that

(A) the Bayeux Tapestry took nearly a decade to complete

(B) William likely asked the Bishop Odo to have the tapestry commissioned

(C) the majority of people will see Halley's Comet twice in their lifetime

(D) on the tapestry, Halley's Comet is depicted as an omen of King Harold's death

(E) the Bayeux Tapestry is the most famous tapestry in Europe

5. What is this passage most likely to discuss next?

(A) the difference between a comet and an asteroid

(B) a tapestry that was commissioned to commemorate the fall of the Berlin Wall

(C) how the telescope changed people's ideas about comets

(D) other reasons for the importance of the Bayeux Tapestry

(E) other naked-eye comets that appear in artworks

The following is an excerpt from Barack Obama's inaugural speech as the 44th President of the United States:

That we are in the midst of crisis is now well understood. Our nation is at war. Our economy is badly weakened, a consequence of greed and irresponsibility on the part of some, but also our collective failure to make hard choices and prepare the nation for a new age. Homes have been lost; jobs

Line 5   shed; businesses shuttered. Our health care is too costly; our schools fail too many; and each day brings further evidence that the ways we use energy strengthen our adversaries and threaten our planet.

At a moment when the outcome of our revolution was most in doubt, the father of our nation ordered these words be read to the people:

10   "Let it be told to the future world, that in the depth of winter, when nothing but hope and virtue could survive, that the city and the country, alarmed at one common danger, came forth to meet it."

America, let us remember these timeless words. With hope and virtue, let us brave once more the icy currents, and endure what storms may come.

15   Let it be said by our children's children that when we were tested we refused to let this journey end, that we did not turn back nor did we falter; and with eyes fixed on the horizon and God's grace upon us, we carried forth that great gift of freedom and delivered it safely to future generations.

6. Which of the following would be a good title for this passage?

(A) The Future is Now
(B) Stand Up For Your Beliefs
(C) We are All American
(D) Let Us Have Courage
(E) The Worst is Over

7. Which of the following adversities does President Obama NOT mention in the passage?

(A) The environment has been damaged by energy production.
(B) The education system suffers from inadequacies.
(C) The country is at war.
(D) Health care is too expensive.
(E) Americans have lost hope.

8. Which of the following best describes the tone of the passage?

(A) victorious
(B) morose
(C) emboldening
(D) doubtful
(E) fearful

9. Which of the following best conveys the central idea of the passage?

(A) It is more important to be brave than it is to be virtuous.

(B) Americans across the country, and from very different walks of life, have voted for change.

(C) It is part of the American spirit to persevere through hardship.

(D) The United States is great because of its capacity for change.

(E) Better times are just around the corner.

10. President Obama compares the current difficult situation to

(A) a long journey that will never end

(B) the harsh climate of winter

(C) the distant horizon on which our eyes are fixed

(D) a tragic war

(E) a relentless battle against greed and irresponsibility

Ivy Global

George Frederick Handel was born on February 23, 1685. Even before he could speak, little George had shown a remarkable fondness for music, and the only toys he cared for were such as were capable of producing musical sounds. With this love for music, however, the father showed no sympathy whatever;

Line 5 he regarded the art with contempt, as something beneath the serious notice of one who aspired to be a gentleman, and that his child should have expressed an earnest desire to be taught to play only served to make him angry. He had decided that George was to be a lawyer, and in order that nothing should interfere with the carrying out of this intention he refused to allow the boy to

10 attend school, lest his fondness for music should induce someone to teach him his notes. Poor George was therefore compelled to stifle his longing whilst in his father's presence, and content himself with 'making music' in the seclusion of his own chamber. It may seem strange that Handel's mother should not have interposed in order that her boy should be taught music, but there is no

15 doubt that the elderly surgeon ruled his household with a firm hand, which not even his wife's intercession would have made him relax. And how could she have known that her son would grow up to be a great composer?

11. A good title for this passage would be

(A) The Early Years of a Composer
(B) Handel at his Peak
(C) The Cruelest Father
(D) A Miserable Child
(E) 17th Century Families

12. According to the passage, what was the profession of Handel's father?

(A) a lawyer
(B) a surgeon
(C) a gentleman
(D) a property-owner
(E) His profession is not mentioned in the passage.

13. When the author says "with this love for music, however, the father showed no sympathy whatever" (line 4), the author most likely means that

(A) no matter how Handel pleaded, his father would not listen to his compositions
(B) Handel's father's taste in music was different from his son's
(C) Handel's father was generally unkind to his son
(D) Handel's father strongly disapproved of his son's interest in music
(E) Handel's father was deaf and could not enjoy music

14. What is the author most likely to discuss next?

   (A) the relative employability of a surgeon and a musician in Handel's time
   (B) common harmonic progressions in 17th century music
   (C) more details of Handel's boyhood
   (D) how Handel became a lawyer
   (E) Handel's love of painting

15. According to the passage, Handel's father disapproved of his son's love of music for all of the following reasons EXCEPT

   (A) he hated music generally
   (B) he wanted his son to become a lawyer
   (C) he wanted his son to be a gentleman
   (D) he believed that his son was too good for music
   (E) he worried that his son wouldn't make a living as a musician

A myth is any imaginative explanation or interpretation of humanity or of the objects and events in nature outside of humanity, including their appearance, their effects and the still greater mystery of their causes. It may exist in many forms, from a simple myth of explanation to a complicated system of religious myths in which the objects of nature are regarded as gods in human form. As sacred stories, myths are often endorsed by rulers and priests and closely linked to religion or spirituality. In fact, many societies have two categories of traditional narrative: "true stories" or myths, and "false stories" or fables. Myths generally take place in a primordial age, when the world had not yet achieved its current form, and explain how the world gained its current form and how customs, institutions and taboos were established.

Closely related to myth are legend and folktale. Myths, legends, and folktales are different types of traditional story. Unlike myths, folktales can be set in any time and any place, and they are not considered true or sacred by the societies that tell them. Like myths, legends are stories that are traditionally considered true, but they are set in a more recent time, when the world was much as it is today. Legends generally feature humans as their main characters, whereas myths generally focus on superhuman characters. The distinction between myth, legend, and folktale is meant simply as a useful tool for grouping traditional stories. In many cultures, it is hard to draw a sharp line between myths and legends.

16. According to the passage, which of the following best describes a myth's relationship to the truth?

(A) Myths are considered true and sacred by the societies that tell them.

(B) Unlike folktales and legends, myths are completely truthful.

(C) Myths contain no elements of truth, but they are always considered true by those who create them.

(D) In myths, it is impossible to distinguish fact from fiction.

(E) Myths are founded in truths, but these truths become distorted as the myth is passed down to younger generations.

17. What is the purpose of this passage?

(A) to explain why myths are more important than folktales and legends

(B) to keep myths from being forgotten by younger generations

(C) to argue why it is still useful to read and understand mythology

(D) to define a myth and compare it to other forms of storytelling

(E) to show how myths have affected societies through the ages

18. It can be inferred from this passage that

   (A) myths are typically not set in modern time
   (B) myths are less popular than legends
   (C) myths use more antiquated vocabulary than folktales and legends
   (D) myths are a central component of all civilized cultures
   (E) myths would be more memorable if they were entirely truthful

19. A "traditional story" (line 13) is most likely

   (A) a story that deals with serious subject matter and that has been around for hundreds of years
   (B) a story told in formal language on important occasions
   (C) a story connected to the culture or customs of a particular society
   (D) a story that is impossible to forget
   (E) a story that is told aloud

Ivy Global

Isadora Duncan was a dancer considered by many to be the creator of modern dance. Duncan believed that classical ballet, with its strict rules of posture and formation, was "ugly and against nature." She rejected traditional ballet steps, preferring to stress improvisation, emotion, and the human form.

Line 5 She gained a very wide following and set up several schools. Duncan became so celebrated that artists and authors created sculpture, poetry, novels, and even jewelry inspired by her. When the Théâtre des Champs-Élysées was built in 1913, her likeness was included in the bas-relief over the entrance, carved by sculptor Antoine Bourdelle.

10 Duncan restored dance to a high place among the arts. Breaking with convention, she traced the art of dance back to its roots as a sacred art. Within this idea, she developed free and natural movements inspired by the classical Greek arts, folk dances, social dances, nature and natural forces. She also incorporated the new American athleticism, which included skipping, running,

15 jumping, leaping, and tossing.

20. According to the passage, Isadora Duncan's modern dance was inspired by all of the following EXCEPT

(A) the heroines of romantic ballet

(B) the natural human form

(C) American athleticism

(D) emotion

(E) nature

21. A good title for this passage might be

(A) Ballet vs. Modern Dance: The Debate of the Century

(B) A History of Ancient and Modern Dance

(C) An Unforgettable Performer

(D) Breaking with Convention

(E) A Star Is Born

22. As it is used in line 4, "stress" most closely means:

(A) tire

(B) emphasize

(C) rehearse

(D) watch

(E) step

23. A "bas-relief" (line 8) is most likely

(A) an ornamental basin

(B) a type of sculpture or engraving

(C) a type of large basket

(D) clothing made of silk or taffeta

(E) decorative baseboards placed along the floor

24. It can be inferred from the passage that Isadora Duncan is primarily famous because

    (A) she was a skilled historian
    (B) she was an excellent dance teacher and opened several schools
    (C) she inspired thousands of artists to make beautiful jewelry and sculptures
    (D) she invented a new form of dance
    (E) she rescued modern dance from years of neglect and bad reputation

From 1949 to 1990, modern-day Germany was split into two states: the Federal Republic of Germany, or West Germany, and the German Democratic Republic (GDR), or East Germany. Although Berlin was located within East Germany, part of it was designated as belonging to West Germany.

Line 5 The Berlin Wall was a barrier constructed by the government of East Germany in 1961 that completely cut off West Berlin from East Berlin. The barrier included guard towers placed along two large concrete walls, with a wide area—later known as the "death strip"—between them. The leaders of East Germany claimed that the Wall was erected to protect its population from

10 enemies conspiring to prevent the "will of the people" in building a socialist state in East Germany. In practice, the Wall served to prevent people from leaving East Germany.

In 1989, a radical series of political changes occurred in East Germany. After several weeks of unrest on the streets, the East German government

15 announced on November 9, 1989 that all GDR citizens could visit West Germany and West Berlin. Crowds of East Germans crossed and climbed onto the wall, joined by West Germans on the other side in a celebratory atmosphere. Over the next few weeks, a euphoric public and souvenir hunters chipped away parts of the wall; the governments later used industrial

20 equipment to remove most of the rest. The fall of the Berlin Wall paved the way for German reunification, which was formally concluded on 3 October 1990.

25. According to the passage, the East German Government claimed that

(A) West Germans were planning a terrorist attack on their East German neighbors

(B) a socialist state in East Germany is what the East Germans wanted

(C) the area between the concrete walls should not be controlled by either government

(D) East Germans were free to visit West Germany during the day

(E) East Germans had asked them to build a wall to commemorate "the will of the people"

26. All of the following questions are answered in the passage EXCEPT

(A) What was the German Democratic Republic?

(B) What material was the Berlin wall made from?

(C) Why did Berliners long for German reunification?

(D) How did the governments of East and West Germany take the wall down?

(E) What did the wall prevent East Berliners from doing?

27. It can be inferred from the passage that

    (A) the GDR put limitations on its citizens' freedom

    (B) the leaders of West Germany did everything they could to have the wall removed

    (C) most citizens of East Berlin tried to climb over the wall

    (D) guards shot at thousands of people who approached the wall

    (E) no citizens of East Germany supported the construction of the wall

28. This passage would most likely be found in

    (A) a book on the most beautiful parks in Berlin

    (B) a guide to the history of Berlin

    (C) a government press release

    (D) an anthology of German stories

    (E) a book on ancient German architecture

UPPER-LEVEL CHALLENGE PASSAGES

Use these questions to practice the most challenging passages that you might see in an Upper Level reading section. These passages would very rarely appear in a Middle Level section.

> *The following was written by Helen Keller, who was both blind and deaf due to a childhood illness.*
>
> Most people measure their happiness in terms of physical pleasure and material possession. Could they win some visible goal which they have set on the horizon, how happy they would be! Lacking this gift or that circumstance, they would be miserable. If happiness is to be so measured, I who cannot hear
>
> Line 5 or see have every reason to sit in a corner with folded hands and weep. If I am happy in spite of my deprivations, if my happiness is so deep that it is a faith, so thoughtful that it becomes a philosophy of life—if, in short, I am an optimist, my testimony to the creed of optimism is worth hearing. As sinners stand up in meeting and testify to the goodness of God, so one who is called afflicted may
>
> 10 rise up in gladness of conviction and testify to the goodness of life.

1. A good title for this passage might be

   (A) Life is Good
   (B) The Life of Helen Keller
   (C) Material Happiness
   (D) The Deaf Speak
   (E) The Sin of Resentfulness

2. The "gift" and "circumstance" the author refers to in line 3 are

   (A) spiritual desires
   (B) the basic necessities of life
   (C) the five senses
   (D) awards from the community
   (E) material pleasures

3. The author would probably agree that

   (A) some people need expensive things to be happy
   (B) sinners cannot testify to the goodness of God
   (C) it is possible to be happy even in terrible situations
   (D) no one could have a worse life than she does
   (E) it is sinful to think that happiness is found in material things

4. According to the author, the "creed of optimism" (line 7) is a belief

(A) in the goodness of strangers

(B) in the goodness of life

(C) that good things will come to those who wait

(D) that philosophy has more answers than religion

(E) that people who suffer more are happier

5. The tone of this passage could be described as

(A) harsh

(B) aloof

(C) upbeat

(D) jolly

(E) self-indulgent

November

There is wind where the rose was,
Cold rain where sweet grass was,
And clouds like sheep
Stream o'er the steep
Line 5   Grey skies where the lark was.

Nought warm where your hand was,
Nought gold where your hair was,
But phantom, forlorn,
Beneath the thorn,
10   Your ghost where your face was.

Cold wind where your voice was,
Tears, tears where my heart was,
And ever with me,
Child, ever with me,
15   Silence where hope was.

6. Which of the following best summarizes the meaning of the poem?

(A) November has come and the terrible weather dampens the poet's mood.

(B) November is over and hope will return as soon as sun and warmth replace the seasonal greyness.

(C) The poet has lost someone dear to him, and sees his loss reflected in the season of November.

(D) The poet cannot find his child because it is so dark and windy outside.

(E) The poet longs to escape from the awful season of November.

7. What is the most likely meaning of the word "nought" as it appears in lines 6 and 7?

(A) enough
(B) do not
(C) although
(D) even more
(E) nothing

8. To what does the poet compare the clouds?

(A) the lark
(B) sheep sitting still
(C) running sheep
(D) grey skies
(E) his unhappiness

9. In the last stanza, the poet suggests that

(A) his life is sad now, but it will improve eventually

(B) he has lost all hope forever

(C) he would feel hopeless if it weren't for the presence of his child

(D) if the child stays with him forever, he may learn to love again

(E) he wishes the child would stop crying

The following is a translation of a part of an address by Mr. Tsa Yuan-Pei, Chancellor of the Government University of Peking and formerly Minister of Education in the first Republican Cabinet, delivered on March 3rd, 1917.

I am a scholar and not a practical politician. Therefore I can only give you my views as a man of letters. As I see it, the War in Europe is really one between Right and Might, or in other words, between Morality and Savagery. Our proverbs run to this effect: "Every one should sweep the snow in front of

Line 5 his door and leave alone the frost on the roof of his neighbor," and that "when the neighbors are fighting, close your door." These proverbs have been used by the anti-war party in China as arguments against China's entrance into the War. The War in Europe, however, is not the "frost on the roof of our neighbor," but rather the "snow right in front of our door." It is not a "fight

10 between neighbors," but rather a quarrel within the family—the family of Nations. China therefore cannot remain indifferent. For, if Germany should eventually win the War, it would mean the triumph of Might over Right, and the world would be without moral principles. Should this occur, it would endanger the future of China. It is therefore necessary for China to cast her lot

15 with the Right.

10. What is the purpose of this passage?

(A) to argue that China should embrace peace and not become involved in the War in Europe

(B) to convince the reader to join the anti-war party of China

(C) to insist that China must become involved in the War in Europe

(D) to explain the difference between Right and Might

(E) to expose Germany as the greatest enemy to world peace

11. The tone of this passage could be best described as

(A) ambivalent

(B) hostile

(C) rueful

(D) serious

(E) mocking

12. What does the speaker mean when he says "it is not a fight between neighbors but rather a quarrel within the family" (lines 9-10)?

   (A) The world is like a family and China, as a member of this family, has a responsibility to help its relatives.

   (B) China must intervene in the war because many Chinese citizens have relatives in Europe and North America.

   (C) In truth, China played a role in causing the war, and therefore should help to end it.

   (D) People are only accountable to their families, not to their neighbors.

   (E) China is not part of the network of nations involved in the war.

13. Which of the following does the speaker NOT use as a reason for China to enter the war?

   (A) Chinese culture has a tradition of bravery.

   (B) German victory would endanger the future of China.

   (C) Joining the war is China's moral duty.

   (D) Inaction might mean the triumph of Might over Right.

   (E) Indifference could lead to a world without moral principles.

14. Why might the speaker have stated: "I am a scholar and not a practical politician" (line 1)?

   (A) He isn't absolutely sure that his opinion is the right one.

   (B) He doesn't necessarily want everyone to take him seriously.

   (C) He thinks that politicians are corrupt and ineffective.

   (D) He wants to stress that he is speaking from a perspective of honesty and careful thought.

   (E) He is worried that the audience may not recognize him.

Pluto is the second-most-massive known dwarf planet in the Solar System. From its discovery in 1930 until 2006, Pluto was classified as a planet. In the late 1970s, following the discovery of minor planet 2060 Chiron in the outer Solar System and the recognition of Pluto's relatively low mass, Pluto's

Line 5 status as a major planet began to be questioned. In the early 21st century, many objects similar to Pluto were discovered in the outer Solar System, notably the scattered disc object Eris in 2005, which is 27% more massive than Pluto. In 2006, the International Astronomical Union (IAU) defined what it means to be a "planet" within the Solar System. This definition excluded

10 Pluto as a planet and added it as a member of the new category "dwarf planet" along with Eris. A number of scientists hold that Pluto should continue to be classified as a planet.

Researchers on both sides of the debate gathered in 2008 for a conference called "The Great Planet Debate." The conference published a post-

15 conference press release indicating that scientists could not come to a consensus about the definition of a planet. Some members of the public have also rejected the new IAU classification, citing the disagreement within the scientific community on the issue or their own sentimental reasons: they maintain that they have always known Pluto as a planet and will continue to

20 do so regardless of the IAU decision.

15. With which of the following statements would the author most likely agree?

(A) Pluto should keep its new categorization as a dwarf planet.

(B) Pluto should revert to its original categorization as a regular planet.

(C) It is foolish to be sentimentally attached to Pluto's categorization as a planet.

(D) The IAU should take public opinion into account.

(E) The debate around Pluto's categorization remains unresolved.

16. According to the passage, the most massive known dwarf planet in the Solar System is

(A) Pluto

(B) 2060 Chiron

(C) Eris

(D) Earth

(E) It is impossible to tell from the passage.

17. What is the central idea of this passage?

   (A) Many planets are difficult to categorize with the IAU's new criteria.

   (B) It is crucial that we reach a consensus about Pluto's categorization.

   (C) Many mysteries remain in the field of astronomy.

   (D) Pluto is officially a dwarf planet, but not everyone agrees.

   (E) Many of the solar system's current planets should be classified as dwarf planets.

18. According to the passage, which event originally cast doubt on Pluto's status as a planet?

   (A) the discovery of another minor planet

   (B) the realization that Eris was 27% more massive than Pluto

   (C) the IAU's 2006 redefinition of a planet

   (D) the discovery that Pluto was much smaller than scientists originally believed

   (E) the realization that 2060 Chiron was actually bigger than Pluto

19. According to the passage, in 2006 the International Astronomical Union

   (A) excluded Pluto as a planet, because they didn't like it

   (B) excluded Pluto as a planet, because it never should have been considered a planet in the first place

   (C) named the newly-discovered scattered disc object "Eris"

   (D) could not come to an agreement about what a "planet" is

   (E) came up with an official definition of what can be called a "planet"

There are several kinds of stories, but only one difficult kind—the humorous. I will talk mainly about that one. The humorous story is American, the comic story is English, the witty story is French. The humorous story depends for its effect upon the MANNER of the telling; the comic story and the

Line 5   witty story upon the MATTER.

The humorous story may be spun out to great length, and may wander around as much as it pleases, and arrive nowhere in particular; but the comic and witty stories must be brief and end with a point. The humorous story bubbles gently along, the others burst.

10   The humorous story is told gravely; the teller does his best to conceal the fact that he even dimly suspects that there is anything funny about it; but the teller of the comic story tells you beforehand that it is one of the funniest things he has ever heard, then tells it with eager delight, and is the first person to laugh when he gets through.

20. What best describes the main purpose of this passage?

(A) to explain the difficulties of story-telling

(B) to list the qualities of a successful story-teller

(C) to give a history of American story-telling

(D) to compare and contrast a few specific types of stories

(E) to explain what makes a story funny

21. According to the passage, humorous stories differ from witty and comic stories in

I.   they way in which they are told

II.   their length

III. their level of difficulty

(A) I only

(B) II only

(C) III only

(D) I and II only

(E) I, II, and III

22. According to the passage, what makes comic and witty stories successful?

(A) They are told in both English and French.

(B) Their subject matter is funny.

(C) The story-tellers laugh as they tell their stories.

(D) They ramble without direction.

(E) They are hard to understand.

23. What does the author mean when he says "the humorous story bubbles gently along, the others burst" (line 7)?

(A) Humorous stories are more light-hearted.

(B) Comic and witty stories are more likely to fail.

(C) Humorous stories are less direct and more subtle.

(D) Humorous stories are funnier.

(E) Comic and witty stories are more violent.

24. The meaning of the word "gravely" as it is used in line 8 is closest to

(A) seriously

(B) menacingly

(C) deeply

(D) abrasively

(E) comically

THE WRITING SAMPLE

CHAPTER 5

ABOUT THE WRITING SAMPLE

PART 1

INTRODUCTION

The SSAT includes a 25-minute Writing Sample of one to two pages in length. Middle Level students will be asked to write a story starting with a phrase or a sentence provided by the test. Upper Level students will be asked to choose between writing a story and writing an essay in response to a question. The essay topics tend to be broad and varied. In some cases, you will be asked to take a side on an issue (in other words, you will be asked to write a persuasive essay). In some cases, you will be asked to offer a description or show cause and effect (in other words, you will be asked to write an informative essay).

Your story or essay will not be scored, but will be sent to the admissions officer of the schools to which you are applying. Although the Writing Sample will not affect your SSAT score, admissions officers consider your Writing Sample an important component of your application. They will look for a strong writing style free from spelling, punctuation, and grammar mistakes. They will also try to get a sense of who you are as a person. With this in mind, choose subjects you would be comfortable talking about during an interview with a principal or admissions officer. Avoid overly dark, violent, or inappropriate subject matter.

WRITING BASICS

APPROACHING THE WRITING SAMPLE

Here are some general tips for all students approaching the SSAT Writing Sample. For more specific tips and exercises tailored to your level, work your way through the later sections on creative and essay writing strategies.

TIME MANAGEMENT

Regardless of your approach or level, you will need **to budget your time**. Plan to spend no more than a few minutes choosing your prompt, brainstorming, and planning, and save a few minutes at the end to edit. Don't spend too long on any one paragraph.

MANAGING YOUR TIME	
Time	**Goal**
1 – 2 minutes	Choose your topic and plan your essay or story
4 – 5 minutes	Write your first paragraph
4 – 5 minutes	Write your second paragraph
4 – 5 minutes	Write your third paragraph
4 – 5 minutes	Write your conclusion
2 – 3 minutes	Re-read or edit your essay or story
Total: 25 minutes	Complete essay or story

Here are some more specific guidelines for the length of your Writing Sample:

- Stories should have a beginning (first paragraph), middle (second and third paragraphs), and end (fourth paragraph).
- Essays should have an introduction (first paragraph), body (second and third paragraphs), and conclusion (fourth paragraph).
- Some Upper Level essays will require a five-paragraph format. In that case, reserve four minutes writing time per paragraph.

WRITE NEATLY

Write legibly in either cursive or print, whichever is neater. Neatly cross out any errors you make. Using legible, medium-sized writing, fill up the entirety of the lined pages given. Use the other parts of your student response sheet for your outline and notes. Indent to make sure it is clear where a new paragraph begins. Use standard punctuation and indentation for dialogue. See the section on Cleaning up your Grammar for more information on proper punctuation.

BE CONCISE AND SPECIFIC

Keep your writing clear and to the point. Avoid rambling or repeating yourself. Use specific, precise vocabulary instead of vague words and phrases. Use sophisticated vocabulary, but make sure you use words properly. Use vivid language that incorporates the five senses: sight, smell, taste, touch, and sound.

EDIT YOUR WORK

Remember to edit for spelling, punctuation, and grammar. Read the section on Cleaning up your Grammar for more information.

WRITING DESCRIPTIVELY

Like playing an instrument or learning a new sport, writing is a skill acquired through practice. A strong piece of writing is the product of critical thinking. In order to improve your writing and critical thinking skills, make a commitment to read and write daily.

In this section, you'll find some techniques and exercises for building your writing skills. These techniques are suitable for all students, but the specific approach you will use will vary depending on whether you are an Upper Level or a Middle Level student. Middle Level students should additionally study the Creative Writing section, while Upper Level students should study the Creative Writing, Persuasive Writing, and Informative Writing sections. All students should read the Grammar section.

Whether you are writing a short story, a persuasive essay, or an informative essay, you will need to learn how to **write descriptively**. You can make your writing more descriptive by:

- using the sensory descriptions of smell, touch and even taste in addition to sight and sound
- identifying key characteristics of your subject
- being able to describe and explain causes and effects

In addition to the writing exercises offered in this section, here are some daily writing ideas:

- Keep a daily journal where you record your thoughts and observations.
- Write "fan fiction" involving characters or events from novels you are reading.
- Write opinion pieces in response to news articles you read.
- Work on writing your very own novel!
- If you get stuck, the internet offers a plethora of writing ideas.

USING YOUR FIVE SENSES

How do writers bring stories and ideas to life? They write sentences that employ the five senses.

Here's an example of descriptive writing from a work of fiction:

> "Toto was not gray; he was a little black dog, with long silky hair and small black eyes that twinkled merrily on either side of his funny, wee nose."
>
> - L. Frank Baum, *The Wizard of Oz*

Look at all the sensory imagery! We can see the dog because we are told he is "little" and "black." He has eyes that "twinkle." We can also get a sense of what it would be like to touch him. He has "silky hair."

Here's another example from an essay:

> "The whistle of the locomotive penetrates my woods summer and winter, sounding like the scream of a hawk sailing over some farmer's yard, informing me that many restless city merchants are arriving within the circle of the town, or adventurous country traders from the other side."
>
> -Henry David Thoreau, *Walden*

This is a description we can hear! First we hear the "whistle" of the train, only to learn that it sounds like a "scream." And, it's not just any scream, but the "scream of a hawk"! Thoreau provides us with many fine visual descriptions: the hawk the author hears is "sailing." The author also makes the suggestion that the town has a shape. Merchants arrive "within the circle of the town."

To get started writing with your five senses, try using some of the following words:

DESCRIPTIVE WORDS	
Sensory Perception	**Description**
Sight words	Color, shape, light, dark, bright, dim…
Smell words	Sweet, acrid, fetid, fragrant, musty, musky, perfumed, pungent, rancid, stinky…
Touch words	Cold, damp, dry, furry, hot, lumpy, rough, sharp, slimy, smooth, sticky, wet…
Hearing words	Bang, chime, chirp, clash, crunch, fizz, jingle, ping, rattle, roar, sizzle, slam, tap, thud…
Taste words	Bitter, sweet, sour, salty, juicy, fruity, rich, sharp, sugary, succulent, tangy, tart, zesty…

Exercise #1: To practice bringing the reader into your story with vivid sensory descriptions, re-write the following sentences to make them more interesting by using one of the five senses. Have a trusted reader check your work.

1. Alisha and Sam were at the seashore. *(taste)*

   Alisha and Sam could taste the salt in the fresh sea air.

2. I saw a car go by. *(sound)*

3. It was sunset. *(sight)*

4. Robin went into the woods. *(smell)*

5. I walked down the street. *(touch)*

6. They sat down to lunch. *(taste)*

IDENTIFY KEY CHARACTERISTICS

Identifying and defining key characteristics is another way to make your writing stronger. Let's go back to the Thoreau example:

> "The whistle of the locomotive penetrates my woods summer and winter, sounding like the scream of a hawk sailing over some farmer's yard, informing me that many restless city merchants are arriving within the circle of the town, or adventurous country traders from the other side."
>
> -Henry David Thoreau, *Walden*

Thoreau use sensory imagery and he also identifies the key characteristics of the locomotive. The locomotive seems to serve two functions: (1) it is a noisy distraction, and (2) it informs the author that merchants will soon arrive.

Being able to vividly describe characteristics of people, places, and things is a good skill to keep in mind when writing stories or essays.

Let's try a few together:

What are some characteristics of a good teacher? Can you think of a third?

- *Expertise*
- *Organization*
- _____

Exercise #2: Identify and describe some characteristics on your own. Have a trusted reader check your work.

1. List three characteristics of a good friend:

   (1)

   (2)

   (3)

2. List three characteristics of a helpful person:

   (1)

   (2)

   (3)

3. What is your favorite book? List three qualities that make it interesting:

   (1)

   (2)

   (3)

4. What three things make for a good student?

   (1)

   (2)

   (3)

5. What is your favorite hobby? List three qualities that make it enjoyable:

   (1)

   (2)

   (3)

6. What are three words you'd use to describe yourself?

   (1)

   (2)

   (3)

Ivy Global

WRITING ABOUT CAUSES AND EFFECTS

Whether you are writing an essay about how you can help prevent climate change or a short story about an alien invasion, you will need to be able to write vividly about cause and effect.

Let's say you are trying to write an essay about how you can help slow down climate change. Before you can start writing, you will need to think about causes and effects. In other words, if you don't know the causes of climate change, how can you possibly write about stemming, or eliminating, the effects? Since you already know the effect, namely, climate change, you just need to identify some of the causes:

- Car pollution
- Manufacturing
- Burning of coal for electricity

Now that you have listed some of the causes, you can better write about ways you can prevent climate change. For instance, carpooling reduces car pollution, and turning off lights when you leave the room means electric companies need to use fewer coal resources to keep power plants going. By evaluating causes and effects, you are better able to plan a more thorough, clear, and detailed essay.

Now, let's say you're writing a short story about that alien invasion. Here, you'll need to invent your own causes and effects.

- *Possible Cause*: Aliens want to come to earth to harvest pebbles.
- *Possible Effect*: Earth leaders draft a peace treaty in which the aliens are allowed to harvest certain types of pebbles at certain locations on earth.

- *Possible Cause*: The aliens are lost in space. Fortunately, they are philanthropic and help teach one lucky school of fifth graders Einstein's theory of relativity.
- *Possible Effect*: One of the brilliant fifth graders builds a rocket capable of getting the stranded aliens home.

Exercise #3: List some causes and effects. Have a trusted reader check your work.

1. A girl wakes up on Saturday morning only to realize that the sun hasn't risen.

    Causes:

    Effects:

2. A boy wakes up to discover his dog can speak to him.

Causes:

Effects:

3. A city street is empty.

   Causes:

   Effects:

4. A stranger arrives in town.

   Causes:

   Effects:

5. Someone needs help.

   Causes:

   Effects:

6. You need to try something a second time.

   Causes:

   Effects:

7. Your school proposes that bullying become a criminal offense.

   Causes:

   Effects:

Ivy Global

CLEANING UP YOUR GRAMMAR

Use this section to review basic grammar rules and style conventions for creative and essay writing. These concepts will help make your SSAT writing samples as clean and understandable as possible.

USE COMMON CONVENTIONS

Conventions are customs or rules we follow. When writing your SSAT essay, there are some common writing conventions you'll want to make sure you follow:

Indent your paragraphs: make sure the first line of each new paragraph starts a few spaces over to the right. This helps your reader see where each new paragraph begins.

Capitalize the first word in each sentence. Also capitalize proper nouns, which are words that name specific people, places, organizations, or events. For example:

- Suzanne turned in her homework to Mrs. Williams.
- We had a lot of fun on our trip to Honolulu, Hawaii.
- The violinist gave his first recital at Carnegie Hall.
- The World Health Organization released a new report.
- The Revolutionary War was a turning point in American history.

Underline the titles of novels, newspapers, and magazines. For example:

- <u>The Giver</u>
- <u>The Lion, the Witch, and the Wardrobe</u>
- <u>The New York Times</u>

Put quotation marks around short stories, poems, or article titles. For example:

- "To Build a Fire"
- "Yankees Win the Pennant"
- "The Raven"

When you first mention a novel, story, poem, or article, provide the author's full name. For example:

- <u>The Lion, the Witch, and the Wardrobe</u> by C.S. Lewis
- "The Raven" by Edgar Allan Poe
- "To Build a Fire" by Jack London

When you mention a novel, story, poem, or article for the second, third, fourth, or hundredth time, you only need to use the author's last name. However, *always* use the full name of the novel, story, poem, or article every time!

- In <u>The Lion, the Witch and the Wardrobe</u>, Lewis writes . . .
- Poe shows in "The Raven" . . .
- We see in London's "To Build a Fire" . . .

Finally, avoid using phrases like "a lot" and "really." Your writing will be stronger if you omit these words.

AVOID THE PASSIVE VOICE

The **passive voice** re-orders your sentence so it sounds clunky and impersonal. Using the **active voice** instead of the passive voice will strengthen your writing. For every sentence, make sure the "doer" of the verb (or the person performing the action) comes first. See the following chart:

PASSIVE VOICE VS. ACTIVE VOICE	
Passive Voice	**Active Voice**
The soup was heated.	I heated the soup.
The essay was written by Joe.	Joe wrote the essay.
The computer was being used by Alice.	Alice was using the computer.

Exercise #4: Re-write the following sentences in the active voice. Then, check your answers in the answer key that follows.

1. The cookie was eaten by Amanda.

2. The dishes were washed by my brother.

3. My homework was eaten by my dog.

4. The mistake was made by me.

AVOID RUN-ON SENTENCES

A **run-on sentence** joins together too many complete sentences in a row. Break up these long sentences into shorter sentences. You can also avoid run-on sentences by using words like "and," "or," "but," "so," "if," "because," and "when." These words can properly join together otherwise complete sentences. However, don't use too many of them in a row, or you'll still have a run-on sentence! Here are some examples:

FIXING RUN-ON SENTENCES	
Incorrect	**Correct**
It is cold outside, don't forget your jacket.	It is cold outside. Don't forget your jacket.
It was cold and windy and raining outside, so my mother told me to wear a jacket but I forgot so I was cold.	Because it was cold, windy, and raining outside, my mother told me to wear a jacket. Unfortunately, I didn't heed her warning. As a result, I was cold.
I sang, the crowd applauded.	When I sang, the crowd applauded.
I'll finish my homework then I'll read then I'll walk the dog then I'll have dinner.	After I finish my homework, I will read. Then, I will walk the dog and have dinner.

Exercise #5: Correct the following run-on sentences. Then, check your answers in the answer key at the end of the section.

1. I like to ski, it makes me happy.

2. James went home then did his homework then went to bed.

3. Don't forget to bring your folder it is important.

4. The strangest thing happened on my way to school, our school bus broke down and they made us all get out through the back door and we had to wait beside the road for another bus to pick us up, but it took a long time to come so we were late.

WATCH OUT FOR HOMOPHONES

Homophones are words that sound the same, but are spelled differently and have different meanings. Students often make errors with homophones by substituting one homophone for another. Study the following chart for common homophones and their uses. When using these words in your essay, make sure you are spelling the word correctly for a given context.

COMMON HOMOPHONES		
Homophone	**Meaning**	**Examples**
Too	Excessive	Too much, too fast
Two	Number	Two apples, two cars
To	Direction: went to the store	Went to the store
There	Location	Stay right there, go there
Their	Belonging to them	Their cat, their essays
They're	Contraction for "they are"	They're ready!
By	Author or place	By the lake, by C.S. Lewis
Buy	Purchase	Buy some food
Bye	Farewell	Bye, I'll see you tomorrow!
Here	Location	Right here, come here
Hear	Listen	Hear a song, hear a noise
Whether	Doubt or choice	Whether to go, whether to stay
Weather	Climate	The weather is nice today.
Principal	Leader of a school	The principal's office
Principle	Truth or belief	I stick to my principles.

Its	Belonging to something	Turn the book on its side.
It's	Contraction for "it is"	It's raining outside.
Your	Belonging to you	Your car, your homework
You're	Contraction for "you are"	You're coming tonight.
Than	Comparison	An elephant is bigger than a dog.
Then	Time	Then, I went home.

Exercise #6: The following sentences may contain one, many, or no homophone errors. Rewrite the sentences to make them error free. Answers are provided at the end of this section.

1. "To Build a Fire" was written bye Jack London.

2. Jack borrowed too pens. Than he went home.

3. There coming to our house tomorrow.

4. Your waiting to long to answer.

5. My mother told me to wait they're.

6. Their right hear. Can't you see them?

7. My school has a great principle.

8. Your not serious!

9. The whether is nice outside.

10. I need to bye three binders too take to school. Its important.

PUT APOSTROPHES IN THE RIGHT PLACE

Apostrophes are used to signify **possession**, or when something belongs to something else. To make a **singular noun** possessive, add apostrophe and the letter "s." For example:

- Joe's fish
- My uncle's car
- My mother's friend

For a **plural noun ending in the letter "s,"** add an apostrophe to the end of the word, but do not add another "s." For example:

- Boys' cars
- Ladies' hats
- Heroes' victories

For all **plural nouns not ending in the letter "s,"** add apostrophe and "s." For example:

- Women's hats
- Children's ideas
- People's Republic

Exercise #7: Correct the following sentences. Check your answers at the end of this section.

1. Mikes dog is sweet.

2. The mens suits were elegant.

3. All the partiers hats fell off.

4. Is this someones pencil?

THE SHORT STORY

PART 2

INTRODUCTION

A well-written story engages its readers and brings them into the world of the characters. Your challenge is to establish a character and to tell a story that matches the prompt given. When reading the prompt, think about the causes that may have contributed to the scenario presented. What are some potential effects? There shouldn't be too much happening in your story. One conflict is usually sufficient.

If you are writing a short story on the SSAT, the prompt must be the first sentence of the story, so pay attention to the words in it. What is the tense? Is it written from the first person or second person point of view? Who might this character be? Is there more than one character? What setting or situation is suggested?

Show, don't tell. Employ your descriptive writing skills: use your five senses, identify key characteristics, and establish cause and effect. Let yourself be imaginative. Your story can be based on an actual event or completely made up. You can set it somewhere you've been or somewhere you've never been; your characters can be people from anywhere, who do whatever you want them to do. They don't have to be people at all! Be yourself and write a story you would want to read.

WRITING A SHORT STORY

SECTION 2

There are many things to think about when writing a short story. You'll want to consider point of view, tense, plot structure, conflict, sentence structure, punctuation, and the level of detail you put into the writing itself. Finally, Upper Level and advanced students will want to consider elements of style.

Sounds like a lot? Don't stress. Take a deep breath and take a lesson from Imhotep who lived in ancient Egypt. Whenever we find a statue of him, he's always depicted writing! He was an engineer, architect, and physician and he knew that you couldn't build a pyramid without a sound foundation. The same is true for writing short stories.

Take a look at the pyramid below. We'll start with the foundation and work our way up. The concepts on the bottom are the most important and as we move higher on the pyramid, the skills become more stylistic.

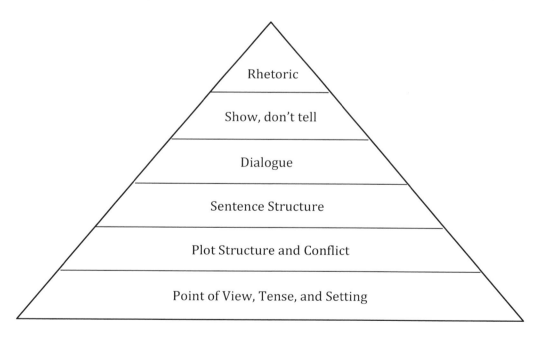

HOW TO BEGIN

In this section, we'll look at the very first questions you should consider when starting your story. These concepts form the foundation of your creative writing pyramid.

POINT OF VIEW, TENSE, AND SETTING

Before you start writing, decide on a **point of view**: who is telling the story? Sometimes the point of view is established by the sentence provided. For the purposes of this short story, you'll have to choose between two distinct points of view: **first person** and **third person** point of view.

- First person point of view uses "I": "I couldn't believe my eyes."
- Third person point of view uses "he", "she", "they", or "it": "He couldn't believe his eyes."

You'll also want to decide what **tense** you will use for your story: is it taking place right now, or sometime in the past? Sometimes the tense is established by the sentence provided. For the purposes of this short story, you'll have to choose between two distinct tenses: **past tense** and **present tense**.

- Past tense: "I went," "I saw, I did."
- Present tense (rarer and more difficult to maintain): "I go," "I see," "I do."

Once you've decided on the point of view and the tense, you'll need to establish the setting: where and when is the story taking place? Sometimes the setting has been suggested by the prompt. Sometimes you'll have to invent one on your own. Whatever you do, you will want to describe the setting using vivid description involving the five senses.

Exercise #1: Identify whether the following sentences are written in present tense, past tense, first person, or third person. Answers to these questions are provided at the end of this section. Then, write a few sentences in which you maintain a consistent tense and point of view that helps establish the setting. The first exercise has been completed for you. Have a trusted reader check your work.

1. He didn't want to go.

    Point of View: Third Person

    Tense: Past Tense

    Establish the setting: He didn't want to go to his grandparents' house. Mario's grandfather always made him work in the garden to help protect it from the constant assault of vermin and rodents.

2. I saw the car speed away.

   Point of View:

   Tense:

   Establish the setting:

3. I know I can't do it alone.

   Point of View:

   Tense:

   Establish the setting:

4. She can't believe she can fly!

   Point of View:

   Tense:

   Establish the setting:

5. I thought about the problem.

   Point of View:

   Tense:

   Establish the setting:

6. I tell my mother I will be right back.

   Point of View:

   Tense:

   Establish the setting:

7. He finds it.

   Point of View:

   Tense:

Establish the setting:

8. She had the strangest dream.

    Point of View:

    Tense:

    Establish the setting:

Exercise #2: The following passages are written incorrectly. The tense and point of view shifts as the passages unfold. Rewrite the passages so that they employ the tense and point of view indicated. Check your answers at the end of this section.

1. Re-write this passage so it is consistently in the past tense:

    When she was two years old, she was playing in a garden, and she plucks a flower. She looked rather happy. Her mother wonders where she found the flower.

2. Re-write this passage so it is consistently in the present tense:

    Marley was dead. There is no doubt about it. We all know. The death certificate was signed by the clerk, the undertaker, and the chief mourner. Even Scrooge signed it.

3. Re-write this passage so it is consistently in the first person:

    When I was left alone, I began to feel hungry. She went to the cupboard and cut herself some bread. I gave some to my dog and, taking a pail from the cupboard, she carried it down to the brook and filled it with clear sparkling water.

4. Re-write this passage so it is consistently in the third person:

    She opened the door and saw that it led to a small passage, no smaller than a rat-hole. I knelt down and looked into the prettiest garden I ever saw. I longed to wander through those flower beds! She could not get her head through the doorway.

ESTABLISHING THE CONFLICT

In addition to establishing the tense, the point of view, and the setting, you will want to establish the **conflict** of your story. Conflict, put generally, is the problem, difficulty, or challenge facing the main character.

Certain kinds of conflict recur throughout literature and short stories. Listed below are some of the more common conflicts:

COMMON CONFLICTS		
Type of Conflict	**Description**	**Examples**
Main Character vs. Other People	The main character faces a daunting foe, struggles against a cruel oppressor, or fights a powerful figure in order to attain a certain goal.	*Matilda* by Roald Dahl, *Peter Pan* by J.M Barrie
Good vs. Evil	The main character, often representing a force of good, faces a force of evil that threatens the character or the character's family, friends, society, or world.	*The Wizard of Oz* by L. Frank Baum, *The Lion, the Witch, and the Wardrobe* by C.S. Lewis, the *Harry Potter* series by J.K. Rowling, *A Wrinkle in Time* by Madeline L'Engle
Main Character vs. Society	The main character fights to overthrow or overcome an oppressive society or government.	*The Giver* by Lois Lowry, *The Hunger Games* by Suzanne Collins
Main Character vs. Nature	The main character goes out into the wild and faces the dangers of weather, wilderness, and beasts.	"To Build a Fire" by Jack London, *The Lord of the Flies* by William Golding
Main Character vs. Self	The character struggles to overcome personal flaws or weaknesses in order to achieve a goal.	*The Secret Garden* by Francis Hodgson Burnett, *Ramona Quimby, Age Eight* by Beverly Cleary

SSAT prompts are often vague. If you have a sense of what kinds of stories you are interested in writing for each of the traditional conflicts, you'll save time when you write the test. Being prepared to write on the following conflicts can help you. Sometimes the sentence will suggest a certain kind of conflict and sometimes you'll have to interpret the sentence yourself. Arrive at the test prepared with some ideas!

Exercise #3: For each of the following conflicts, can you think of some short story ideas of your own? Have a trusted reader check your work!

1. Main Character vs. Other People:

2. Good vs. Evil:

3. Main Character vs. Society:

4. Main Character vs. Nature:

5. Main Character vs. Self:

PLOT STRUCTURE

Put very simply, every story should have a beginning, middle, and end. It is also helpful to know classic short story structure. Most stories have:

- a **beginning** that establishes the setting, tense, point of view, and conflict
- **rising action** in which the main character devises a plan to resolve the conflict
- a **climax**, or the moment right before we learn whether the plan works
- **falling action**, in which the problem is resolved
- a **conclusion** in which all loose ends are tied up

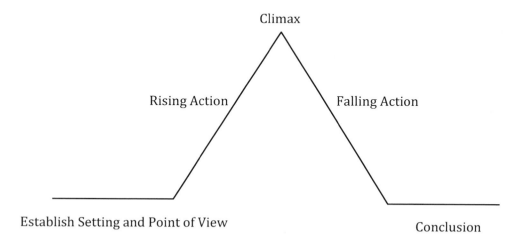

At the **beginning** of your story, use the techniques we outlined earlier in this section to introduce your setting, point of view, and the main conflict of your story.

During the **rising action**, describe the conflict in detail and have your character develop a plan to overcome the conflict. For example:

- A girl trapped in a tower plans to grow out her hair in order to escape.
- In order to defeat a despotic ogre, a valiant knight rallies up an army.
- A character lost in the wilderness on a cold day plans to build a fire.

The **climax** is the moment in the story of greatest uncertainty. It is the moment when the forces working against the main character (other people, evil, society, nature) seem most likely to make the character fail. For example:

- The character throws her hair out the window, but the prince is nowhere to be seen.
- The evil ogre rallies an army of his own; the army seems likely to defeat the knight's army.
- The twigs are all damp and won't light. The character thinks she will freeze.

The **falling action** is the description of the outcome. Your character has set the plan into motion, and now the plan either fails or succeeds. For example:

- We learn that the prince, who had been delayed by a dragon, arrives just in time.
- The knight's army forms a phalanx and defeats the ogre's disorganized army.
- The resourceful character cuts a patch from her sweater and lights it on fire. The heat produced dries the twigs, allowing them to light.

The **conclusion** is the end of your story. You want to make sure to tie up all loose ends. Make sure your story doesn't just stop. The conclusion should resolve your story. In many cases, a good way to show the reader that the conflict has been resolved is to describe a character's reaction to it. This also gives the reader a feeling for why the event was important. Another good thing to do is to refer back to what happened in the beginning to show what has changed. In other words, has the conflict been resolved? For example:

- The girl who had been trapped in tower becomes the queen.
- The ogre and his army is banished to Antarctica.
- The sun rises, the day warms up, and the character finds her way home out of the wilderness.

As you think of ways to end your story, ask yourself the following questions:

- Does it have to end this way? Sometimes the most interesting story is one that doesn't end the way we expect it to.
- Do I need to say that? Don't feel you need to end with a moral lesson or a "happier ever after." Just ending your main event is enough.
- What questions would my reader ask now? Your reader might be left wondering what will happen to your characters in the future, but he or she should not be

wondering what just happened, who those people were, or why any of it was important.

Exercise #4: In Exercise #1, you established the setting and point of view for a story. Now, we're going to take another look at those sentences in order to establish conflict, rising action (your character's plan to overcome the conflict), climax, falling action, and conclusion. Make a plan for the following topics using this plot structure. You might need to use another sheet of paper. Have a trusted reader look over your responses.

1. Prompt: He didn't want to go

   Conflict: Mario didn't want to spend all day working in his grandfather's garden. His fortunes changed when a big meteorite landed right in the middle of the yard. He noticed a door in the meteorite but he didn't know what to do.

   Rising Action: Mario decided to investigate the door. Inside, he discovered two squid-like aliens who informed him that his parents were in danger because their cruise ship might hit a reef. Mario decided to help the squid in a plan to save his parents.

   Climax: Mario was left alone to steer the meteorite spaceship while the squid dove into the sea to try to save his parents.

   Falling Action: The squid created a whirlpool in the ocean that diverted the cruise ship from the perilous reef. The squid then returned to the meteorite and helped Mario get back to his grandparents' house.

   Conclusion: After dropping Mario off at home, the aliens returned to their own home planet. Mario's parents returned from their vacation, none the wiser about their son's adventure.

2. Prompt: I saw the car speed away.

   Conflict:

   Rising Action:

   Climax:

   Falling Action:

   Conclusion:

3. Prompt: I know I can't do it alone.

   Conflict:

   Rising Action:

   Climax:

   Falling Action:

   Conclusion:

4. Prompt: She can't believe she can fly!

   Conflict:

   Rising Action:

   Climax:

   Falling Action:

   Conclusion:

5. Prompt: I thought about the problem.

   Conflict:

   Rising Action:

   Climax:

Falling Action:

Conclusion:

6. Prompt: I tell my mother I will be right back.

   Conflict:

   Rising Action:

   Climax:

   Falling Action:

   Conclusion:

7. Prompt: He finds it.

   Conflict:

   Rising Action:

   Climax:

   Falling Action:

   Conclusion:

8. Prompt: She had the strangest dream.

   Conflict:

Rising Action:

Climax:

Falling Action:

Conclusion:

ORGANIZE YOURSELF

Once you understand how to plan for content, planning how you will structure your story actually becomes rather easy:

STORY STRUCTURE	
Paragraph	**Content**
First paragraph	Establish tense, setting, point of view, and conflict.
Second paragraph	Show rising action (character devises a plan).
Third paragraph	Character sets the plan into motion.
Fourth paragraph	Conclude the story. Show whether the plan works or doesn't work and explain why.

If you get stuck, here are some questions you can ask yourself to stay focused:

- Who will be in the story?
- When does it take place?
- Where does it take place?
- What conflict will my characters face?
- What plan should my characters develop in order to deal with the conflict?
- Will my characters succeed or fail?

POLISHING YOUR WRITING

Before we go any further, let's return to the pyramid with which we began.

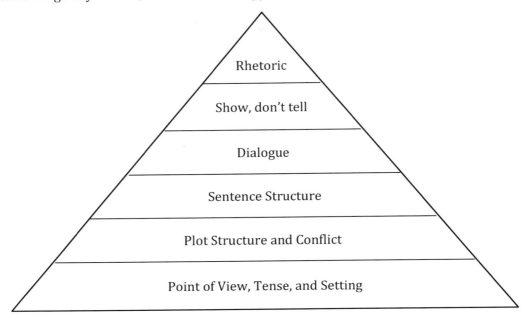

We've covered the foundation: point of view, tense, setting, conflict, and plot structure. This foundation provides the basic components of your story. Now, we're going to move toward the upper parts of the pyramid and discuss how to polish your storytelling technique—how to make a story engaging and interesting to read.

SENTENCE STRUCTURE

You should aim to vary your sentence structure. Study the following chart and compare the sentences to your own. Are your sentences as varied as they could be?

If you find yourself writing the same type and length of sentence over and over again, try to write a different one. If you are using the same words repeatedly, see if you can come up with another word to use.

SENTENCE STRUCTURE	
Sentence Type	**Example**
Short	What a long day at school! Jane was hungry. She opened the refrigerator. Whoosh! Three birds flew out.
Medium	After a long day at school, Jane was hungry. When she opened the refrigerator (whoosh), three birds flew out.
Long	After a long day at school, a rather hungry Jane opened her refrigerator door and – whoosh – three birds flew out!
Combination	After a long day at school, a rather hungry Jane opened her refrigerator door. Whoosh! Three birds flew out.

DIALOGUE

In short stories involving more than one character, you might find it natural to include **dialogue** to further develop your story. Dialogue occurs when two or more characters speak to one another.

When you quote a character, you want to make sure you always let your reader know who is speaking. You can do this by writing "he said" or "she said" before or after the quotation.

Dialogue is easy to write once you learn how to properly punctuate it. When writing dialogue, begin a new paragraph when the speaker changes. If you are quoting a complete sentence, you always capitalize the first word within the quotation—just like a normal sentence. If the sentence you are quoting is incomplete, you do not need to capitalize the first word within the quotation marks. Use commas to divide "he said" or "she said" from the quoted text. Study the following examples:

	SENTENCE EXAMPLES	
Sentence Type	**Explanation**	**Examples**
Questions or exclamations	When you are quoting a complete sentence and the sentence is a question or an exclamation, the question mark or exclamation point always belongs within the quotes. Note that nothing changes when "he said" or "she said" goes before or after the quoted text.	"Where is my mother?" asked Joe. Joe asked, "Where is my mother?" Jane shouted, "Charge!" "Charge!" shouted Jane. Jane asked, "Where can I find the office?" "Where is everyone?" wondered Mike.
Complete sentences	When the quote is a complete sentence, punctuation varies. If "he said" or "she said" comes *before* the complete sentence, the period belongs within the quotation. If "he said" or "she said" comes *after* the complete sentence, you do not use a period within the quotation. Instead you place a comma within the quotation marks and follow with the attribution.	Mike sighed and said, "I love you." "I love you," Mike said. Jane said, "I saw where he went." "I saw where he went," Jane said. Lois said, "I think I understand now." "I think I understand now," Lois said.
Incomplete sentences	When the quoted text is not a complete sentence, punctuation at the end of the sentence goes outside the quotation. Commas go inside the quotation when the quoted text is followed by either a new quote or the "he said." Commas are also always used to divide clauses in the sentence through normal grammar rules. When a quotation ends a sentence, the period belongs inside the quotation.	Did Joe really say, "I do not know the way home"? "Well," said Joe, pausing to think, "we need to go," but he was interrupted by Jane who had an idea. Jane read the list. "James," "Mike," and "Laurie" were included. What does it mean to "calculate the perimeter"? The test asked me to "find the area of a triangle."

Ivy Global

Exercise #5: The following quotes are not punctuated or capitalized. Rewrite the quotes using proper punctuation and capitalization. Answers are provided at the end of this section.

1. Did Anne really say I don't know how to tie my shoe laces

2. I know where to go Mario said

3. Marina said I will find the right book

4. Incredible exclaimed Ismaeel

5. Well he said it makes sense

6. I heard her say go but I didn't hear her say stop

7. Where is the park asked Samuel

8. Maria asked can I borrow this book

SHOW, DON'T TELL

Remember to use language that uses the five senses: sight, smell, taste, hearing, and touch. When describing people, places, or things, identify and describe key characteristics. Finally, make sure that for every action in your story, there is a proper reaction. In other words, you should establish clear causes and effects. Actions should be followed by consequences and your characters should react to events in your story in a logical, believable manner. Review the basics of descriptive writing covered earlier in this chapter.

RHETORIC

So far we've covered the essential elements of strong writing. It is important to maintain a consistent point of view and tense. You'll want to establish a setting for your story using your five senses and ensure that your story has a clear plot structure. You'll also want to practice developing interesting conflicts for your characters. It's important to also vary the length of your sentences while working to write vividly in a way that shows rather than tells.

Once you've mastered these skills, you'll also want to think about employing rhetorical devices in your writing. **Similes**, **metaphors**, and **personification** can bring your writing to life.

A **simile** compares two different things using the words "like" or "as":

- The moon is like a boat in the sky.
- The road was as twisted as a snake.

A **metaphor** compares two different things without using "like" or "as":

- The moon is a boat in the sky.
- The road was a snake that wound through the mountains.

When you use human qualities to describe things and animals, you are using **personification**:

- The moon smiled in the sky.
- The hawk studied the mountains for signs of prey.

Rhetorical devices help bring your writing to life. Strong writing often vividly employs rhetorical devices. Next time you write, try incorporating rhetorical devices into your writing.

Ivy Global

SAMPLE STORIES AND PROMPTS

Look at the following sample stories to see how these writers have used the strategies outlined in this chapter. Then, try writing your own stories using the sample prompts at the end of the section.

SAMPLE STORIES

The following **sample stories** expand upon the given prompt in the first sentence, and use vivid descriptive language to illustrate one main event. As you read, look for the setting, characters, and main event, and see if you can find the beginning, middle, and end.

SAMPLE STORY 1

Prompt: He didn't want to go.

He didn't want to go. The first day of sixth grade was not something Joey was looking forward to. There were too many new people to meet and get to know.

He was able to get through the first three periods without talking to anyone, but then it was lunchtime. The cafeteria was a sea of unfamiliar faces. It smelled of meatloaf and cleaning fluid. Joey couldn't find an empty table at which to sit, so he found the closest thing—a table with a tray on it, but nobody sitting there. He hoped that maybe the person wouldn't come back.

He was part-way through trying to enjoy his meatloaf when the person did come back: a tall girl in a purple sweater. She sat down without saying anything. Joey looked back at his meatloaf.

"I just hope they're not trying to impress us with this."

Joey looked back up at the girl. "Uh ... what?"

"I just hope they're not trying to impress us with this meatloaf. I mean, if it gets worse from here, we've got a rough year ahead of us." Joey glanced down at his meatloaf again. He had to agree with her. "Here," she said, pulling a paper bag out of her backpack and depositing it on the table between them. "I came prepared." She tore the paper away to reveal a pineapple.

Joey couldn't help but laugh. "What are you going to do with that?"

"Well, eat it." She looked at the pineapple, which sat up proudly on the table like a cross between a pet hedgehog and a palm tree. "Or ... try to."

Though they attacked it with every utensil the cafeteria made available to them, they could not break down the pineapple's spiky defenses. But by the time the bell rang for next period, they were laughing too hard to be too disappointed.

Joey looked forward to whatever exotic lunch substitute his new friend would bring tomorrow.

Exercise #6: Analyze the sample story above.

1. Identify the

   Point of view:

   Tense:

   Setting:

2. Underline and label the point where the writer establishes the:

   - Conflict
   - Rising Action
   - Climax
   - Falling Action
   - Conclusion

3. Circle and label rhetorical devices the author uses. Extra credit if you can name whether the device is a metaphor, simile, or personification.

4. Do you have any other ideas about how this story could end? Try writing a different ending for this story on a separate piece of paper.

SAMPLE STORY 2

Prompt: He didn't want to go.

He didn't want to go. Visiting his grandparents in the boring countryside wasn't Mario's idea of how he wanted to spend his spring break. But Mario had no choice. His parents were going on a cruise to the Bahamas and were leaving him with his grandparents. He knew Grandpa was going to make him work in the garden. Last year, Mario spent hours rigging the trees with chicken wire to protect his grandfather's precious garden from the constant assault of rabbits, squirrels, and foxes. Yet, when Mario's parents left, Grandpa's face hardened into an inscrutable expression of concern.

"Grandson, this year we have a bigger problem," said Grandpa, handing Mario a shovel.

"What do you mean?" said Mario.

"You'll see," said Grandpa.

A rock the size of an elephant sat smoldering in the area where the garden had been.

"What's this?" said Mario.

"It fell two nights ago," Grandpa said.

All day, Mario worked to help his grandfather dig out the rock. On the third day of work, Mario noticed a groove in the rock that looked like a door. Mario decided not to tell his grandfather about his discovery. Later that night, when Grandpa and Grandma were fast asleep, Mario approached the door. It glowed in the darkness. Mario held his breath and tapped on it, and to his utter shock, the door slid open. He couldn't believe what he saw next. Two green creatures that looked like giant squid peered out of the portal. Mario slowly backed away from them. His hands trembled and he dropped his flashlight. One of the creatures spoke first. "Your parents are in grave danger. Tomorrow their cruise ship will hit a reef and sink. We need you to come with us, to help save them." Again, Mario could not believe his ears, but he realized that he had no choice. If his parents were in danger, he'd do anything to help. He passed through the portal.

When the door slid closed, Mario felt the rock spin beneath him and he felt like he was on a ride at a carnival. When the door opened again a few moments later, he saw a ship coasting serenely on an electric blue tropical sea. "We need you to steer the machine while we work," the creatures said. They showed him how to steer the rock so that it would hover in place just over the water. Then, the creatures slid into the ocean. Mario couldn't believe what he saw next. The creatures formed a whirlpool in front of the ship, causing it to change its course. They returned to the ship moments later.

"Well, our work here is done!"

"Will everything be okay?" asked Mario, still concerned.

"Yes. We've diverted them from the reef."

The creatures took Mario home and the rock disappeared from Grandpa's yard the following day. The creatures were gone. A week later, Mario's parents arrived at Grandma and Grandpa's doorstep, tanned from the sun. "Did you have a good time, Mario?" they asked.

Mario smiled. "You cannot imagine," he said.

Exercise #7: Analyze the sample story above.

1. Identify the following:

    Point of view:

    Tense:

    Setting:

2. Underline and label the point where the writer establishes the:

    - Conflict
    - Rising Action
    - Climax
    - Falling Action
    - Conclusion

3. Circle and label rhetorical devices the author uses. Extra credit if you can name whether the device is a metaphor, simile, or personification.

4. Do you have any other ideas about how this story could end? Try writing a different ending for this story on a separate piece of paper.

SAMPLE PROMPTS

On a separate sheet of paper, practice brainstorming and writing stories using the following **sample prompts**. Have a trusted reader evaluate your work.

1. She waved goodbye.
2. The telephone rang.
3. There was a loud noise in the other room.
4. He didn't understand it.
5. The door was ajar.
6. She went to the window and saw...
7. I was suddenly woken up by...
8. There was nowhere to go except...
9. I couldn't believe that...
10. I was almost ready to go when...

THE ESSAY:
UPPER LEVEL ONLY

The SSAT requires Upper-Level students to write either a short story or an essay in twenty-five minutes. The essay topics tend to be broad and varied. In some cases, you will be asked to take a side on an issue (in other words, you will be asked to write a **persuasive essay**). In some cases, you will be asked to offer a description or to show cause and effect (in other words, you will be asked to write an **informative essay**). Two sentences will be provided, and students are asked to select the sentence they find most interesting and to use it as the basis for an essay or a story.

Students should be prepared to write a short story, a persuasive essay, or an informative essay. Work through the preceding section for short story strategies. The short story prompts for Upper Level students tend to be more serious and formal than the Middle Level prompts (they might present a moral dilemma or suggest a more narrowly defined conflict or setting). The essay prompt will usually ask you to reflect on your own life, thoughts, and values, or on a current issue. The question will ask you to state an opinion, to share an experience, to offer a definition, or to present a description.

UNDERSTAND YOUR MISSION

The Upper Level essay section is particularly challenging because it requires you to know the difference between persuasive writing, informative writing, and creative writing. In order to write a successful essay, it is important to practice differentiating between different types of writing.

CREATIVE WRITING

A **creative writing** prompt presents an open-ended scenario. While a conflict or a dilemma may be established, the prompt won't necessarily ask you to write about yourself.

Some examples of creative writing prompts include:

- He would have to try again.

- It was the biggest challenge he would have to face.

PERSUASIVE WRITING

Persuasive writing requires you to state an opinion. You may be asked to argue for or against an idea, to urge the reader to act a certain way, or to urge the reader to agree to a certain position on an issue. In short, persuasive writing will require you to take a side on an issue.

Some examples of persuasive writing prompts include:

- Is it more important to learn from mistakes or successes?
- Which are more important, arts and music or sports and athletics?

INFORMATIVE WRITING

Informative writing is rather broadly defined. The purpose of informative writing is to describe, to define characteristics and qualities, to provide an extended definition, to explain, to inform, or to show cause and effect.

Some examples of informative writing prompts include:

- What three qualities define a good student?
- What is the most important issue facing the world today and what would you do to contribute to solving this issue?

Exercise #1: Identify whether the topics presented below are creative writing, persuasive, or informative prompts. Answers are provided at the end of this section.

1. What three qualities make for a good school?

2. They had to make a plan.

3. One rule that should never be broken is . . .

4. Which is more important, science or literature?

5. Should students be required to wear uniforms to school?

6. He solved the problem.

7. If I saw a student cheating on a test, I would . . .

KNOW YOUR STRENGTHS

Once you know the difference between creative writing, persuasive, and informative prompts, you'll want to practice responding to each in timed settings. Consider starting by practicing using some of the prompts provided for Exercise #1. Show your writing to a trusted reader. Are you stronger at one kind of writing? Are you more comfortable with one type of writing? Knowing where you excel will help you more easily choose a prompt on test day. Knowing yourself better will also help you choose a prompt that will best highlight your strengths.

You'll still want to know how to respond to creative, persuasive, and informative prompts because it is hard to predict what kind of prompts the test writers will ask you to write on test day.

We've already covered creative writing in the preceding section. Now we'll take a closer look at persuasive and informative writing.

PERSUASIVE ESSAYS

Persuasive writing will ask you to state an opinion. When writing persuasively, you'll want to:

- Clearly state your position on the prompt or issue presented. This will be your thesis statement. The thesis statement should let your reader clearly know what opinion you hold. Your entire essay should support your thesis statement.

- Explain why you hold the position you hold. Take a side. Don't sit on the fence.

- Use concrete examples to support your position: History, science, literature, or current event examples work best. Well-described personal examples can also be effective.

- Conclude your essay by refuting (disproving) a counterexample.

STRUCTURE

A four-paragraph essay works well for most persuasive prompts. The essay should contain an introduction in which you state your position and introduce your supporting examples, two body paragraphs explaining and supporting your opinion, and a conclusion paragraph that includes a counterexample.

Note: for some prompts, it may be useful to provide three reasons for your opinion, in which case you should write three shorter body paragraphs.

ESSAY STRUCTURE	
Paragraph Type	**Content**
Introduction Paragraph	Take a side on the issue presented. The sentence that explains your position is your **thesis statement**. Introduce two reasons why you believe what you believe.

Body Paragraph: Evidence/Support	Introduce your first supporting reason with a clear topic sentence. Provide 2 – 3 sentences that offer clear details about this reason. Make sure your concluding sentence clearly relates this example back to your thesis.
Body Paragraph: Evidence/Support	**Transition** from your first reason to your second reason. Provide 2 – 3 sentences that offer clear details about this reason. Make sure your concluding sentence explains how this reason supports your thesis.
Conclusion Paragraph: Counterexample/ Summary	Introduce a **counterexample** and refute or disprove it, ideally using reasoning from your body paragraphs. If you cannot think of a counterexample, make sure you summarize your reasons and your thesis.

PLAN AHEAD

A successful essay needs strong specific examples or reasons to demonstrate your position or opinion. The best examples are "big picture" examples from history, literature, or current events. Examples from your personal life can be effective, but these examples can be more difficult to clearly narrate in the limited time provided.

Think about important people or events that you have studied in history class, in books you have read recently, or events you have read about in newspapers. Consider your knowledge of government and politics. Be as specific as possible—for instance, instead of discussing "wars" in general, discuss a specific war or battle. Make sure you select topics about which you know a great deal. Make sure you are able to provide names, places, dates, and other detailed background information for every example you choose.

Before you start writing, take a few minutes to brainstorm examples for both sides of the argument. Then, pick the side that has the stronger examples—it doesn't necessarily have to be the side you agree with.

Let's say you choose the following topic: *Do we learn more from our mistakes or from our successes?*

Let's brainstorm!

BRAINSTORMING EXERCISE	
We learn more from our mistakes because…	**We learn more from our successes because…**
Only 705 of the Titanic's 2,224 passengers and crew survived when the ship hit an iceberg in 1912. The ship didn't have enough lifeboats for every passenger. The disaster led to better regulation later, with governments in both Britain and America requiring all ships to have enough lifeboats to accommodate all passengers.	Gregor Mendel set out to study variation in plants. He cultivated pea plants in his monastery and, as a result of his observations, he was able to develop his important Laws of Inheritance. For every trait, an individual possesses two alleles. Only one allele is passed on to offspring from each parent. This discovery helps account for genetic variation in individuals.
Alexander Fleming was a brilliant researcher, but he wasn't tidy. Before going on vacation, he stacked his Petri dishes on a bench in his laboratory. When he returned, he noticed that one of the dishes had been mistakenly left without a lid and had grown a mold. The mold killed the bacteria in the Petri dish. Fleming had discovered Penicillin, a lifesaving antibiotic.	Early success often has a positive impact on later success. Wolfgang Amadeus Mozart was a child prodigy. By age five, he was proficient on the piano and had already begun to compose music. His early experience allowed him to develop into a lifelong learner. In his maturity, he became a musician capable of composing the *Requiem*.
Last year, I wrote an article for the school newspaper that won a district award. Yet, before I wrote the winning story, I wrote several drafts with which I wasn't pleased. I revised my work and showed it to teachers. Finally, after several attempts, I wrote a story with which I was pleased. This story went on to win the district award.	In grade five I made it my summer goal to read a complete play by Shakespeare in the original Early Modern English. I worked very hard, and by the end of the summer, I completed *Romeo and Juliet*. I gained the confidence after the summer to try to read challenging books during the school year. I am now working on reading H.G. Wells' *The Time Machine*.

Exercise #2: Practice brainstorming on the following prompts. Think of two "big picture" examples for each side of the issue. Decide which side has the stronger examples. Have a trusted reader review your work.

1. Do you prefer group work or individual work?

    I prefer group work because . . .

    Example One:

Example Two:

I prefer individual work because . . .
Example One:

Example Two:

2. Do you think money is important to a happy life? Why or why not?

I think money is important to a happy life because . . .
Example One:

Example Two:

I think money is not important to a happy life because . . .
Example One:

Example Two:

3. Which do you think is more important, kindness or intelligence?

Kindness is more important than intelligence because . . .
Example One:

Example Two:

Intelligence is more important than kindness because . . .
Example One:

Example Two:

4. Does technology make people's lives better? Why or why not?

Technology makes people's lives better because . . .
Example One:

Example Two:

Technology makes people's lives more difficult because . . .

   Example One:

   Example Two:

5. In your opinion, what is the most important school rule?

   Think of a first school rule:

     One reason why this rule is important:

     Another reason why this rule is important:

   Think of a second school rule:

     One reason why this rule is important:

     Another reason why this rule is important:

6. If you had the power to read your best friend's mind, would you use it? Why or why not?

   I would choose to read my best friend's mind because . . .

     Example One:

     Example Two:

   I would not choose to read my best friend's mind because . . .

     Example One:

     Example Two:

WHAT TO INCLUDE IN AN INTRODUCTION

After you decide what position you will take to answer the prompt, use the first paragraph of your essay to introduce your reader to this position. Start by explaining the issue in your own words to show that you understand the prompt. Don't begin with "Yes, I agree" or "No, I don't agree"– make sure that you are using full sentences! After you have explained the issue, take a side. The sentence where you explain your own position on the issue is called your **thesis** statement. After your thesis statement, use the last one or two sentences of your introduction to briefly introduce the reasons or examples that you will be using to demonstrate your position.

WHAT TO INCLUDE IN A BODY PARAGRAPH

After your first paragraph introduces your position, the next two paragraphs are your body paragraphs supporting your position. Your body paragraphs should each have an example with specific and relevant **details**. Give enough background information that your example would make sense to a reader who knows nothing at all about it. Explain the "who," "what," "when," "where," "why," and "how." In one or two sentences, analyze how your example supports your position. This is the "aha!" part of your essay—your reader should say, "Aha! That is why this example is important!" End each body paragraph with a concluding sentence summarizing your example and connecting it clearly back to your main point.

WRITING A COUNTERARGUMENT

Students often wonder how to conclude essays. One way to effectively conclude your essay is to include a counterargument. In a **counterargument**, you identify an objection to your thesis or position and then refute or disprove that objection.

When developing a counterargument, you will want to imagine an intelligent skeptic reading your essay. If a friend held an opposing view to yours, how would he or she respond to your argument? Express your counterargument fairly. A strong, fairly presented, well-refuted counterargument lends credibility to your writing and can make the difference between an acceptable essay and an excellent one.

Let's say you've just finished writing a stellar essay about the benefits of wearing school uniforms. You've argued your position using strong examples and now it's time to conclude your essay. But, before you set your pen to page, imagine what would happen if you showed your essay to a friend who doesn't believe students should have to wear school uniforms. What would your friend say? You friend might say, "Uniforms make students less creative; less able to express themselves."

Or, let's say you show your essay to a school principal who doesn't believe students should be asked to wear uniforms. Your principal might say, "Uniforms promote elitism."

Or, let's say you show your essay to a mother who doesn't believe her child should wear uniforms. The parent might say, "Uniforms are too expensive."

The responses above are objections to your position. A strong counterargument presents an objection and responds to it.

There are several ways you can respond to an objection. The following chart provides a few counterarguments you might use to defend your position on uniforms:

COUNTERARGUMENT EXAMPLES		
Objection	How to respond	Counterargument
Uniforms make students less creative; less able to express themselves.	Show ways in which the objection is valid, but not important.	*While adolescents require opportunities to express themselves, clothing is neither the best nor the only medium.*
Uniforms promote elitism	Show ways in which the objection is flawed.	*Some have gone as far as to claim that uniforms promote elitism, but elitism is a mental state. Mental states can be occasioned by many factors, clothing being only one factor among many.*
Uniforms are too expensive	Minimize the objection or compare and contrast it to your	*While uniforms can indeed be costly, everyday clothes can sometimes be even more expensive.*

Exercise #3: Practice writing counterarguments for the following prompts. Have a trusted reader evaluate your work.

1. Do you prefer group work or individual work?

    My opinion:

    One objection to my opinion:

    My response to this objection:

2. Do you think money is important to a happy life?

    My opinion:

    One objection to my opinion:

    My response to this objection:

3. Which do you think is more important, kindness or intelligence?

    My opinion:

    One objection to my opinion:

    My response to this objection:

4. Does technology make people's lives better? Why or why not?

    My opinion:

    One objection to my opinion:

    My response to this objection:

5. In your opinion, what is the most important school rule?

    My opinion:

    One objection to my opinion:

    My response to this objection:

6. If you had the power to read your best friend's mind, would you use it? Why or why not?

    My opinion:

    One objection to my opinion:

    My response to this objection:

Ivy Global

SAMPLE PERSUASIVE ESSAY

In the following sample persuasive essay, the author gives a specific answer to the prompt using two main reasons. As you read, observe how the writer follows the structure we learned about above.

Prompt: *Do we learn more from our mistakes or from our successes?*

While success is the result of mastery and learning, learning itself is often the result of a willingness to learn from errors or mistakes. People grow when they are given the opportunity to properly evaluate and correct for their failures. This is evident in the sciences, but it is also true in my life. Alexander Fleming invented Penicillin because he was able to properly evaluate the repercussions from an error he made. In my own life, my ability to evaluate my own shortcomings has helped me to develop as a writer.

Alexander Fleming was a brilliant researcher, but he wasn't very tidy. Before going on vacation, he stacked his Petri dishes on a bench in his laboratory. However, he made a crucial mistake: he failed to cover one of the dishes with a lid. The dishes contained strains of Staphylococci. Staphylococci are sometimes harmless bacteria, but pathogenic strains can cause food poisoning and respiratory disease. When Fleming returned home from his vacation, he noticed that one of the lidless dishes had grown a mold. Where the mold grew, the Staphylococci had been eradicated. Fleming had made the error of not properly storing his Petri dishes. Yet, Fleming's willingness to explore the implications of the mold on his Petri dishes led to the discovery of Penicillin, a life-saving antibiotic. In this case, a careless mistake led to a discovery that changed medicine forever.

In the sciences, errors can sometimes lead to discovery; the same is true for those who work in language arts. I often write for my school newspaper. Last year, I wrote several drafts for an important story about school uniforms, but I wasn't pleased with any of my drafts. The structure wasn't quite right and I didn't like how the story ended. My advisor told me to revise my work. I knew I needed to work harder. Finally, after several false starts and a couple of outright failures, I wrote a draft with which I was pleased. This story went on to win a district journalism award. In this case, my ability to learn from failure allowed me to write a better story.

Some might claim that early success has a lasting effect on later success, and for this reason failure at all cost should be avoided. This claim might seem valid at first. For example, Wolfgang Amadeus Mozart was a child prodigy whose early successes allowed him to become a successful composer at a young age. Yet Mozart was no stranger to failure. As an adult, he failed to accept many good appointments and fell into debt. However, this time of failure was essential to Mozart's growth as an artist.

During this time he wrote important pieces, most notably Symphony Number 31. Mistakes, failures, errors, and difficulties create opportunities for learning. In the sciences, Fleming discovered Penicillin, a life-saving drug. Failure also tempers those who work in the arts. One doesn't have to be Mozart to learn this lesson; I learned its value as a writer for my school paper.

Exercise #4: Evaluate the sample essay. Have a trusted reader evaluate your summary.

1. What is the author's opinion?

2. What is the author's first reason and evidence?

3. What is the author's second reason and evidence?

4. What is one objection the author presents?

5. What is the author's response to the objection?

SAMPLE PERSUASIVE ESSAY PROMPTS

Now, try your hand at writing your own essays using the prompts we've explored earlier in this section. For each of the following **sample prompts**, on a separate sheet of paper, write a practice 25-minute essay using the structure and brainstorming exercises completed earlier. Have a trusted reader evaluate your work.

1. Do you prefer group work or individual work?
2. Do you think money is important to a happy life? Why or why not?
3. Which do you think is more important, kindness or intelligence?
4. Does technology make people's lives better? Why or why not?
5. In your opinion, what is the most important school rule?
6. If you had the power to read your best friend's mind, would you use it? Why or why not?

INFORMATIVE ESSAYS

For an **informative essay**, you may be asked to describe or characterize something, offer an explanation, or show cause and effect.

There are two main types of informative essays that you may be required to write:

1. A **descriptive essay** requires you to describe or define characteristics or qualities. Prompts might include:

   - Describe one thing you do well.
   - What do you want to be when you grow up?
   - What three qualities make for a good teacher?
   - Everyone has a person he or she admires. Write about this person and list three characteristics this person possesses that makes him or her admirable.

2. A **cause and effect essay** requires you to describe a situation and analyze its possible causes and effects. Prompts might include:

   - What would you do if you saw a student bullying another student?
   - What is one problem facing the world today and what is one thing you can do to help solve this problem?
   - What is the most important lesson you have learned? How have you changed as a result?

We'll discuss approaches to each of these essays in this section.

WRITING A DESCRIPTIVE ESSAY

When writing a **descriptive essay**, or an essay that asks you to **define characteristics and qualities**, stick to topics you know. The topics are defined broadly, so the specific subject matter is largely up to you to decide. For example, if you are asked to write about your favorite subject in school, it makes sense to choose a subject you know well.

Before you start writing, choose two or three qualities you'd like to discuss (and think of the reasons why you chose the subject you chose). Some prompts will specify how many characteristics or qualities you are required to find (in some cases you'll be asked to identify two qualities, in some cases, you'll be asked to identify three qualities). In your body paragraphs you'll want to explain the importance of the qualities you select and explain how these qualities relate to your subject. Descriptive writing is similar to persuasive writing. You must persuade your reader through vivid description that the qualities you have selected to define a specific topic are apt.

The following chart offers one way you can structure a descriptive essay.

DESCRIPTIVE ESSAY STRUCTURE	
Prompt: Which three qualities make a good teacher?	
Introduction Paragraph	Establish the three qualities you'd like to discuss: *I admire teachers who set ambitious goals. Teachers who show expertise and organization place their students in a position to succeed.*
Body Paragraph 1	Establish why one of these qualities is important: *A teacher must have expertise. Joshua Bell developed mastery of the violin by learning from the expert violin master, Josef Gingold …*
Body Paragraph 2	Establish why the second of these qualities is important: *In order to learn, we must be organized. Watson and Crick's discovery of DNA was the result of the scientists' attempt to organize and understand the work of other scientists …*
Body Paragraph 3	Establish why the third of these qualities is important: *Teachers should set ambitious goals. Had John F. Kennedy not set the ambitious goal of sending people to the moon, the Apollo missions would never have taken place …*
Conclusion Paragraph	Summarize your description: *While there are other important qualities that make a good teacher, the most important qualities, in my view, are ambition, organization, and expertise.*

Exercise #5: For each topic, identify your subject, some qualities you'd like to discuss, and why each quality is important. Have a trusted reader evaluate your work.

1. Describe one thing you do well.

    Identify the subject (name one thing you do well):

    Explain one way in which you excel in this area:

    Explain why this is important:

    Name another way in which you excel in this area:

    Explain why this is important:

2. What do you want to be when you grow up?

    Identify the subject (name what you want to be when you grow up):

    One reason why I aspire to this goal:

    Explain why this is important:

    Second reason why I aspire to this goal:

    Explain why this is important:

3. Everyone has a person he or she admires. Write about this person and list three characteristics this person possesses that makes him or her admirable.

    Identify the subject (the person you admire):

    Name one characteristic this person possesses:

    Explain why this is important:

    Name another characteristic this person possesses:

Explain why this is important:

Name a third characteristic this person possesses:

Explain why this is important:

4. What is your favorite subject in school? What characteristics make this subject appealing?

   Identify the subject:

   Name one characteristic:

   Explain why this is important:

   Name a second characteristic:

   Explain why this is important:

5. Tell us about a time you did something you are proud of.

   Identify the subject (name the thing that makes you proud):

   Name one reason why this is important:

   Name a second reason why this is important:

SAMPLE DESCRIPTIVE ESSAY

In the following **sample descriptive essay**, the author gives a specific answer to the prompt using two main reasons. As you read, look for the main structure of the essay (introduction, body paragraphs, and conclusion), and identify how the author uses supporting details as evidence for her opinion.

Prompt: *Whom do you admire, and why?*

I admire my grandmother for her creativity and for her independent-mindedness. She showed her creativity in the countless paintings and other artwork she made throughout her life, and she showed her independent mind by going back to work while she was still raising her children.

My grandmother's creativity is apparent in the many beautiful paintings that adorn the walls in the homes of her four children. My aunt's dining room boasts a large oil painting of herself and her siblings playing in a stream; in my bedroom, I have a small watercolor of an African violet, my grandmother's favorite flower. She was able to evoke the fuzz of the violet's leaves by painting a fine sheen of gray over the green. My grandmother also made the beautiful quilt on my bed. As an aspiring artist, I am inspired by my grandmother's creative work.

In addition to being creative, my grandmother was also very independent. When she was raising my mother and her siblings in the 1960s, it was unusual in her community for a mother to work outside the home. My grandmother was not happy working only as a wife and mother, however, so she took a job as a teacher at the local elementary school. Her friends and even her husband were surprised by this choice. They didn't understand why she would want to devote so much time to a job when my grandfather made enough money to support their family comfortably. The work made her happy, however, so she did it in spite of others' objections. I admire her choice to pursue her own happiness even when that led her down an unusual path.

My grandmother enjoyed using her creativity to make beautiful things, and she was able to reap the rewards of a teaching career due to her independent-mindedness. I admire her for these qualities, and hope that I share them.

Exercise #6: Analyze the sample essay above. What are the author's subject, characteristics, and reasons?

1. Identify the subject:

2. Identify the first characteristic the author describes:

3. Explain why this is important:

4. Identify the second characteristic the author describes:

5. Explain why this is important:

Let's take a closer look at how to structure a **body paragraph** using the second paragraph from the sample essay. Remember that a body paragraph should include specific and relevant details to explain the author's reason or example, and should also include an "aha!" statement that shows why this example supports the author's position.

My grandmother's creativity is apparent in the many beautiful paintings that adorn the walls in the homes of her four children. *(In the first sentence, the author introduces the first reason that she admires her grandmother: her creativity.)* My aunt's dining room boasts a large oil painting of herself and her siblings playing in a stream; in my bedroom, I have a small watercolor of an African violet, my grandmother's favorite flower. She was able to evoke the fuzz of the violet's leaves by painting a fine sheen of gray over the green. My grandmother also made the beautiful quilt on my bed. *(In the next three sentences, the author provides specific details as evidence of her grandmother's creativity.)* As an aspiring artist, I am inspired by my grandmother's creative work. *(The last sentence is the "aha!" statement: this is why the author admires her grandmother's creativity.)*

WRITING A CAUSE AND EFFECT ESSAY

Writing a strong **cause and effect essay** will require you to employ all the skills you have learned thus far. Put simply, you'll need to identify causes, explain effects, and offer solutions.

In other words, this essay will require you to describe, explain, and narrate. Before you start writing, you'll want to make sure you narrow the topic sufficiently to ensure that you can respond adequately in twenty-five minutes. For instance, if you have been asked to identify ways you can help your community, it probably doesn't make sense to choose a big unfeasible topic like eliminating homelessness. Instead, you might choose to write about how you would like to volunteer at a soup kitchen.

Include an introduction that provides clear background information and adequately identifies both the causes and effects of an issue. Before you explain how your solution (your desire to volunteer at a soup kitchen) relates to the issue, you'll also want to describe and explain some of the causes and effects of homelessness.

Sometimes the prompt will only present the effects of an issue and it is your job to establish the causes. In some cases, the prompt will present you with a problem and ask you to develop a solution. Even if you have only been asked to develop a solution, a strong essay will explain the causes and effects that led you to decide on a particular course of action.

After you have adequately framed the causes and effects relating to a given issue, you'll want to offer solutions or explain how things can be done differently to improve the situation. Here, you'll want to employ not only your critical thinking skills, but also your ability to narrate possibilities and show potential outcomes.

Cause and effect essays require advanced writing abilities. How you structure your writing will depend on the requirements of the topic. Your goal should be to write an essay that is both logical and clear.

Let's plan a cause and effect essay together:

CAUSE AND EFFECT ESSAY STRUCTURE	
Prompt: What are some things you could start doing today to prevent climate change?	
Establish causes	Climate change is the result of greenhouse gas emissions. These emissions are caused by energy use. I use quite a bit of energy. For instance, sometimes I forget to turn off the light when I leave a room.
Establish effects	Leaving the lights on has negative consequences for the environment. Climate change results in more severe storms, like Hurricane Sandy. It also destroys polar ice, which affects many species.
Offer solutions	By remembering to turn off the lights when I leave the room, I can make a small but important positive impact on the environment. By biking to soccer practice instead of having my parents drive me, I can help prevent climate change.

Exercise #7: For the following topics, establish causes, effects, and offer solutions. Have a trusted reader look over your responses.

1. What would you do if you saw a student bullying another student?

   Establish causes:

   Establish effects:

   Offer solutions:

2. What is one problem facing the world today and what is one thing you can do to help solve this problem?

   Name the problem:

   Establish causes:

   Establish effects:

   Offer solutions:

3. What is the most important lesson you have learned? How have you changed as a result?

Name the lesson:

Establish causes:

Establish effects:

Offer solutions:

SAMPLE CAUSE AND EFFECT ESSAY

In the following **sample cause and effect essay**, the author identifies causes, effects, and offers a solution to a problem. As you read, look at how the author the author identifies causes, effects, and a solution to a problem.

Prompt: *What are some things you could start doing today to prevent continued climate change?*

Human industrial activity has led to the 20th century being the warmest in recorded history. Scientific consensus links the recent trend of increased global temperature to the release of carbon dioxide into the atmosphere. The burning of fossil fuels in industry and for personal uses further exacerbates a problem many scientists currently deem irreversible. Societies will have to limit their output of carbon dioxide if we hope to see the global temperature stop increasing over the next century. Individuals can help mitigate the problem by being conscientious of their energy use.

Climate change is a problem worth addressing because it holds negative consequences for both people and the environment. Increased global temperatures are linked to more severe storms, like hurricanes Katrina and Sandy. The economic costs of these storms is in the billions of dollars and there is no measuring the toll of human suffering when one considers the thousands who have lost homes, businesses, and loved ones due to these weather events. Climate change also increases the rate at which species go extinct. Besides the obvious loss of arctic habitat for penguins and polar bears, animals in other regions of the world suffer from changed habitats. Ignoring climate change means sanctioning the loss of an ecological heritage humanity cannot stand to lose.

There are several things I can do to help play a role in preventing further climate change. Leaving on lights when I am not using them has negative consequences for the environment. Power plants burn fossil fuels so that we may use electricity. Using more electricity means that power plants must burn more fossil fuels, meaning more carbon dioxide is released into the atmosphere. Therefore, turning off lights when I am not in the room or using them is a small but important way I can play a role in preventing further climate change. Another way I can help is by biking to soccer practice instead of having my parents drive me. I can also take public transit on the weekends rather than choosing to drive. Fewer cars on the road means fewer sources of carbon dioxide.

Resolving climate change permanently will clearly require global cooperation between governments and industry. While the problem might seem initially unmanageably large, there are definitely measures I can take in my daily life to play a role in resolving this incredibly important global issue.

Exercise #8: Analyze the sample essay above. What are the author's causes, effects, and solutions?

1. What causes does the author establish?

2. What effects does the author name?

3. What solutions does the author provide?

SAMPLE INFORMATIVE ESSAY PROMPTS

It's important to remember that there is some overlap between a descriptive and a cause/effect essay. There are many ways you can go about planning and writing an informative essay, and the ways outlined in this chapter are just intended to get you started.

For each of the following sample prompts, on a separate sheet of paper, write a practice 25-minute essay. If you need additional topics, use the prompts from the exercises in this section. Show your work to a trusted reader.

1. What is one problem that you have faced, and how did you solve it?
2. If you could do something over again, what would it be, and why?
3. What is one book that has changed the way you think about something?
4. Tell us about a time when you did something you are proud of.
5. Tell us about something you learned from a friend. Why was it a valuable lesson?

VOCABULARY BUILDING

CHAPTER 6

INTRODUCTION

Vocabulary building is the best long-term way to improve your English score. In this chapter, learn some effective and fun strategies for learning SSAT-level words. Although this process might seem intimidating at first, learning words can be fun when you make some of these activities a regular part of your study schedule. And remember that vocabulary building is not just helpful for the SSAT—learning words will help you improve your reading, writing, and speaking skills in school and beyond!

VOCABULARY BUILDING STRATEGIES

The words you will encounter on the SSAT are commonly found in middle- and high-school level academic texts, but some words may be more advanced or less familiar depending on your age. The best way to expose yourself to more advanced vocabulary is to read as much as possible. Read a wide variety of genres—fiction, nonfiction, poetry, newspaper articles— and look up words you don't know. Pay attention to any words that are unfamiliar in the SSAT practice exercises you are working on, and look them up as well.

At the end of this section, you will also find a list of 500 words that will help you start preparing for the level of vocabulary that commonly appears on the SSAT. Use these words as a starting point, and supplement this list with your own personal words from your reading and practice exercises. In order to make this process more fun and effective, use the following strategies when you are learning and reviewing new words.

LEARN THE DEFINITION WITH A PERSONAL TRIGGER

When you learn a new word, the first step is to learn its definition. Some words have more than one meaning, and sometimes the SSAT will ask you to identify a less common meaning for a word. Therefore, make sure you learn **all possible meanings** for any new word you look up.

When you learn a word's definition, it is just as important to learn how a word is **used in a sentence**. Pay attention to any sample sentences that demonstrate how the word is used, and look up more examples in a dictionary or online.

Finally, come up with a **personal trigger** to help you build a personal connection with the word. This can be as simple as writing your own personal sentence for the word. The more personal, the better—if the sentence relates to your own personal life, you'll have an easier time remembering it! For example, if your word is "irritable," you might write a personal sentence like "My aunt Martha is sometimes irritable and grouchy." This way, when you think of the word "irritable," you'll think of your grouchy aunt!

If you can't think of a personal story to connect with your word, see if you can come up with **a wacky way to remember the word** based on what it sounds like. For example, "confluence" means convergence or coming together. A wacky way to remember confluence might be to think of the flu. If one person in a group has the flu and then all of the people come together, chances are they will all get the flu!

KEEP A VOCABULARY JOURNAL

Keep your own personal vocabulary journal as you work your way through this book's word list and as you do your own outside reading. A vocabulary journal is the best way to personalize your vocabulary learning because it allows you to keep track of any words that are new to you. Any time you come across a new word in this book's word list, in an SSAT practice test, or in your own reading, write it down in your journal. Include the definition and an example. It is also sometimes helpful to note the context in which you first encountered the word. For particularly difficult words include a personal trigger or wacky association. Make sure you also understand whether the word is a noun, verb, adjective, or adverb (see page 88 for a review of these types of words). If you find it helpful, you can write "N" for noun, "V" for verb, "Adj" for adjective, and "Adv" for adverb.

Use the following sample entries as a model to start your own journal.

My Vocabulary Journal
Date: _____

Abduct

Definition: to kidnap

Sentence: Susan was abducted by aliens and taken to a faraway planet.

Personal trigger: Think of the word "duck," as to crouch down. If you see an alien ship coming to abduct you, you'd better duck!

Abscond

Definition: to depart in a sudden and secret manner, particularly to avoid capture or legal prosecution

Sentence: The cashier absconded with the money.

Personal trigger: Abscond has "scon" in it, which is close to "scone." Think of a baker absconding from the bakery and bringing lots of scones with him.

Akimbo

Definition: with hands on hips and elbows extending outwards

Sentence: Jeremy stood with arms akimbo, looking very cross.

Personal trigger: Akimbo rhymes with limbo. It certainly wouldn't be easy to do the limbo with arms akimbo!

MAKE FLASHCARDS

Make **flashcards** to help you practice the words in this book's word list and in your own vocabulary journal. Write the word on the front and the definition, type of word, and personal example sentence or trigger on the back. Here is an example:

Front	*Back*
Unique	*Definition: (Adj) the only one of its kind* *Sentence: Marjorie has a unique sense of style – she comes up with clothing combinations that I've never seen anyone else wear.*

If a word has multiple meanings, make sure you include all of these on your flashcard. For example:

Front	Back
Grave	(1) Definition: (N) a place of burial for the dead Sentence: Bill remembers his grandfather by visiting his grave every year. (2) Definition: (Adj.) serious, solemn, alarming Sentence: As the ground began to shake beneath them, they realized that they were in grave danger.

Take your flashcards with you throughout the day, and flip through them during your spare time as you're waiting in line or riding in the car, bus, or train. After you have mastered a word and can remember it easily, put it in a different pile and test yourself just on the words you have more difficulty remembering. As you learn new words, go back to your previous flashcard piles every so often and make sure you still remember your old words.

PRACTICE USING NEW WORDS

As you learn new words, practice using them as frequently as you can in your daily life. Use them when you talk with friends and parents and look out for them in your reading. Some students find it helpful (and fun!) to write a short story using as many vocabulary words as they can think of. You can keep the story going on for as long as you like, and keep adding new words each day.

Take a look at the following sample short story, which uses many of the words from this book's vocabulary list:

Yesterday morning, my parents told me that our family would be taking a surprise vacation to Hawaii. We had all been working too hard, and they could see that we were **fatigued**. I have very **compassionate** parents! I was very excited about the trip, but my older brother, Jim, was **apathetic**. "I've been to Hawaii already," he told me, "so I don't really care if I go again." When I told my best friend about the trip, I thought she would be happy for me, but instead she was irate. "Without me?!" she yelled. "You're taking a trip and leaving me here alone!?" My best friend is very **fickle**. Just that morning she had been in such a good mood. Usually when she gets angry like this, I become **meek** and **submissive**, and do whatever she says. But this time, I decided to stand up for what I wanted. I've always wanted to visit Hawaii, and am **resolute** about going on this trip.

As you work through the vocabulary list and add to your own journal, try finishing this story, or come up with your own!

CREATE A STUDY SCHEDULE

When you learn new words, remember that practice makes perfect! The more you repeat and review your words, the better you will remember them. Aim to work consistently, learning a small number of words on a daily basis, so you don't become overwhelmed. Creating a structured study schedule will help you set goals and track your progress. If you have a structured schedule to follow, you'll be more likely to stick with it. Set a goal for the number of words you would like to learn before your test, and divide this number by the days you have available. It may be helpful to set aside certain days of the week, like Saturdays or Sundays, to review the new and old words you have been learning.

Here is a sample study schedule for three weeks:

Week	Monday	Tuesday	Wednesday	Thursday	Friday	Saturday	Sunday
1	5 words	5 words	5 words	5 words	5 words	Review Week 1 words	Break
2	5 words	5 words	5 words	5 words	5 words	Review Week 2 words	Review Week 1 and 2 words
3	5 words	5 words	5 words	5 words	5 words	Review Week 3 words	Review Week 1, 2, & 3 words

If you keep up this schedule, you'll learn 75 words in 3 weeks, 150 words in 6 weeks, and 300 words in 12 weeks! Adjust the number of words you learn per night to fit the amount of time you have before your test, but make sure you are working at a pace that is feasible for you. If you are an older student, you may be able to remember 10 or more words per night. Don't forget to review both your new and your old words on a regular basis.

WORD ROOTS, PREFIXES AND SUFFIXES

In English grammar, many words can be broken into basic parts. Learning these basic parts will help you decipher unfamiliar vocabulary and speed up your vocabulary building process. Learning only 30 key word parts can help you decode over 10,000 words!

In this section, learn about the basic parts that make up English words and practice breaking down words into these parts. Learn some of the most common word parts by working your way through the list at the end of this section.

WORD ROOTS

The **root** of a word is the main building block that carries a specific meaning. If different words have the same root, they are related in meaning. Therefore, looking for a word's root or thinking of other words that have the same root can help you guess at a word's meaning. Knowledge of French, Spanish, German, or Latin can be helpful here, because many English word roots are similar to words in these languages.

For example, you might guess that the word root "act" means "to do." The words ACTION, ACTOR, and ACTIVE all involve doing things because they all have this same word root.

For a more advanced example, look at the word AMIABLE. If you know that "ami" in French and "amigo" in Spanish mean "friend," you can guess that this word might have something to do with friends. In fact, AMIABLE means "friendly."

This is because AMIABLE contains the word root "am," which has to do with love or liking. Can you think of some other words with the roots "am," "ami," or "amor," which relate to love or liking? Here is a list to get started:

- AMICABLE: friendly
- AMITY: friendly or peaceful relations
- ENAMOR: to fill with love

As another example, consider the word BENEFICENT, which contains the word root "ben." This root is related to the words "bien" in French and "bene" in Italian, which mean "good." We can guess that BENEFICENT means something good. In fact, it means "performing acts of kindness or charity."

Here are some other English words with the root "ben":

- BENEFICIAL: favorable, resulting in good
- BENEVOLENT: kind, well-meaning
- BENIGN: gentle, kind, not harmful

Exercise #1: Look at the list of word roots at the end of this section to find the meaning of the underlined roots below. Then, look up the definition of each word in a good dictionary. Notice how the root influences the meaning of the word! The first word has been filled out for you.

WORD	ROOT MEANING	DEFINITION OF WORD
bibliography	biblio: related to books	a list of books referred to in a scholarly work
carnivore		
chronology		
civilian		
fidelity		
juvenile		
mortuary		
potential		
sacred		
vacuous		
eloquent		

PREFIXES

Sometimes a word has a **prefix**, which is a small component that comes before the root. Not all words have prefixes—in fact, as you saw in Exercise #1, many words start with roots. However, when a word has a prefix, the prefix can significantly change the word's meaning.

For example, the word UNHAPPY has two parts: the prefix "un" and the root "happy." The prefix "un" means "not," so UNHAPPY means "not happy."

As a more advanced example, consider the word INCORRIGIBLE. "In" is another prefix that often means "not"—for instance, "inadequate" means "not adequate." So, INCORRIGIBLE means "not corrigible."

What does "corrigible" mean? We can think of another word with the root "corr": "correct." "Corrigible" means "able to be corrected" or "correctable." Therefore, INCORRIGIBLE means "not able to be corrected." It is often used to describe a person who is so bad or so stubborn that his or her behavior cannot be improved!

Exercise #2: Look at the list of prefixes at the end of this section to find the meaning of the underlined prefixes below. Then, look up the definition of each word in a good dictionary. Notice how the prefix influences the meaning of the word! The first word has been filled out for you.

WORD	PREFIX MEANING	DEFINITION OF WORD
<u>amphi</u>bian	*amphi: both*	*an animal that can live both in water and on land*
<u>circum</u>ference		
<u>contra</u>dict		
<u>dys</u>functional		
<u>inter</u>mediate		
<u>poly</u>gon		
<u>peri</u>meter		
<u>trans</u>parent		

SUFFIXES

A word might also have a **suffix**, which is a small component that comes at the end of a word. Not all words have suffixes. However, when they do, the suffix frequently changes the word's meaning or function. A suffix might change a word to a noun, verb, adjective, or adverb.

Take a moment to review the definitions of nouns, verbs, adjectives, and adverbs:

TYPES OF WORDS			
Word Type	**Definition**	**Examples**	**Sample Sentence**
Noun	a person, place, or thing: "things" can also include qualities or categories that you might not be able to touch or see	teacher, lawyer, city, Italy, animal, car, water, tool, hunger, comfort, curiosity, trust, emotion, science, art, biology	The young puppy ran quickly.
Verb	an action word: what the subject of the sentence (the main noun) is "doing"	run, hit, dig, carve, learn, hear, enjoy, understand, become, be	The young puppy ran quickly.
Adjective	a word that describes, identifies, or defines a noun	soft, sharp, green, full, loud, wet, happy, thoughtful, diligent, humorous, good	The young puppy ran quickly.
Adverb	a word that describes a verb, adjective, or another adverb: often ends in "-ly"	quickly, desperately, sadly, suddenly, freely, quietly, strangely, well	The young puppy ran quickly.

Notice how many of the adverb examples in the chart above end with the suffix "-ly." This is because the suffix "-ly" is a very common way to change an adjective into an adverb. For example, if you start with the adjective QUICK and add "-ly," you'll have the adverb QUICKLY.

As another example, let's start with the adjective MUSIC. If we add the suffix "-al," we'll get the adjective MUSICAL, which means "related to music." The suffix "-al" can change a noun to an adjective. Here are some other English words that use this suffix:

- ACCIDENTAL: by accident

- FUNCTIONAL: working, relating to a specific function
- GLOBAL: relating to the whole world (the globe)

Suffixes can be added to other suffixes to create longer and longer words! For example, if we start with the adjective GLOBAL and add the suffix "-ize," we'll have the verb GLOBALIZE. If we then add the suffix "-ation," we'll have the noun GLOBALIZATION.

Exercise #3: Look at the list of suffixes at the end of this section to find the meaning of the underlined suffixes below. Then, look up the definition of each word in a good dictionary. Notice how the suffix influences the meaning of the word! The first word has been filled out for you.

WORD	PREFIX MEANING	DEFINITION OF WORD
manage<u>able</u>	*able: capable of*	*able to be managed or controlled*
critic<u>ize</u>		
apt<u>itude</u>		
aer<u>ate</u>		
defens<u>ible</u>		
futil<u>ity</u>		
tens<u>ion</u>		
triumph<u>ant</u>		
eco<u>logy</u>		

CHALLENGE TACTIC: PUTTING IT ALL TOGETHER

Now that you know the meaning of some common roots, prefixes, and suffixes, let's look at how you would break down a complicated word with several of these parts in combination. For example, consider the word COLLABORATE. You probably know that this word means "to work together," but did you know that you could break it into a prefix, root, and suffix?

- "col" is a prefix that means "with"
- "labor" is a root that means "work"
- "ate" is a suffix that turns a word into a verb

Therefore, we can break down COLLABORATE as follows:

$$COL + LABOR + ATE$$

with   work   verb

From these parts, we see that COLLABORATE is a verb that literally means to work with someone else.

Exercise #4: Look at the list of roots, prefixes, and suffixes at the end of this section. Use this information or your own knowledge to break the following words into parts and guess at their combined meaning. Then, check your answer with the answer key that follows. The first word has been filled in for you.

#	WORD	WORD PARTS	MEANING
1.	prenatal	*pre + nat + al*	*before birth (adjective)*
2.	inaudible		
3.	amorphous		
4.	synchronize		
5.	rejuvenate		
6.	incredulous		
7.	ambivalent		

8.	philanthropy		
9.	vivisection		
10.	retrospective		

COMMON WORD ROOTS, PREFIXES, AND SUFFIXES

Here is a list of some of the most common roots, prefixes, and suffixes that make up words in the English language. Remember that roots carry a word's basic meaning, prefixes come before a root and change its meaning, and suffixes come at the end of words and tell you whether they are nouns, verbs, adjectives, or adverbs. Start learning some of these basic word parts to cement your vocabulary knowledge and help decipher new, unfamiliar vocabulary.

COMMON ROOTS		
ag, act	do	action, activity, agent
ambul	walk, move	ambulance, ambulatory, amble
ami, amo	love	amiable, amorous
anim	mind, soul, spirit	animal, animate, unanimous
anthro	human	anthropology, philanthropy
aud, audit	hear	audible, auditorium, audience
auto	self	automobile, autobiography, autograph
belli	war	belligerent, rebellious, bellicose
ben	good	benefactor, beneficial, benevolence
biblio	book	bibliography, Bible

bio	life	biography, biology
carn	flesh, meat	carnivore, carnal, incarnate
chron	time	chronic, chronology, synchronize
cid, cis	cut, kill	incision, homicide, insecticide
civi	citizen	civilization, civilian, civil
corp	body	corporation, corporeal, corpse
dem	people	democracy, demographic
dic, dict	speak	dictate, contradict, prediction, verdict
domin	master	dominant, domain, domineering
err	wander	error, erratic, errand
eu	good, beautiful	eulogize, euphoria, euphemism
fall, fals	deceive	fallacious, infallible, falsify
fid	faith	fidelity, confide, confidence
graph, gram	writing	grammar, telegram, graphite
loqu, locut	talk	soliloquy, loquacious, elocution
luc	light	elucidate, lucid, translucent
magn	great	magnify, magnate, magnanimous
mal	bad	malevolent, malediction, malicious
mori, mort	die	mortuary, immortal
morph	shape, form	amorphous, metamorphosis
nat	born	innate, natal, nativity

nom	name	misnomer, nominal
nov	new	novice, innovate, renovate, novelty
omni	all	omniscient, omnipotent, omnivorous
pac, pas, pax	peace	pacify, pacific, pacifist
path, pass	disease, feeling	pathology, sympathetic, apathy, antipathy
phil	love	philanthropist, philosophy, philanderer
port	carry	portable, porter, transport, export
poten	able, powerful	potential, omnipotent, potentate, impotent
psych	mind	psyche, psychology, psychosis, psychopath
reg, rect	rule	regicide, regime, regent, insurrection
sacr, secr	holy	sacred, sacrilegious, sacrament, consecrate
scribe, script	write	scribe, describe, script
somn	sleep	insomnia, somnolent, somnambulist
spec, spic	see, look	spectators, spectacles, retrospect
tang, tact, ting	touch	tactile, tangent, contact, contingent
terr	land	terrain, terrestrial, subterranean
urb	city	urban, urbane, suburban
vac	empty	vacation, vacuous, evacuate, vacant
ver	truth	veracity, verify, veracious
verb	word	verbose, verbatim, proverb
viv, vit	alive	revival, vivacious, vitality

COMMON PREFIXES		
ambi, amphi	both	ambidextrous, ambiguous, ambivalent
an, a	without	anarchy, anemia, amoral
anti	against	antibody, antipathy, antisocial
circum	around	circumnavigate, circumspect, circumscribe
co, col, com, con	with, together	coauthor, collaborate, composition, commerce
contra, contro	against	contradict, contravene, controversy
di, dif, dis	not, apart	digress, discord, differ, disparity
dia	through, across	diagonal, diameter, dialogue
dys	abnormal, bad	dysfunction, dyslexia, dystopia
e, ex, extra, extro	out, beyond	expel, excavate, eject, extrovert
in, il, im, ir (1)	not	inefficient, inarticulate, illegible, irrepressible
in, il, im, ir (2)	in, upon	invite, incite, impression, illuminate
inter	between, among	intervene, international, interjection, intercept
intra	within	intramural, introvert, intravenous
mis	bad, hatred	misdemeanor, mischance, misanthrope
mono	one	monarchy, monologue, monotheism
non	not, without	noncommittal, nonentity, nondescript
pan	all, every	panacea, panorama, pandemic
peri	around, near	perimeter, periphery, periscope

poly	many	polygon, polygamist, polyglot
post	after	postpone, posterity, postscript, posthumous
pre	before	preamble, prefix, premonition, prediction
pro	forward, for, before	propulsive, proponent, prologue, prophet
re, retro	again, back	reiterate, reimburse, react, retrogress
sub, suc, sup, sus	under, less	subway, subjugate, suppress
super, sur	over, above	superior, supernatural, supervise, surtax
syn, sym, syl , sys	with, together	symmetry, synchronize, synthesize, sympathize
trans	across	transfer, transport, transpose
un	not	unabridged, unkempt, unwitting

COMMON SUFFIXES		
able, ible	ADJ: capable of	edible, presentable, legible
ac, ic, ical	ADJ: like, related	cardiac, mythic, dramatic, musical
acious, icious	ADJ: full of	malicious, audacious
ant, ent	ADJ/N: full of	eloquent, verdant
ate	V: make, become	consecrate, enervate, eradicate
en	V: make, become	awaken, strengthen, soften
er (1)	ADJ: more	bigger, wiser, happier
er (2)	N: a person who does	teacher, baker, announcer
cy, ty, ity	N: state of being	democracy, accuracy, veracity
ful	ADJ: full of	respectful, cheerful, wonderful
fy	V: to make	magnify, petrify, beautify
ism	N: doctrine, belief	monotheism, fanaticism, egotism
ist	N: dealer, doer	fascist, realist, artist
ize, ise	V: make	victimize, rationalize, harmonize
logy	N: study of	biology, geology, neurology
oid	ADJ: resembling	ovoid, anthropoid, spheroid
ose/ous	ADJ: full of	verbose, lachrymose, nauseous, gaseous
osis	N: condition	psychosis, neurosis, hypnosis
tion, sion	N: state of being	exasperation, irritation, transition, concession
tude	N: state of	fortitude, beatitude, certitude

SSAT CORE VOCABULARY

The following words will help you prepare for the vocabulary you will encounter on the Middle and Upper levels of the SSAT. These words are sorted by subject category to help you learn groups of words with similar or related definitions. When you learn a word, pay attention to its part of speech (is it a noun, verb, adjective, or adverb?) and to other possible definitions of the word. The level of the word approximately corresponds to your grade level, but you should still study all of these words because any level of vocabulary could appear on the SSAT.

Use this section as a study aid and write your own personal sentence for each word to help you remember it. To help cement your learning, try making separate flashcards for each word, writing the word on the front, and writing all of its definitions and your own personal sentence on the back. In order to master as many words as possible before your SSAT exam, create a daily schedule and make sure to review old words while you are learning new ones.

#	WORD	LEVEL	DEFINITION	SAMPLE SENTENCE	GROUP
1	colleague	6	N: a co-worker or fellow classmate	The young doctor impressed his colleagues with the difficult diagnosis.	Relationships & Emotions
2	compatible	7	ADJ: capable of getting along well with other people or things	George and Larry seem to have compatible personalities, as they get along quite well.	Relationships & Emotions

3	accommodate	8	V: (1) to be agreeable, acceptable, suitable, (2) to adapt. ADJ: accommodating	(1) This table is meant to accommodate six diners. (2) Jose worked to accommodate himself to the difficult economic times.	Relationships & Emotions
4	amiable	10	ADJ: friendly, kind, likeable	Kelly was an amiable hostess, friendly and welcoming to all of her guests.	Relationships & Emotions
5	congenial	10	ADJ: friendly, sociable, suited to one's needs	The college aimed to create a congenial atmosphere for both professors and students.	Relationships & Emotions
6	aloof	10	ADJ: emotionally distant	The grandfather was generally aloof and uninterested in playing with his grandchildren.	Relationships & Emotions
7	nonchalant	9	ADJ: casual, calm, unconcerned	The mayor's nonchalant attitude toward the disaster lost him many supporters.	Relationships & Emotions
8	apathetic	8	ADJ: showing no interest or concern. N: apathy	Politicians are wondering why voters are so apathetic this election year.	Relationships & Emotions
9	indifferent	8	ADJ: showing no interest or concern. N: indifference	I really don't care where we go for dinner tonight-- I am entirely indifferent.	Relationships & Emotions
10	sentimental	6	ADJ: overly emotional	Although he had long outgrown it, Neil felt a sentimental attachment to his baby blanket.	Relationships & Emotions

11	hysterical	8	ADJ: having excessive and uncontrollable emotion. N: hysteria	When she heard the news, Susan reacted with hysterical sobbing.	Relationships & Emotions
12	benevolent	10	ADJ: kind, generous. N: benevolence	Queen Elizabeth was a benevolent ruler, generous and responsive to the needs of her people.	Relationships & Emotions
13	compassionate	5	ADJ: kind, sympathetic. N: compassion	Mrs. White was a firm instructor but also compassionate towards her students.	Relationships & Emotions
14	empathy	6	N: understanding another's feelings. ADJ: empathetic	Caring and considerate, Liam always expressed deep empathy towards others.	Relationships & Emotions
15	charismatic	8	ADJ: charming. N: charisma	With his naturally magnetic and charming personality, he was a charismatic leader.	Relationships & Emotions
16	engaging	6	ADJ: interesting, charming, attractive	The students found the hands-on activity more engaging than simply reading a textbook.	Relationships & Emotions
17	gracious	7	ADJ: charming, generous, polite	Always a good sport, the losing player was still gracious in defeat.	Relationships & Emotions
18	courteous	6	ADJ: polite. N: courtesy	The staff was courteous and helpful when asked for advice.	Relationships & Emotions

Ivy Global

19	cordial	9	ADJ: polite, friendly	The president extended a cordial invitation to the Chinese and Korean ambassadors.	Relationships & Emotions
20	tact	7	N: consideration and sensitivity in dealing with others. ADJ: tactful	Diplomats must display tact when dealing with sensitive issues between nations.	Relationships & Emotions
21	emulate	8	V: to copy or imitate, to look up to	An excellent team player, Christine is a role model whom everyone should emulate.	Relationships & Emotions
22	flatter	6	V: to praise excessively or dishonestly. N: flattery	At first flattered by his employee's compliments, the boss realized that she was only angling for a pay raise.	Relationships & Emotions
23	fidelity	8	N: faithfulness, loyalty	The knight served his king with utmost fidelity.	Relationships & Emotions
24	steadfast	8	ADJ: determined, loyal, steady	Maria's steadfast commitment to the cause won her great recognition.	Relationships & Emotions
25	fickle	7	ADJ: not reliable or dependable, changing opinions frequently	The fans were fickle, abandoning the team whenever it began to lose.	Relationships & Emotions
26	headstrong	6	ADJ: stubborn, disobedient	Elizabeth showed a headstrong determination to do things her own way.	Relationships & Emotions

27	obstinate	8	ADJ: stubborn, disobedient. N: obstinacy	Despite evidence to the contrary, Alex obstinately refused to admit he had made a mistake.	Relationships & Emotions
28	exasperate	6	V: to annoy, irritate. ADJ: exasperating	The mother was exasperated by her daughter's whining.	Relationships & Emotions
29	infuriate	7	V: to anger or enrage. ADJ: infuriating	The judge's decision against him infuriated the defendant.	Relationships & Emotions
30	indignant	10	ADJ: outraged, angry at something unjust.	The new ruling inspired an onslaught of indignant letters of protest.	Relationships & Emotions
31	mock	6	V: to ridicule or make fun of. N: mockery	The newcomer was mocked for his foreign accent.	Relationships & Emotions
32	malicious	7	ADJ: intending to harm or cause suffering N: malice	Jenny was deeply hurt by the malicious rumors spread about her.	Relationships & Emotions
33	exploit	6	(1) V: to take advantage of, (2) N: a bold action or deed	(1) The drug company exploited the system by abusing the patients' trust. (2) The daring exploits of Robin Hood are legendary.	Relationships & Emotions
34	belittle	7	V: to put someone down, to express a negative opinion	People would not belittle the disabled if they got to know them better.	Relationships & Emotions
35	jeer	7	V: to laugh at with scorn, N: a scornful laugh	When Ryan first got braces, the school bullies jeered at him.	Relationships & Emotions

36	snub	8	V: to behave coldly towards, to ignore	Mary could not understand why her friends now snubbed her and ignored her in the hall.	Relationships & Emotions
37	condescend	6	V: to look down on, to display arrogance. ADJ: condescending	The arrogant judge finally condescended to speak with the poor woman.	Relationships & Emotions
38	disdain	6	N: arrogance, scorn, V: to display scorn. ADJ: disdainful	The criminal showed disdain for the law.	Relationships & Emotions
39	hypocrite	7	N: someone who says one thing and does another. ADJ: hypocritical	Sam's father forced all of his children to eat their vegetables, but he hypocritically never ate his own.	Relationships & Emotions
40	admonish	8	V: to scold or warn strongly	The players were admonished for not paying close enough attention during the game.	Relationships & Emotions
41	reprimand	8	(1) V: to scold or warn strongly. (2) N: a strong warning	(1) The policeman reprimanded the careless driver but did not issue a ticket. (2) The student received a strong reprimand from the teacher for forgetting his homework.	Relationships & Emotions
42	vivacious	9	ADJ: lively, spirited	Catherine's vivacious and enthusiastic personality made her a great team member.	Relationships & Emotions

Ivy Global

43	animated	7	ADJ: lively, spirited. N: animation	She approached the challenge with an energetic, animated attitude.	Relationships & Emotions
44	extrovert	8	N: a sociable, outgoing person. ADJ: extroverted	Outgoing and sociable, Elaine is a true extrovert.	Relationships & Emotions
45	introvert	8	N: a person who has a quiet, reserved personality. ADJ: introverted	James is friendly but introverted, keeping his thoughts and feelings to himself.	Relationships & Emotions
46	reserved	8	ADJ: quiet, shy, not showing one's feelings. N: reservation	Mark is a reserved person, not likely to share his feelings openly.	Relationships & Emotions
47	timid	6	ADJ: shy, lacking confidence	The timid animals ran away as we approached.	Relationships & Emotions
48	meek	7	ADJ: humble, tame	Despite his meek attitude, he was actually a courageous opponent.	Relationships & Emotions
49	docile	9	ADJ: obedient, tame	Sarah was a docile and obedient student who never questioned what the teacher said.	Relationships & Emotions
50	subdued	8	ADJ: quiet, low-key, hushed. V: subdue	The painting should be displayed in a room with soft, subdued lighting.	Relationships & Emotions
51	submissive	7	ADJ: giving in to orders, obedient. V: submit	Nova was an overly submissive dog, easily dominated by more assertive animals.	Relationships & Emotions

52	passive	8	ADJ: lacking in energy or will, submissive	Gordon is a passive group member, preferring to let others take charge and make decisions.	Relationships & Emotions
53	cynical	8	ADJ: believing the worst about people or events	Many young voters are cynical about politicians and their campaign promises.	Overcoming Obstacles
54	dejected	9	ADJ: depressed, sad. N: dejection	Eric was dejected after hearing the bad news.	Overcoming Obstacles
55	initiate	6	V: to begin	Customers can use the online forum to initiate discussion about the product.	Overcoming Obstacles
56	fatigue	7	N: exhaustion, tiredness. ADJ: fatigued	After his third night with little sleep, Michael was suffering from severe fatigue.	Overcoming Obstacles
57	feeble	6	ADJ: weak, faint, lacking strength	Aaron gave a rather feeble excuse for why he forgot his homework.	Overcoming Obstacles
58	diligent	7	ADJ: steadily persevering to complete a task. N: diligence	Mary is a diligent student, studying every day to improve her grades.	Overcoming Obstacles
59	industrial	7	ADJ: (1) diligent, hardworking, (2) related to making goods and services. N: industry	(1) The group approached the project with industry, working hard at each task until it was complete. (2) Factories and new inventions boomed during the Industrial Revolution.	Overcoming Obstacles

Ivy Global

60	valiant	8	ADJ: showing courage or determination. N: valor	Although it was defeated, the team made a valiant effort during the soccer match.	Overcoming Obstacles
61	resolute	7	ADJ: determined, firm, unyielding. N/V: resolve	Martia's hard work and resolute determination earned her great success in her career.	Overcoming Obstacles
62	emphatic	7	ADJ: forceful, spoken with emphasis	When asked whether he would change his mind, Peter made an emphatic refusal.	Overcoming Obstacles
63	endeavor	7	V: to make an attempt, N: an attempt	Scientists are currently endeavoring to find a cure for cancer.	Overcoming Obstacles
64	endure	5	V: to suffer, to put up with something unpleasant. N: endurance	Residents of Siberia have to endure extremely cold, dark winters.	Overcoming Obstacles
65	withstand	7	V: to resist, to stand up to something	Strong as they were, the walls of the fortress could not withstand the attack.	Overcoming Obstacles
66	resilient	8	ADJ: springing back, recovering quickly	Policemen have to be resilient in order to cope with and bounce back from the stress of their work.	Overcoming Obstacles
67	robust	9	ADJ: strong, sturdy	There are few plants robust enough to survive the arctic climate.	Overcoming Obstacles
68	pragmatic	9	ADJ: practical, useful. N: pragmatist	The software's pragmatic design was intended to make it easier to use.	Overcoming Obstacles

69	fret	8	V: to worry unnecessarily	Relax, enjoy, and don't fret the small stuff!	Overcoming Obstacles
70	adversity	8	N: hardship, difficulty, misfortune. ADJ: adverse	Martin Luther King, Jr. had to overcome great adversity in his struggle for racial equality.	Overcoming Obstacles
71	plight	7	N: a difficult or extremely unpleasant situation	After the earthquake, the world was concerned about the plight of the citizens of Haiti.	Overcoming Obstacles
72	predicament	6	N: a difficult or extremely unpleasant situation	The doctor was faced with a difficult predicament: how could he treat the patient's infection if the patient was allergic to antibiotics?	Overcoming Obstacles
73	rigor	8	N: something very hard to endure. ADJ: rigorous	The rigorous curriculum was designed to challenge the students and teach them how to manage a heavy workload.	Overcoming Obstacles
74	strenuous	7	ADJ: requiring hard effort or energy	Mountain climbing is a strenuous activity, requiring strength as well as endurance.	Overcoming Obstacles
75	toil	6	V: to labor, to work hard N: hard work	At noon, the farmhands came back for lunch and a chance to rest from their toil under the hot sun.	Overcoming Obstacles

76	tedious	8	ADJ: boring, tiring, long	The chapters in the textbook were long and stuffed with so much information that they were tedious to read.	Overcoming Obstacles
77	trek	6	N: a very long journey on foot	The guide took us on a long trek through the jungle in order to reach the village.	Overcoming Obstacles
78	grimace	7	N: a facial expression indicating pain, V: to contort one's face in pain	We grimaced as the frigid gust of December air whipped across our faces.	Overcoming Obstacles
79	wince	6	V: to flinch in fear or pain	Jose winced as the doctor touched his swollen, bruised ankle.	Overcoming Obstacles
80	daunting	8	ADJ: discouraging, inspiring fear	Balancing the budget appeared a daunting task, but it was the new president's goal.	Overcoming Obstacles
81	bleak	6	ADJ: hopeless, depressing, bare	After the stock market crash, the future of the economy looked bleak.	Overcoming Obstacles
82	dread	5	N: great fear, terror, V: to feel great fear or terror	The students dreaded the approaching exam week.	Overcoming Obstacles

83	grim	7	ADJ: (1) gloomy, dark, bleak, (2) relentless, unyielding	(1) The earthquake destroyed the village so thoroughly that its hopes of recovery look grim. (2) With grim determination, he plodded forward through the blowing snow.	Overcoming Obstacles
84	ail	8	V: to be ill or unwell. N: ailment	The government proposed a bailout to rescue the ailing car manufacturers.	Overcoming Obstacles
85	deteriorate	6	V: to become worse, to disintegrate	The abandoned house had deteriorated after years of exposure to harsh weather.	Overcoming Obstacles
86	falter	8	V: to be unsteady or weak, to stumble	After keeping up his pace for ten kilometers, the runner began to falter.	Overcoming Obstacles
87	relinquish	6	V: to give up, abandon, release	After several days of bombardments, the rebels relinquished control of the military base.	Overcoming Obstacles
88	concede	9	V: (1) to yield or surrender, to give in, (2) to admit to be true. N: concession	(1) The losing candidate graciously conceded defeat and congratulated his opponent. (2) The journalist conceded that his report may have been influenced by his own personal opinions.	Overcoming Obstacles

89	pessimist	6	N: a person who expects a bad outcome. ADJ: pessimistic	Always a pessimist, Andrew expected to fail the test.	Overcoming Obstacles
90	optimist	6	N: a person who expects a good outcome. ADJ: optimistic	Despite the rough start to the season, the coach was optimistic about the team's improvement.	Overcoming Obstacles
91	versatile	7	ADJ: having a wide variety of skills, flexible. N: versatility	Susan was a versatile actress, able to adapt easily from theatre to film acting.	Overcoming Obstacles
92	apt	8	ADJ: able, skillful, fitting. N: aptitude	The poems are accompanied by humorous and apt illustrations.	Overcoming Obstacles
93	capacity	7	N: (1) the capability to perform, produce, or hold, (2) the maximum amount that can be produced or held	(1) With continued training, Mark will have the capacity to become a successful athlete. (2) The theatre has a capacity of 450 audience members.	Overcoming Obstacles
94	merit	6	N: (1) excellence in achievement or performance, (2) deserving of aid or recognition. V: to deserve aid or recognition	(1) Scholarships will be given based on financial need and academic merit. (2) The environmental program merits further consideration by the government.	Overcoming Obstacles

95	surpass	7	V: to exceed	With their popular new blockbuster, the filmmakers aim to surpass their previous record of success.	Overcoming Obstacles
96	feat	7	N: a great achievement	The heroes were rewarded for their feats of bravery.	Overcoming Obstacles
97	exuberance	8	N: joyful enthusiasm. ADJ: exuberant	His youthful exuberance always keeps his parents on their toes.	Overcoming Obstacles
98	bliss	8	N: extreme happiness. ADJ: blissful	As the child stuffed the cake into his mouth, his face showed pure bliss.	Overcoming Obstacles
99	ecstasy	8	N: extreme happiness. ADJ: ecstatic	For some, sky-diving is ecstasy; for me, it is terrifying.	Overcoming Obstacles
100	elation	8	N: extreme happiness. ADJ: elated	The elation you feel when you cross the finish line makes running a marathon worth all the difficulty.	Overcoming Obstacles
101	jubilation	8	N: extreme happiness. ADJ: jubilant	When the team scored the winning goal, the crowd exploded with jubilation.	Overcoming Obstacles
102	awe	6	N: wonder, respect, admiration	We felt a sense of awe as we gazed at the Grand Canyon.	Overcoming Obstacles

Ivy Global

103	acclaim	9	N: praise, approval. V: to praise or approve	The author's first novel received widespread public acclaim, and we eagerly await her second book.	Overcoming Obstacles
104	exalt	9	V: to praise, glorify, honor, to heighten. N: exaltation	Salvador Dali's paintings are works of art that exalt the imagination.	Overcoming Obstacles
105	astute	10	ADJ: intelligent, smart, sharp	Michael was an astute businessman with an excellent sense of timing.	Language & Intellect
106	keen	6	ADJ: (1) sharp, intelligent, (2) cutting, painful, (3) eager	(1) Jordan's keen eyesight was able to spot the eagle from many yards away. (2) Having not eaten for many days, the prisoner felt a keen pang of hunger. (3) We are keen to hear the report from the new committee.	Language & Intellect
107	methodical	7	ADJ: in a careful, organized manner	The experiment was conducted in a very organized, methodical fashion.	Language & Intellect
108	meticulous	9	ADJ: paying strict attention to detail	Amy was meticulous about hygiene and took every precaution to keep her house sanitized.	Language & Intellect
109	impeccable	9	ADJ: perfect, without fault	Although the new immigrants had just recently arrived in Canada, they spoke impeccable English.	Language & Intellect

110	immaculate	9	ADJ: without fault or error, completely clean or perfect	The new car looked immaculate sitting in the driveway; it was shining and spotless.	Language & Intellect
111	omniscient	9	ADJ: all-knowing, infinitely wise. N: omniscience	Many religions believe in an omniscient, all-knowing god.	Language & Intellect
112	profound	8	ADJ: deep, significant, important	The Battle of Gettysburg had a profound effect on the rest of the Civil War.	Language & Intellect
113	superficial	8	ADJ: not deep, not significant	The wound was only superficial and did not require stitches.	Language & Intellect
114	prolific	10	ADJ: producing a lot of offspring or materials quickly	Karen was a prolific writer and published a new book almost every year.	Language & Intellect
115	ornament	6	N: a decoration, V: to decorate.	The shield was ornamented with gold and gemstones.	Language & Intellect
116	embellish	7	V: (1) to decorate or add detail to, (2) to make something look or sound better than it actually is	(1) The scarf was embellished with embroidery and beads. (2) Tony said he hadn't actually lied, but had only embellished the truth.	Language & Intellect
117	ornate	8	ADJ: flowery, highly decorated or ornamented	The castle's ornate decorations were overwhelming.	Language & Intellect
118	vivid	5	ADJ: bright, striking, intense, graphic	Vincent Van Gogh used vivid yellows, oranges and reds in his paintings.	Language & Intellect

119	thesis	7	N: the central argument that an author proves through evidence	The thesis of the essay argued that technology makes our lives easier but not necessarily better.	Language & Intellect
120	ambivalent	10	ADJ: having mixed feelings about a topic or a person. N: ambivalence	Leo felt ambivalent towards his newborn baby sister, unsure whether he liked the new addition to the family.	Language & Intellect
121	articulate	8	(1) V: to put into words, (2) ADJ: well-spoken, using elegant language	(1) Overwhelmed by emotion, Samantha struggled to articulate what she was feeling. (2) Abraham Lincoln was a highly articulate and persuasive speaker.	Language & Intellect
122	eloquent	8	ADJ: well-spoken, using elegant language	The author's eloquent language makes the novel a pleasure to read.	Language & Intellect
123	monotonous	7	ADJ: flat, all the same, lacking in variety	Nobody likes to listen to flat, monotonous voices.	Language & Intellect
124	concise	7	ADJ: brief and to the point. N: concision	Good writers avoid wordiness and use concise language to make their point.	Language & Intellect
125	succinct	8	ADJ: brief and to the point	Your summary should be succinct and should not exceed 200 words.	Language & Intellect
126	elaborate	6	V: to add detail to, to make complex, ADJ: complex, detailed	As his story began to unravel, Joseph's elaborate lie was revealed.	Language & Intellect

127	redundant	7	ADJ: more than is needed, overly repetitive. N: redundancy	The phrase "in the near future" is redundant and should be avoided.	Language & Intellect
128	extraneous	8	ADJ: extra, unnecessary	Monica cleared all of the extraneous clothes out of her closet.	Language & Intellect
129	cliché	6	N: an overused phrase or remark	The phrase "to think outside the box" is a cliché and highly overused.	Language & Intellect
130	vulgar	8	ADJ: coarse, common, rude	Edward was sent to the principal's office for his vulgar behavior.	Language & Intellect
131	profane	7	ADJ: rude, vulgar, unholy. N: profanity	The book was banned from school libraries for its profane language.	Language & Intellect
132	coherent	7	ADJ: logical and orderly. N: coherence	The play had a highly coherent plot, making it easy for the audience to follow.	Language & Intellect
133	legible	6	ADJ: able to be read	Work to keep your handwriting clear and legible.	Language & Intellect
134	cite	8	V: to mention, make reference to. N: citation	In a research paper, it is important to cite the sources you use.	Language & Intellect

135	document	7	(1) V: to record in detail, (2) N: writing that provides information	(1) The film documents the devastation and recovery efforts of Port-au-Prince, Haiti, after the earthquake. (2) A contract is a document that outlines a legal agreement between two parties.	Language & Intellect
136	inquire	7	V: to ask about. N: inquiry	The doctor inquired about the medical history of the patient.	Language & Intellect
137	orate	8	V: to give a speech. N: oration, orator	Stephen was a fine orator who could make even the longest speech interesting.	Language & Intellect
138	monologue	7	N: a dramatic speech by one character	Drama students applying to the program must memorize and recite a monologue.	Language & Intellect
139	soliloquy	9	N: a speech where a character talks out loud to himself	Hamlet's speech to himself is one of Shakespeare's most recognizable soliloquies.	Language & Intellect
140	prologue	7	N: an introduction to a play or book	The novel's prologue sets the scene and provides interesting background information.	Language & Intellect
141	epilogue	7	N: a short piece of writing at the end of a play or book	In the story's epilogue, we see a glimpse of the characters' lives thirty years in the future.	Language & Intellect

142	excerpt	7	N: a selection from a larger literary work, V: to take a selection from a larger work	The Critical Reading portion of the test contains many excerpts from short stories and poems.	Language & Intellect
143	synopsis	7	N: a summary or outline	Can you give a short synopsis of the movie's plot without spoiling the ending for me?	Language & Intellect
144	genre	8	N: a style of literature or art	Students must identify the genre of the passage and answer questions about style.	Language & Intellect
145	memoir	7	N: an autobiography	At the age of 80, Grandma decided it was time to write her memoirs.	Language & Intellect
146	narrative	6	N: a story	Dickens's Christmas Carol is a narrative of greed, sorrow, and making amends.	Language & Intellect
147	epic	6	(1) N: a very long poem about a hero's adventures, (2) ADJ: long and impressive	(1) Homer's Odyssey is an epic about the adventures of Odysseus. (2) Frodo Baggins undertook an epic journey to Mount Doom.	Language & Intellect
148	saga	7	N: a story telling the adventures of a hero	The Vikings enjoyed playing music and telling sagas of their gods and heroes.	Language & Intellect

149	parody	9	N: a spoof, a humorous imitation	"Weird Al" Yankovic creates parodies of popular songs.	Language & Intellect
150	protagonist	7	N: the main character in a story	Leonardo DiCaprio played the protagonist of the movie Inception.	Language & Intellect
151	metaphor	7	N: a poetic or symbolic comparison between two objects or ideas. ADJ: metaphorical	The poem used the metaphor of the changing seasons to represent human life and death.	Language & Intellect
152	parallel	6	ADJ: (1) similar, related, (2) two lines that will never meet	(1) The newspaper noticed that the two wars were strikingly parallel. (2) The pinstripe tie had a pattern of parallel lines.	Language & Intellect
153	abstract	7	(1) ADJ: existing only in ideas or theory, not concrete, (2) a short summary of a scientific article	(1) The only way to test an abstract theory is to put it into practice in the real world. (2) The scientists submitted an abstract of their experiment to the journal.	Language & Intellect
154	anonymous	7	ADJ: having no name or known identity	The police received an anonymous phone call with information about the crime.	Language & Intellect
155	counsel	9	(1) V: to give advice. (2) N: advice	(1) The Cabinet counsels the President on issues of domestic and international policy. (2) The elders provided wise counsel to the young leaders.	Law & Politics

156	advocate	8	(1) V: to argue in favor of a person or idea, (2) N: a lawyer	(1) Health experts advocate moderation when consuming alcohol. (2) He has a strong reputation as an advocate for women and children's rights.	Law & Politics
157	champion	6	(1) N: a hero, someone who holds first place. (2) V: to fight for a cause	(1) The Junior Girls Volleyball Team was the district champion this year. (2) Susan B. Anthony championed early on the cause of women's rights.	Law & Politics
158	contemplation	7	N: long and thoughtful observation. V: contemplate	The poet spent a week in the wilderness in the contemplation of nature's beauty.	Law & Politics
159	objective	6	(1) ADJ: based on evidence, not influenced by personal experience or emotion, (2) N: a goal	(1) The scientists were asked to provide objective evidence for their claims. (2) The team's objective was to score more goals in the second half.	Law & Politics
160	subjective	6	ADJ: based on personal experience or emotion	The novel gives a highly subjective, personal account of the Vietnam War.	Law & Politics
161	bias	5	N: prejudice, unequal favor to one side, V: to make prejudiced. ADJ: biased	The judge was accused of being biased in his decision.	Law & Politics

162	legislate	7	V: to pass a law. N: legislation	The committee legislated the new health care reform bill.	Law & Politics
163	ratify	8	V: to formally approve, sign off on. N: ratification	191 nations have formally ratified the Kyoto Protocol on climate change.	Law & Politics
164	decree	7	V: to order, N: an order	The king decreed that no commoner would be allowed to wear purple, the color of royalty.	Law & Politics
165	coerce	8	V: to force someone to do something through threats and intimidation. N: coercion	The king coerced his citizens into paying higher taxes.	Law & Politics
166	comply	8	V: to act according to someone's laws or commands	Robin Hood refused to comply with King John's harsh tax policy.	Law & Politics
167	censor	7	V: to forbid the distribution of material considered harmful or inappropriate	Wartime letters are censored to remove sensitive military information.	Law & Politics
168	prohibit	6	V: to ban or forbid. N: prohibition	School rules prohibit the use of cell phones during class.	Law & Politics
169	felon	6	N: someone who has been convicted of a serious crime	The notorious felon was sentenced to life in prison.	Law & Politics
170	lethal	5	ADJ: deadly	Chocolate can be lethal to dogs.	Law & Politics

171	plead	7	V: to humbly request help. N: plea	Knowing he was defeated, the enemy knight pleaded for mercy.	Law & Politics
172	pardon	6	V: to forgive, N: formal forgiveness	The convict was ordered to kneel before the king and beg pardon for his crime.	Law & Politics
173	condone	8	V: to forgive or excuse	The teacher could not condone such rude behavior in her classroom.	Law & Politics
174	thwart	9	V: to prevent someone from doing something	George's parents thwarted his winter vacation plans by insisting that he study for three hours every day.	Law & Politics
175	mediate	10	V: to resolve differences between conflicting sides. N: mediator	The U.N. sent peacekeepers to mediate between the warring groups.	Law & Politics
176	righteous	8	ADJ: following just and moral principles. N: righteousness	Defending the homeless man was a righteous act.	Law & Politics
177	virtuous	6	ADJ: morally excellent	A truly virtuous person performs acts of kindness for their own sake, not for recognition.	Law & Politics
178	notorious	8	ADJ: having a bad reputation, well-known for bad reasons	The government was notorious for its human rights abuses.	Law & Politics

179	repress	8	V: to put down by force or intimidation	The government was quick to repress the rebellion.	Law & Politics
180	oppression	7	N: keeping down by force or authority	Many countries around the world still oppress their citizens and deny them their rights.	Law & Politics
181	authoritarian	9	ADJ: requiring absolute obedience, enforcing strong or oppressive policies	The authoritarian government restricted public debate and opposition.	Law & Politics
182	tyrant	8	N: a cruel and oppressive ruler. ADJ: tyrannical	Hitler is known as one of the most ruthless tyrants of the 20th century.	Law & Politics
183	lax	8	ADJ: loose, not strict. N: lassitude	A lax attitude towards airport security could put all passengers in danger.	Law & Politics
184	resign	8	V: (1) to accept a hopeless situation, (2) to step down from a position of power. N: resignation, ADJ: resigned	(1) As the game came to a close, the team resigned itself to defeat. (2) Richard Nixon was the first US President to resign from office.	Law & Politics
185	endorse	9	V: to give support or approval	The board endorsed the decisions recommended by the paper.	Law & Politics
186	novice	7	N: a beginner	Although a novice to the sport, Sarah showed a great potential for soccer.	Law & Politics

187	naïve	8	ADJ: inexperienced, lacking knowledge of the world. N: naïveté	The citizens were naïve to believe that the new mayor would be better than the old one.	Law & Politics
188	diplomacy	8	N: negotiations between nations or groups. ADJ: diplomatic	Peacemakers hoped that successful diplomacy would keep the two countries from going to war.	Law & Politics
189	allegiance	6	N: loyalty, commitment	In order to gain citizenship, immigrants must pledge allegiance to their new country.	Law & Politics
190	intervene	6	V: to come between or get involved, often to prevent an action	When the industry was on the brink of failure, the government intervened to save the economy.	Law & Politics
191	autonomous	9	ADJ: independent, self-ruling. N: autonomy	India became an autonomous nation in 1947 after many years of British rule.	Law & Politics
192	sovereign	8	(1) N: a ruler or head of government. (2) ADJ: independent, self-ruling. N: sovereignty	(1) The Queen used to be the sovereign of England, but in modern times she has a mostly ceremonial role. (2) The United States Constitution united the sovereign states into one federal government.	Law & Politics
193	convene	7	V: to gather, to hold a meeting	The committee will convene every month.	Law & Politics

194	converge	9	V: to come together	The city was founded where the two rivers converged.	Law & Politics
195	consensus	7	N: general agreement	The jury arrived at the consensus that the defendant was guilty.	Law & Politics
196	dissent	8	(1) V: to protest or disagree. (2) N: disagreement or protest	(1) The jury was almost unanimous in their decision; only one juror dissented. (2) A strong democratic government should be able to tolerate non-violent dissent.	Law & Politics
197	transgress	8	V: to violate a law, boundary, or duty. N: transgression	The leader was accused of transgressing the appropriate limits of his power.	Law & Politics
198	explicit	7	ADJ: very specifically and clearly stated	Parents must give their explicit consent for students to attend the field trip.	Law & Politics
199	overt	8	ADJ: open and observable, not secret or concealed	There was overt hostility between the two leaders; it was clear that they hated each other.	Law & Politics
200	negligent	9	ADJ: neglectful, careless, irresponsible. N: negligence	Alan demonstrated negligent behavior by talking on his cell phone while driving.	Law & Politics
201	inadvertent	9	ADJ: accidental, unintentional	Susan was embarrassed when she inadvertently mispronounced the teacher's name.	Law & Politics

202	universal	8	ADJ: characteristic of all people, nationalities, or ethnicities. N: universality	Many wonder whether we can ever agree on a universal standard for right and wrong.	Law & Politics
203	venerate	10	V: to respect or admire greatly, to worship. ADJ: venerable	The town was venerated as the birthplace of an important saint.	Status & Conduct
204	revere	7	V: to idolize or worship. N: reverence	Mahatma Gandhi was revered by many as the leader of the Indian Independence Movement.	Status & Conduct
205	pompous	8	ADJ: arrogant and self-important	His arrogant speech made the politician seem pompous and stuck-up.	Status & Conduct
206	pretentious	7	ADJ: arrogant and self-important	Allan tried to avoid sounding pretentious while describing his accomplishments.	Status & Conduct
207	haughty	6	ADJ: arrogant, scornful, feeling superior to others. N: haughtiness	The duchess showed a haughty attitude towards members of the lower class.	Status & Conduct
208	unruly	8	ADJ: wild, uncontrollable, disobedient	The substitute teacher found the class unruly and disrespectful of her authority.	Status & Conduct
209	insolent	10	ADJ: rude or disrespectful to authority. N: insolence	The student was sent to the principal's office for his insolence towards the teacher.	Status & Conduct

Ivy Global

210	conceited	6	ADJ: self-centered	They were concerned that her success was causing Karen to become conceited.	Status & Conduct
211	vain	5	ADJ: (1) self-centered, (2) useless, without effect. N: vanity	(1) Elaine was so vain that she admired her reflection every time she passed by a shiny surface. (2) The police tried in vain to catch the criminal, but had no success.	Status & Conduct
212	smug	7	ADJ: pleased with oneself, self-satisfied	Knowing he was right, Paul gave a smug grin.	Status & Conduct
213	refined	7	ADJ: polished, highly developed, purified. N: refinement	Marie developed a refined taste for French wine after her year abroad.	Status & Conduct
214	prominent	7	ADJ: important, well-known. N: prominence	Martin Luther King, Jr. was a prominent leader of the Civil Rights Movement.	Status & Conduct
215	renown	8	N: fame. ADJ: renowned	Michael Jackson achieved great renown for his unique musical and performance style.	Status & Conduct
216	affluent	8	ADJ: wealthy. N: affluence	Many feel that the affluent nations should do more to help those less fortunate.	Status & Conduct
217	thrive	7	V: to boom, flourish, grow	A large number of scavenging animals thrive in the city environment.	Status & Conduct

218	prosperous	5	ADJ: thriving, economically well-off. N: prosperity	The now prosperous businessman earned his success over many years of hard work.	Status & Conduct
219	meager	8	ADJ: lacking in amount or quality	The company struggled to survive on its meager budget.	Status & Conduct
220	benefactor	8	N: a person who helps others or other organizations, often by donating money	The gala was held to thank the benefactors who donated to the university.	Status & Conduct
221	charitable	7	ADJ: motivated by generosity, raising funds for the disadvantaged. N: charity	During the holidays, many people consider donating to charitable organizations.	Status & Conduct
222	humanitarian	7	ADJ: devoted to the well-being of other people. N: someone devoted to the well-being of other people	After the earthquake, many countries sent humanitarian aid to Haiti.	Status & Conduct
223	philanthropy	8	N: generous assistance to those in need, devotion to the well-being of other people	Bill Gates has become a well-known philanthropist who has donated much of his personal wealth to charity.	Status & Conduct

224	liberal	6	ADJ: (1) giving freely or loosely, (2) broad or open-minded, progressive	(1) The paper cited many sources and was liberal in its use of quotations. (2) The politician was socially liberal, arguing for more government aid programs for the needy and unemployed.	Status & Conduct
225	miserly	10	N: one who hoards money rather than spending it. ADJ: miserly	Ebenezer Scrooge was miserly and unwilling to share even a cent of his money.	Status & Conduct
226	procure	8	V: to get, acquire or obtain	The fundraiser aimed to raise money to procure new equipment for the hospital.	Status & Conduct
227	vend	7	V: to sell something. N: vendor	You can buy chips and cookies from the vending machine downstairs.	Status & Conduct
228	peddle	7	V: to sell something. N: peddler	The salesman peddled his wares from door to door.	Status & Conduct
229	entrepreneur	8	N: someone who starts a business	The city's small business subsidy was meant to encourage entrepreneurs to move there.	Status & Conduct
230	prudent	9	ADJ: careful and sensible	Jane was prudent in her spending and careful to save for an emergency.	Status & Conduct
231	thrifty	6	ADJ: careful in spending money	During the Great Depression, families had to become thrifty in order to make do with what they had.	Status & Conduct

232	frugal	6	ADJ: avoiding wasteful or excessive spending	University students often have to live a frugal lifestyle.	Status & Conduct
233	extravagant	7	ADJ: excessive, unrestrained, often relating to spending money	The society was known for its extravagant parties, with expensive food and entertainment.	Status & Conduct
234	lush	8	ADJ: extravagant, abundant, rich	The king treated his guests to a lush five-course dinner.	Status & Conduct
235	mediocre	9	ADJ: second-rate, average or inferior in quality	Compared to the great masterpieces of Leonardo Da Vinci and Michelangelo, this painting seems mediocre and second-rate.	Status & Conduct
236	stark	8	ADJ: bare, simple, without decoration or disguise	The landscape was stark and barren of any trees.	Status & Conduct
237	squander	7	V: to waste, to spend carelessly	James won a million dollars through the lottery, and then squandered it all on expensive cars and clothes.	Status & Conduct
238	frivolous	7	ADJ: not serious or sensible, often related to spending money	The government's frivolous spending cost the taxpayers a lot of money.	Status & Conduct
239	spontaneous	6	ADJ: impulsive, without planning	Her art appeared spontaneous, as if she had applied paint in an entirely impulsive, unplanned manner.	Status & Conduct

Ivy Global

240	whim	7	N: an impulse or sudden desire	On a whim, Amanda decided to buy a motorcycle.	Status & Conduct
241	restrained	7	ADJ: held back, kept under control	The elegance of the composition is subtle and restrained, not over the top.	Status & Conduct
242	destitute	9	ADJ: extremely poor	The shelter provided housing for destitute families.	Status & Conduct
243	impoverished	7	ADJ: extremely poor	The region was impoverished by the prolonged drought.	Status & Conduct
244	aristocrat	7	N: a member of the upper class. ADJ: aristocratic	The aristocrats came under attack during the French Revolution.	Status & Conduct
245	elite	8	ADJ, N: upper-class, superior in intellect or status	Many of Rome's wealthy elite owned large estates where they could escape the city.	Status & Conduct
246	eminent	9	ADJ: important, well-known, respected	Einstein was probably the most eminent physicist of the 20th century.	Status & Conduct
247	hierarchy	7	N: organized ranking of status and authority. ADJ: hierarchical	European society during the Middle Ages had a strict social hierarchy.	Status & Conduct
248	promote	6	V: (1) to advertise or support a person or cause, (2) to raise in rank or importance	(1) The group promoted awareness of illiteracy in the community. (2) The employee was promoted to the status of manager.	Status & Conduct

249	demote	7	V: to reduce to a lower rank or position	The boss decided not to fire the employee, but rather to demote him.	Status & Conduct
250	subordinate	7	(1) N: lower in rank or importance, (2) V: to reduce in rank or importance	(1) The states have some degree of independence, but are subordinate to the federal government. (2) Critics argued that the party system subordinated the interests of the general population to the interests of the individual parties.	Status & Conduct
251	suppress	8	V: to hold back, keep down	She suppressed her feelings of disappointment and tried to smile.	Status & Conduct
252	inconsequential	9	ADJ: unimportant, insignificant	The committee frequently spent too much time on inconsequential details instead of dealing with bigger issues.	Status & Conduct
253	creed	7	N: a statement of belief	Many Catholics follow the Nicene creed, a statement of their beliefs that is over 1000 years old.	Time, History, & Tradition
254	conviction	7	N: (1) unshakably strong belief, (2) the final judgment that a person is guilty of a crime	(1) Maria was a lifelong member of the Catholic Church and had strong religious convictions. (2) The defendant appealed to the higher court to overturn his conviction.	Time, History, & Tradition

255	pious	9	ADJ: faithful to one's religious beliefs	Mother Theresa was admired by many for her pious and charitable behavior.	Time, History, & Tradition
256	conform	8	V: to obey customs, rules, or styles. N: conformist, conformity	Students who do not conform to the dress code will not be allowed to attend the dance.	Time, History, & Tradition
257	convention	7	N: (1) a meeting or assembly, (2) a custom or standard. ADJ: conventional	(1) Hundreds of fans attended the Star Trek convention dressed in costume. (2) In many cultures, it is convention that a visitor bring a gift to a sick patient in hospital.	Time, History, & Tradition
258	orthodox	8	ADJ: traditional, customary, conventional	The musician's alternative music was far from orthodox.	Time, History, & Tradition
259	uniform	8	(1) ADJ: always the same, consistent, even. (2) N: a distinctive or official outfit worn by a particular group	(1) The finely woven fabric had a smooth, uniform texture. (2) Our school uniforms are green and white.	Time, History, & Tradition
260	anomaly	8	N: an unusual or unexpected event. ADJ: anomalous	The unusually warm winter was an anomaly in a region known for its snow and freezing temperatures.	Time, History, & Tradition
261	atypical	7	ADJ: unusual or unexpected	Barry's bad mood is atypical; he is generally a very cheerful person.	Time, History, & Tradition

262	radical	8	(1) ADJ: extreme or revolutionary. (2) N: a person who has extreme or revolutionary ideas	(1) The new CEO proposed radical changes in the way the company was structured. (2) Extremists and radicals exist in every major religion.	Time, History, & Tradition
263	chronological	6	ADJ: arranged in order of time. N: chronology	The chart shows a history of events in chronological order.	Time, History, & Tradition
264	contemporary	8	ADJ: belonging to the present or same time	The students were asked to research three contemporary events currently in the news.	Time, History, & Tradition
265	simultaneous	6	ADJ: occurring at the same time	The phone and the doorbell rang simultaneously.	Time, History, & Tradition
266	premonition	8	N: a foreboding, a feeling of evil to come	Jake stocked up on supplies because he had a premonition that a horrible snowstorm was coming.	Time, History, & Tradition
267	ominous	8	ADJ: threatening, menacing, foretelling evil	I had an ominous feeling that something was going to go wrong.	Time, History, & Tradition
268	precursor	8	N: something that comes before and indicates the approach of something or someone	What looks like a harmless skin spot can sometimes be the precursor to a cancerous growth.	Time, History, & Tradition

269	precedent	9	N: a previous act or decision that serves as a guide for later situations	The court considered the case carefully, as it knew that their decision could serve as a precedent for future cases.	Time, History, & Tradition
270	predecessor	8	N: a person who holds an office or position before another	George W. Bush was Barack Obama's predecessor as President of the United States.	Time, History, & Tradition
271	lineage	8	N: an individual's series of ancestors	The family traced its lineage back to the first French traders to settle in North America.	Time, History, & Tradition
272	pedigree	8	N: an individual's or animal's series of ancestors	The puppies share a strong, healthy pedigree.	Time, History, & Tradition
273	residual	9	ADJ: left over, remaining. N: residue	After the building was completed, construction crews cleaned up the residual building material.	Time, History, & Tradition
274	remnant	9	N: a leftover	The land contains only the remnants of the massive forest that once grew there.	Time, History, & Tradition
275	duration	7	N: a time period over which something lasts or continues	Zinc is said to shorten the duration of cold symptoms.	Time, History, & Tradition
276	durable	5	ADJ: lasting for a long time. N: durability	Linda hoped that her boots were durable enough to survive Toronto's winters.	Time, History, & Tradition

277	sustain	7	V: (1) to prolong or extend, (2) to undergo or endure, (3) to provide with necessary nourishment and support. N: sustenance	(1) Janice sustained her cheerful and optimistic attitude even when disaster struck. (2) The plants could not sustain the blistering heat with little water, and they quickly wilted. (3) The emergency supplies will sustain us in case we are snowed in.	Time, History, & Tradition
278	prophesy	7	V: to predict or reveal something before it has happened. ADJ: prophetic, N: prophet	Some claim that the ancient Mayans prophesied the end of the world in 2012.	Time, History, & Tradition
279	foreshadow	8	V: to suggest or indicate what might happen next	The education reform in Poland foreshadows great changes in its school system.	Time, History, & Tradition
280	foresight	8	N: looking ahead, knowing in advance, preparing for the future	The city planners had the foresight to accommodate the need for mass transit in the city's future.	Time, History, & Tradition
281	foretell	7	V: to predict, to tell what is going to happen	Many realized that the economy was unstable, but no one foretold the sudden stock market crash.	Time, History, & Tradition
282	subsequent	8	ADJ: following in time, later	Although first edition of the book contained many printing errors, subsequent editions corrected these mistakes.	Time, History, & Tradition

Ivy Global

283	imminent	10	ADJ: about to happen, occur, take place very soon	The doctors determined that the patient's health was not in imminent danger.	Time, History, & Tradition
284	impending	10	ADJ: about to happen, occur, take place very soon	The hero had only two choices: to embark on the dangerous quest, or to face impending doom.	Time, History, & Tradition
285	inevitable	7	ADJ: unavoidable, unable to be prevented	The team was playing so poorly that everyone knew defeat was inevitable.	Time, History, & Tradition
286	recollect	6	V: to remember. N: recollection	The witness stated that she could not recollect the specific details of the crime.	Time, History, & Tradition
287	reminisce	8	V: to recall the past, particularly pleasant memories. N: recollection	Blaine looked forward to seeing many of his former classmates and reminiscing about the past.	Time, History, & Tradition
288	nostalgia	9	N: longing for the past. ADJ: nostalgic	The film conveys a sense of bittersweet nostalgia for lost youth.	Time, History, & Tradition
289	remorse	8	N: a feeling of deep regret. ADJ: remorseful	Now a changed man, he felt remorse over his past misdeeds.	Time, History, & Tradition
290	commemorate	8	V: to remember through a ceremony or service	Memorial Day commemorates those who lost their lives serving their country.	Time, History, & Tradition

291	homage	10	N: respect, tribute, honor	Remembrance Day events pay homage to those who served in the military.	Time, History, & Tradition
292	antiquated	9	ADJ: old-fashioned, out-of-date	Eliza was happy when her school finally replaced its antiquated computers with newer laptops.	Time, History, & Tradition
293	archaic	8	ADJ: ancient, old-fashioned	Mosaics lined the walls of the ruin, with an unrecognizable archaic script carved underneath.	Time, History, & Tradition
294	obsolete	7	ADJ: not current, no longer in use, out-of-date	Technology is changing so rapidly that new products may become obsolete within a year or even a few months.	Time, History, & Tradition
295	renovate	6	V: to renew, to restore to a better condition. N: renovation	The apartment was recently renovated with all-new kitchen and bathroom appliances.	Time, History, & Tradition
296	innovation	7	N: a new way of doing something, a creation of something new	The general economy is experiencing a fundamental change fuelled by technological innovation.	Time, History, & Tradition
297	novelty	8	N: (1) the state of being new or interesting, (2) a new product	(1) The novelty of the toy quickly wore off, and the child became bored with his birthday present. (2) The store sells wigs, glasses, hats, props, and other novelties.	Time, History, & Tradition

Ivy Global

298	habitual	9	ADJ: usual, regular, according to habit	Matt was not a habitual Mac user and found the different operating system frustrating.	Time, History, & Tradition
299	intermittent	8	ADJ: stopping and starting irregularly	The snow continued lightly into the evening and became intermittent by midnight.	Time, History, & Tradition
300	artifact	7	N: a man-made object	The museum has a display of ancient Egyptian art and artifacts.	Time, History, & Tradition
301	mosaic	7	N: art consisting of glass or stone tiles	The cathedral is decorated by mosaics on the walls, ceiling, and floor.	Time, History, & Tradition
302	intuition	7	N: instinctive, irrational knowledge. ADJ: intuitive	Scientists must rely on both their analytical logic and their well-developed intuition.	Truth & Deception
303	presume	7	V: to assume without proof. ADJ: presumption	Austin was presumed dead in the shipwreck, though his body was never found.	Truth & Deception
304	imply	6	V: to suggest, to state indirectly. N: implication	Although he did not say so directly, the president implied that he did not agree with the military's position.	Truth & Deception
305	insinuate	10	V: to make an indirect, often negative, suggestion	The reporter insinuated that the company had been lying to the public.	Truth & Deception
306	allege	10	V: to declare, report	The defendant alleged temporary insanity.	Truth & Deception

307	assert	7	V: to make a claim, to state as true	Emily was not shy about asserting her opinion.	Truth & Deception
308	testify	6	V: to give evidence for, often in court. N: testimony	The witnessed testified that she had seen the suspect lurking outside of her house.	Truth & Deception
309	certify	8	V: to provide evidence for	The expert certified that the violin was, indeed, an authentic Stradivarius.	Truth & Deception
310	decode	7	V: to figure out, interpret	The language is so ancient and unusual that expert linguists cannot decode it.	Truth & Deception
311	enlighten	8	V: to shed light upon, to make clear	The seminar was meant to enlighten the audience about the application process.	Truth & Deception
312	illuminate	6	V: to shed light upon, to make clear. N: illumination	The paintings on display were illuminated by well-placed lights.	Truth & Deception
313	clarity	7	N: clearness, ability to be understood. V: clarify	A good essay will demonstrate sound logic and clarity.	Truth & Deception
314	fathom	10	(1) V: to come to understand, (2) N: a unit of water depth	(1) We really could not fathom why the singer was so popular. (2) The shipwreck was 130 fathoms underwater.	Truth & Deception
315	feasible	9	ADJ: achievable, possible, able to be done	Sending humans to Mars will likely be possible in the future, but is currently not feasible.	Truth & Deception

316	plausible	9	ADJ: possible, reasonable	The hypothesis sounded plausible but had never been proven.	Truth & Deception
317	credible	8	ADJ: believable	The defense attorney questioned whether the witness was credible.	Truth & Deception
318	legitimate	6	ADJ: legal, authorized, valid V: to make legal, to authorize	Critics wondered whether the election was legitimate, or whether it had been rigged.	Truth & Deception
319	acknowledge	7	V: to notice or accept	The organization's donation to the charity was acknowledged with great thanks.	Truth & Deception
320	frank	9	ADJ: honest, open	The criminal could have shortened his prison sentence by making a full and frank confession.	Truth & Deception
321	integrity	6	N: (1) wholeness, unity, (2) honesty	(1) The engineers ran tests on the bridge to determine its structural integrity. (2) The reporter's deceptive tactics drew questions about his journalistic integrity.	Truth & Deception
322	gullible	8	ADJ: easily deceived or tricked	People should not be so gullible as to believe everything they read in advertisements.	Truth & Deception
323	devise	8	V: to invent, to create a plan	The research team devised a new method of gathering data.	Truth & Deception

324	devious	9	ADJ: misleading, deceitful	Martha deviously managed to trick her opponent.	Truth & Deception
325	crafty	7	ADJ: sly, skilled in deception	Always crafty, Pete fooled his parents into thinking he had eaten his vegetables.	Truth & Deception
326	wily	6	ADJ: sly, skilled in deception	The police hunted for the escaped criminal, but he proved too wily to be caught.	Truth & Deception
327	blatant	6	ADJ: obvious, offensive	John's action showed a blatant disrespect for authority.	Truth & Deception
328	conspicuous	9	ADJ: obvious, easy to notice	Camouflage uniforms are meant to make the army less conspicuous among the trees.	Truth & Deception
329	confide	7	V: to tell a secret to, to entrust	Brian knew he could always confide in his parents.	Truth & Deception
330	discreet	8	ADJ: respectful of privacy or secrecy. N: discretion	I hope you will be discreet and not mention this secret to anyone else.	Truth & Deception
331	subtle	7	ADJ: fine, delicate, not obvious	Mary dropped subtle hints about what she wanted for her birthday, but her boyfriend did not notice.	Truth & Deception

332	oblivious	8	ADJ: lacking awareness, forgetful	Many people are oblivious to the serious dangers of climate change.	Truth & Deception
333	sarcastic	7	ADJ: ridiculing or making fun of	"Oh, of course, you're always right," Amy's mother said in a sarcastic manner when Amy wouldn't admit that she was wrong.	Truth & Deception
334	cryptic	8	ADJ: difficult to understand or decipher	The anonymous message was cryptic and mysterious.	Truth & Deception
335	enigma	8	N: a mystery, a difficult problem. ADJ: enigmatic	The cause of Type 1 diabetes is still an enigma.	Truth & Deception
336	ambiguous	8	ADJ: unclear, having more than one possible meaning	The report is ambiguous about whether health care will be affected by the government's cutbacks.	Truth & Deception
337	dubious	8	ADJ: (1) doubtful, uncertain; (2) disbelieving, not convinced	After losing the election, the senator's political future looked dubious.	Truth & Deception
338	skeptical	6	ADJ: disbelieving, doubting	It is a good idea to be skeptical about the claims made in advertisements.	Truth & Deception
339	absurdity	6	N: something unreasonable, contradictory, ridiculous	Sartre's plays expose the absurdity of everyday life.	Truth & Deception

340	delusion	9	N: a false belief, not real or logical	The man suffered from delusions of grandeur, believing he was destined to save the world.	Truth & Deception
341	mirage	10	N: an illusion	As he walked through the desert he thought he glimpsed a shining oasis on the horizon, but this was just a mirage.	Truth & Deception
342	distort	7	V: (1) to deform or alter an object's original shape, (2) to falsely change the meaning of something	(1) The reflection was distorted as a ripple moved across the water's surface. (2) The media were accused of distorting the facts.	Truth & Deception
343	obscure	6	ADJ: unclear, dark, V: to make dark or unclear	The English class found the poem difficult because of its obscure vocabulary.	Truth & Deception
344	baffling	6	ADJ: puzzling and frustrating. V: baffle	The instructions are absolutely baffling, so confusing that they are impossible to follow.	Truth & Deception
345	perplex	7	V: to confuse, to puzzle. ADJ: perplexed, perplexing	The scientists were perplexed by the odd results of the experiment.	Truth & Deception
346	bewilder	8	V: to confuse, to puzzle	We were bewildered by the government's sudden policy reversal.	Truth & Deception

347	muddle	6	V: to confuse, mix up, N: a confused or disorganized mess. ADJ: muddled	The paper's argument was unclear and muddled.	Truth & Deception
348	convoluted	8	ADJ: complex and intricate	The movie's plot was so convoluted that many viewers could not understand what was happening.	Truth & Deception
349	contend	9	V: (1) to dispute or compete, (2) to claim to be true	(1) The final two teams contended for the championship title. (2) The defendant contended that the judge was biased in his decision.	Truth & Deception
350	contradict	5	V: to oppose or deny	In the second paragraph of your essay, you contradict what you stated in the first paragraph.	Truth & Deception
351	irony	8	N: (1) contradiction between what is expected and what actually occurs, (2) sarcasm	The fireman found it ironic that their own firehouse burned to the ground in the middle of the night.	Truth & Deception
352	erroneous	8	ADJ: wrong, mistaken, in error	After further testing disproved their conclusions, the scientists concluded that their earlier theories were erroneous.	Truth & Deception

353	debunk	9	V: to disprove or expose something as false	The evidence given in this passage debunks the legend that Betsy Ross sewed the first American flag.	Truth & Deception
354	refute	9	V: to disprove or expose something as false	The police force refuted any accusations of wrongdoing.	Truth & Deception
355	mourn	6	V: to feel sadness or sorrow, particularly over a death. ADJ: mournful	Millions mourned the death of Michael Jackson.	War & Conflict
356	woe	7	N: grief, sorrow, suffering	Overspending is a major cause of our financial woes.	War & Conflict
357	melancholy	8	ADJ: depressed, sad, gloomy, N: a depressed or gloomy feeling	The violin's melancholy melody brought the listeners to tears.	War & Conflict
358	morose	9	ADJ: depressed, sad, gloomy	Cheer up-- I hate to see you looking so morose!	War & Conflict
359	somber	8	ADJ: depressing, gloomy, dark	The mood at the funeral was somber.	War & Conflict
360	dismal	7	ADJ: depressing, gloomy	The day outside looked gray, rainy, and dismal.	War & Conflict

361	hail	8	V: (1) to praise, (2) to greet joyfully, (3) to rain small ice particles	(1) The new movie was hailed as a stunning achievement. (2) "Hail Caesar!" cried the crowd as the emperor arrived. (3) The forecast promises rain, wind, and hail.	War & Conflict
362	turmoil	7	N: violent disturbance or protest, disorder	The stock market crash created turmoil in the global economy.	War & Conflict
363	uproar	6	N: a state of noise, excitement, and confusion	The fans were in an uproar over the referee's controversial call.	War & Conflict
364	irate	9	ADJ: extremely angry	The irate passengers had to wait for over an hour for their luggage.	War & Conflict
365	livid	9	ADJ: (1) extremely angry, (2) grayish-blue, bruise-colored	(1) The players' irresponsible behavior made their coach livid with rage. (2) The doctors removed the dressing to reveal the livid wound.	War & Conflict
366	ferocity	7	N: the condition of being wild and fierce	The army displayed great ferocity on the battlefield.	War & Conflict
367	recede	6	V: to withdraw or move back. N: recession	As the tide went out, the waters receded and exposed meters of wet sand.	War & Conflict
368	impasse	10	N: a deadlock, a point that cannot be passed	The two leaders have reached an impasse in their peace talks, and negotiations between the two countries are unable to continue.	War & Conflict

369	impenetrable	7	ADJ: (1) dense, unable to be penetrated, (2) impossible to understand	(1) Entering the cave, we were faced with a deep, impenetrable darkness. (2) The book was so dense and hard to understand that the students complained it was impenetrable.	War & Conflict
370	deft	9	ADJ: skillful, quick in action	With his quick fingers, Mike is a deft mechanic.	War & Conflict
371	haste	8	N: speedy or quick action. V: hasten	In her haste to leave, Sarah forgot her wallet on the table.	War & Conflict
372	denounce	9	V: to speak out against	The traitor was denounced for his disloyalty to his country.	War & Conflict
373	reproach	8	(1) V: to express disapproval or criticism. (2) N: shame, disgrace	(1) The media were reproached for exaggerating the story. (2) Despite the scandal in his company, the CEO claimed to be above reproach and entirely blameless.	War & Conflict
374	ensnare	7	V: to catch or trap	The tiger was ensnared in the hunter's trap.	War & Conflict
375	assail	9	V: to attack violently	The army waited until nightfall to assail the enemy camp.	War & Conflict
376	vulnerable	6	ADJ: capable of being wounded or hurt	A turtle's shell protects its vulnerable midsection and inner organs.	War & Conflict

377	debilitate	8	V: to make weak. ADJ: debilitated	The city was debilitated by the devastating flu epidemic.	War & Conflict
378	impair	8	V: to weaken, diminish, make worse	Alcohol impairs judgment and slows reaction time.	War & Conflict
379	detrimental	8	ADJ: causing harm. N: detriment	Smoking can have detrimental effects on your health.	War & Conflict
380	mangle	6	V: to mutilate, to destroy or injure severely	The mangled wreckage of the building was all that remained from the fire.	War & Conflict
381	obliterate	8	V: to destroy or remove completely	The computer virus rewrote the hard drive, obliterating all of its data.	War & Conflict
382	terminate	5	V: to bring to an end	The renter had the right to terminate his rental agreement by giving two months' written notice.	War & Conflict
383	slay	6	V: to murder	The hero slayed the fearsome dragon.	War & Conflict
384	adversary	7	N: opponent	I was not looking forward to competing against Brian in the chess match because he was such a strong adversary.	War & Conflict
385	animosity	10	N: deep hatred	The revolutionaries felt great animosity towards the oppressive military leaders.	War & Conflict
386	hostile	6	ADJ: very unfriendly. N: hostility	The city seemed strange, cold, and hostile to the new immigrants.	War & Conflict

387	affliction	8	N: great suffering, pain, or distress	When we suffer from bodily pain, there is bound to be mental affliction as well.	War & Conflict
388	anguish	6	N: great suffering, pain, or distress	The woman let out a cry of anguish as she watched her city burn.	War & Conflict
389	lament	8	V: to express sorrow or regret, N: an expression of sorrow or regret	The poor man lamented his sorry fate.	War & Conflict
390	atrocity	8	N: an extremely cruel or unjust act. ADJ: atrocious	The war criminal was brought to international trial for the atrocities he had committed.	War & Conflict
391	bane	8	N: something causing misery or death	Injuries are the bane of any athlete.	War & Conflict
392	hazard	7	(1) N: a danger or risk. ADJ: hazardous. (2) V: to make a guess	(1) The building was inspected for fire hazards. (2) I am unsure of the answer, but will hazard a guess.	War & Conflict
393	volatile	9	ADJ: explosive, likely to change suddenly or violently	The United Nations sent in peacekeepers to help stabilize the volatile region.	War & Conflict
394	calamity	7	N: a tragedy, an event resulting in great loss	Critics were concerned that the new financial policy would bring about economic calamity for the country.	War & Conflict

395	catastrophe	7	N: a disaster, tragedy. ADJ: catastrophic	The Haiti earthquake was a huge catastrophe for the island nation.	War & Conflict
396	sinister	8	ADJ: threatening, menacing, dark	The bombing was revealed to be part of a sinister conspiracy.	War & Conflict
397	evade	7	V: to escape or dodge. N: evasion, ADJ: evasive	The spy evaded capture by the enemy army.	War & Conflict
398	subside	8	V: to die down or wear off	The thunderstorm eventually subsided and the sky began to clear.	War & Conflict
399	fortify	7	V: to strengthen. N: fortification	The city fortified its defenses in preparation for the upcoming attack.	War & Conflict
400	prevail	7	V: to be greater in number, power, or importance	Despite their poor performance during the first three quarters, the team made an amazing comeback and prevailed at the end of the game.	War & Conflict
401	sentry	7	N: a lookout, someone who keeps watch	The checkpoint was guarded by sentries who searched all vehicles that tried to pass through.	War & Conflict
402	vigilant	7	ADJ: carefully observant, on the lookout for possible danger	The army remained vigilant, knowing the enemy could strike at any time.	War & Conflict
403	tactician	8	N: a person who is skilled at planning tactics or strategies	Bruce was an inspiring leader, a brave fighter, and a brilliant tactician.	War & Conflict

404	hypothesis	7	N: an educated guess that has not yet been proven. ADJ: hypothetical	The scientists tried to prove their hypothesis by conducting experiments.	Science & Analysis
405	compile	8	V: to gather together. N: compilation	The new report compiled data from surveys in fifty communities.	Science & Analysis
406	cumulative	8	ADJ: adding together, incorporating everything up to the present	Jason found that the cumulative effects of sleep deprivation were making him unable to concentrate.	Science & Analysis
407	comprehensive	7	ADJ: thorough, covering a wide area, including everything	The book gives a comprehensive history of Chinese culture and politics.	Science & Analysis
408	criterion	7	N: a standard against which other things can be judged. PL: criteria	Amy's application was denied because she did not meet a single criterion or requirement for the job.	Science & Analysis
409	scrutiny	6	N: intense examination or inspection	The legislators will carry out an in-depth scrutiny of the bill before it is passed.	Science & Analysis
410	fundamental	7	ADJ: involving basic or essential principles	The fundamental law of gravity states that what goes up must come down.	Science & Analysis
411	innate	10	ADJ: natural, present at birth	The ability to acquire language is innate in most human beings.	Science & Analysis

412	congenital	7	ADJ: present at birth	Edgar had a congenital heart defect that went undetected for years.	Science & Analysis
413	hereditary	7	ADJ: inherited, passed from parents to children	Cholesterol levels are largely hereditary, though exercise and diet contribute as well.	Science & Analysis
414	heterogeneous	9	ADJ: having many different elements or parts	The study surveyed a heterogeneous sample of patients, differing in age, gender, and ethnicity.	Science & Analysis
415	homogeneous	9	ADJ: all of the same kind, having consistent or identical parts. V: homogenize	The ballet company had a fairly homogenous set of dancers, all the same height, weight, and build.	Science & Analysis
416	saturate	8	V: to fill or soak completely. N: saturation	A wetland is a flat area saturated by water, like a marsh or swamp.	Science & Analysis
417	dilute	5	V: to weaken or lessen in strength, to water down	The dye was too dark, so Erin diluted the color by adding water.	Science & Analysis
418	humid	5	ADJ: damp, having a great deal of water vapor in the air. N: humidity	The rainforest climate is warm and humid.	Science & Analysis
419	irrigate	6	V: to supply with water. N: irrigation	The farmer irrigated his crops with a system of sprinklers and hoses.	Science & Analysis
420	deluge	8	N: a flood or downpour	We were caught in the sudden deluge without an umbrella.	Science & Analysis

421	erosion	7	N: the process of wearing away by water or wind	As the cliffs are being worn away by erosion, visitors should watch out for falling stones and debris.	Science & Analysis
422	corrode	8	V: to cause to deteriorate, to eat away by water, air, or acid. N: corrosion	Old batteries will eventually corrode and should be replaced.	Science & Analysis
423	tarnish	9	V: to make dirty, often a metal through exposure to air	The silver had tarnished over time, but polishing revealed its shiny surface.	Science & Analysis
424	dehydrate	6	V: to remove water, to dry out. N: dehydration	Halfway through the race, Adam started to feel dehydrated and stopped for a drink of water.	Science & Analysis
425	arid	8	ADJ: dry, lacking rainfall	Deserts are highly arid climates that receive very little rainfall.	Science & Analysis
426	parch	8	V: to dry out through heat	As the summer progressed with no rain, the land looked parched.	Science & Analysis
427	altitude	6	N: height, elevation above sea level	Passengers must remain seated until the plane reaches its cruising altitude.	Science & Analysis
428	excavate	6	V: to dig up. N: excavation	The team of archeologists was excavating the ruins of an ancient Roman city.	Science & Analysis

429	incision	9	N: the result of cutting. ADJ: incisive	The surgeon made an incision in the patient's abdomen so he could begin operating.	Science & Analysis
430	apparatus	7	N: equipment	The firefighters used breathing apparatus so they could tackle the flames.	Science & Analysis
431	remedy	8	N: a cure or solution, V: to cure or set right	Currently there are many treatments but no remedy for diabetes.	Science & Analysis
432	phenomenon	7	N: an observable event or occurrence. PL: phenomena	It is an unusual phenomenon that water weighs less as a solid (ice) than as a liquid.	Science & Analysis
433	acoustics	7	N: the study of the properties of sound	The architect of the concert hall had to consider carefully the acoustics of his design so the music could be heard well.	Science & Analysis
434	auditory	7	ADJ: relating to the process of hearing	Sound is received by the ear and carried along the auditory nerve to the brain.	Science & Analysis
435	cacophony	9	N: a loud, harsh, disagreeable noise	There was a cacophony in the band room as all the players warmed up at the same time.	Science & Analysis
436	din	8	N: a loud, harsh, disagreeable noise	We could hardly have a conversation over the din of the leaf blower next door.	Science & Analysis

437	muted	8	ADJ: softened, hushed, quiet	The painter preferred muted purples and blues over brighter colors.	Science & Analysis
438	olfactory	9	ADJ: relating to the sense of smell	Dogs have a much keener olfactory sense than do humans.	Science & Analysis
439	pungent	10	ADJ: having a strong or sharp taste or odor	The French cheese smelled pungent but tasted delicious.	Science & Analysis
440	rancid	9	ADJ: having a sour or stale taste or smell due to decomposition	The meat had been sitting out for too long and had gone rancid.	Science & Analysis
441	entice	8	V: to lure or attract, often through appearance or smell. ADJ: enticing	The enticing smell from the oven summoned us into the kitchen.	Science & Analysis
442	glutton	7	N: a person who is greedy, particularly about eating. ADJ: gluttonous	Augustus Gloop was a glutton who gorged himself on chocolate and candy.	Science & Analysis
443	ravenous	8	ADJ: extremely hungry	It had been so long since breakfast that we were ravenous.	Science & Analysis
444	voracious	9	ADJ: greedy or extremely hungry	Nathan has a voracious appetite; he eats and eats and never seems to get full.	Science & Analysis
445	tactile	8	ADJ: relating to the sense of touch	The sculpture was meant to be tactile; in fact, the display invited visitors to touch it.	Science & Analysis

446	tangible	8	ADJ: able to be felt or touched	The prosecutor knew that he could not win his case without tangible proof.	Science & Analysis
447	audible	7	ADJ: able to be heard	The actor spoke quietly but was still audible from the stage.	Science & Analysis
448	taut	8	ADJ: under tension, stretched tightly	The boat's cover should be stretched taut so it does not collect any water.	Science & Analysis
449	contour	7	N: a smooth, curved outline	The road followed the contours of the countryside, rising and falling along with the hills and valleys.	Science & Analysis
450	amorphous	10	ADJ: having no defined shape	The dress was billowy and amorphous, without a fitted shape or structure.	Science & Analysis
451	translucent	6	ADJ: allowing light to pass through	Amethyst can vary in color from translucent lilac to deep purple.	Science & Analysis
452	hue	6	N: a quality or shade of color	The baby ate so many carrots that his skin took on an orange hue.	Science & Analysis
453	solitary	6	ADJ: alone, by oneself	The prisoners were kept in solitary confinement for three nights.	Size, Location & Motion

454	void	7	(1) ADJ: containing nothing, empty. (2) ADJ: invalid, cancelled, having no legal force. (3) N: emptiness, open space	(1) This argument is entirely nonsensical and void of logic. (2) Josh disassembled his computer himself instead of shipping it back to the company, thereby rendering his warranty void. (3) Many ancient religions state that the earth was once a dark, formless void before life was created.	Size, Location & Motion
455	null	10	ADJ: having no value or force	The contract was declared null and void.	Size, Location & Motion
456	equivalent	7	ADJ: of equal value or size	The recipe calls for 150 milliliters of cream, or the equivalent.	Size, Location & Motion
457	ample	7	ADJ: large, more than enough	Aunt Christie piled our plates high with ample servings of turkey.	Size, Location & Motion
458	plentiful	8	ADJ: in full supply, in large amounts	It had been a good growing season, and the harvest was plentiful.	Size, Location & Motion
459	bounty	7	N: (1) a large or generous amount of something, (2) a reward for catching a criminal	(1) After the harvest, they gathered to give thanks for nature's bounty. (2) The bounty hunter captured the fugitive and received his reward.	Size, Location & Motion
460	foster	8	V: to help grow, to nurture or promote	The pep rally was meant to foster team spirit.	Size, Location & Motion

461	pervasive	8	ADJ: spreading throughout, penetrating or affecting everything	The internet is pervasive in business, education, and entertainment.	Size, Location & Motion
462	prevalent	8	ADJ: frequent, common, widespread	After coming home from Cuba, Carrie missed the street music and dancing so prevalent in that culture.	Size, Location & Motion
463	transcend	9	V: to exceed, to go beyond limitations, to excel	Music is a universal language, able to transcend national and cultural boundaries.	Size, Location & Motion
464	elongate	6	V: to make longer, stretch out	Pluto has an elongated, oval-shaped orbit.	Size, Location & Motion
465	constraint	8	N: a restriction, something that limits or holds back	You are free to be as creative as you wish within the constraints of the assignment.	Size, Location & Motion
466	minute	9	(1) ADJ: small and detailed, (2) N: a unit of time.	The minute details of this painting are very impressive.	Size, Location & Motion
467	dearth	10	N: a lack or insufficiency	Ontario is suffering from a dearth of qualified doctors.	Size, Location & Motion
468	deficient	7	ADJ: inadequate, lacking	Anna's blood tests revealed that she was deficient in iron.	Size, Location & Motion
469	meager	8	ADJ: lacking in amount or quality	The company struggled to survive on its meager budget.	Size, Location & Motion

470	scant	9	ADJ: lacking, in short supply	The available data is too scant to allow a full understanding of the issue.	Size, Location & Motion
471	scarce	8	ADJ: lacking, inadequate, not enough	Fresh water is quickly becoming scarce in many regions of the world.	Size, Location & Motion
472	deficit	8	N: a lack, where need or expenses are greater than supply or income	Scientists are concerned that we may face an energy deficit in upcoming years.	Size, Location & Motion
473	wane	7	V: to decline, grow smaller	Our enthusiasm waned as we realized that the task would be very difficult.	Size, Location & Motion
474	sparse	6	ADJ: scattered, not dense	The region is largely bare, with sparse vegetation.	Size, Location & Motion
475	sporadic	10	ADJ: scattered, irregular, infrequent	The city's development was sporadic, occurring in starts and stops over the years.	Size, Location & Motion
476	aimless	8	ADJ: without purpose or direction	Unsure what direction to take, they wandered in an aimless manner through the forest.	Size, Location & Motion
477	meander	8	V: to ramble without direction	The river meandered slowly through the countryside, winding its way to the ocean.	Size, Location & Motion
478	fluctuate	9	V: to change irregularly, to have unpredictable ups and downs	Ian was tired all the time because his sleep schedule fluctuated greatly.	Size, Location & Motion

Ivy Global

479	arbitrary	6	ADJ: random	The teams for this competition were created arbitrarily and are meant to be entirely random.	Size, Location & Motion
480	kinetic	8	ADJ: relating to motion	The wind turbine turns the wind's kinetic energy into electricity.	Size, Location & Motion
481	dynamic	6	ADJ: active, moving, changing	New members are necessary to keep the organization growing and dynamic.	Size, Location & Motion
482	fluid	6	ADJ: (1) flowing, changing, N: (2) a substance that flows and changes shape according to its container	The dancer leapt forward in a fluid, graceful motion.	Size, Location & Motion
483	limber	8	ADJ: flexible, moving quickly and lightly	Kate is a skilled and limber soccer player.	Size, Location & Motion
484	agile	8	ADJ: graceful, moving quickly and lightly	Border collies are known as a quick and agile breed.	Size, Location & Motion
485	nimble	6	ADJ: graceful, moving quickly and lightly	Jack's nimble leap cleared the obstacle.	Size, Location & Motion
486	vigor	8	N: energy, strength	After half-time, the team charged onto the field with renewed vigor.	Size, Location & Motion

487	invigorate	8	V: to make lively and energetic	They were feeling tired and thought a walk in the fresh air might invigorate them.	Size, Location & Motion
488	dormant	7	ADJ: inactive, asleep	Volcanoes may lie dormant for hundreds of years before suddenly erupting.	Size, Location & Motion
489	sedate	9	ADJ: (1) calm, quiet, V: (2) to calm down	After sprinting for the first mile, Matt continued at a more sedate pace.	Size, Location & Motion
490	serene	7	ADJ: calm, peaceful	Susan gave a serene smile, calmly unaffected by the commotion around her.	Size, Location & Motion
491	tranquil	8	ADJ: calm, peaceful	The lake was perfectly tranquil, with no wind to ruffle the still waters.	Size, Location & Motion
492	remote	7	ADJ: distant, located far away	The shipwrecked sailor was stranded on a remote island.	Size, Location & Motion
493	vacant	7	ADJ: (1) empty, not occupied; ADJ: (2) empty of thought or interest	When the aging president suddenly suffered a heart attack, his position was left vacant.	Size, Location & Motion
494	abyss	9	N: a bottomless gulf or pit	The bridge across the abyss appeared rickety and about to fall apart.	Size, Location & Motion
495	chasm	7	N: a deep gorge or valley	The spectacular waterfalls are located where the river hurls itself into a deep chasm.	Size, Location & Motion

Ivy Global

496	evacuate	6	V: to empty completely	Residents were instructed to evacuate the building when the fire alarm sounded.	Size, Location & Motion
497	inhabit	7	V: to live or reside in some place	No people and very few animals inhabit Antarctica.	Size, Location & Motion
498	domestic	7	ADJ: (1) relating to the home, (2) relating to the internal affairs of a nation	The store sells refrigerators, washing machines, and other domestic appliances.	Size, Location & Motion
499	rural	6	ADJ: relating to the countryside	The area is largely rural, comprised of farmland and very few major towns.	Size, Location & Motion
500	rustic	7	ADJ: characteristic of country life, rough or unfinished	The cabins were rustic, with wood fire stoves and no indoor plumbing.	Size, Location & Motion

ANSWER KEYS

CHAPTER 7

THE VERBAL SECTION

CHAPTER 3

SYNONYM STRATEGIES

EXERCISE #3: WORD CONNOTATIONS (PAGES 41-43)

2. –

3. +

4. There are two possible meanings for this word, one positive and one weather-related (neutral).

5. –

6. –

7. +

8. –

9. +

10. –

11. +

12. –

SYNONYM PRACTICE QUESTIONS

WARM-UP QUESTIONS (PAGES 44-45)

1. C
2. B
3. E
4. B
5. C
6. A
7. C
8. B
9. E
10. C

BASIC QUESTIONS (PAGES 46-49)

1. D
2. C
3. E
4. B
5. D
6. E
7. C
8. D
9. C
10. E
11. B
12. B
13. A
14. A
15. D
16. A
17. E
18. B
19. A
20. B

21. C	24. C	27. B	30. D
22. B	25. E	28. A	31. C
23. A	26. E	29. D	32. E

MEDIUM QUESTIONS (PAGES 50-56)

1. C	13. C	25. B	37. D	49. A
2. A	14. E	26. B	38. C	50. B
3. B	15. D	27. C	39. A	51. E
4. D	16. E	28. B	40. B	52. D
5. A	17. B	29. D	41. B	53. D
6. B	18. C	30. E	42. C	54. D
7. C	19. D	31. B	43. D	55. D
8. B	20. D	32. C	44. B	56. A
9. D	21. A	33. A	45. E	57. C
10. E	22. B	34. E	46. A	58. A
11. B	23. E	35. B	47. C	59. D
12. B	24. A	36. A	48. B	60. D

DIFFICULT QUESTIONS (PAGES 57-62)

1. B	13. A	25. C	37. D	49. D
2. C	14. B	26. B	38. C	50. A
3. D	15. C	27. B	39. B	51. E
4. E	16. B	28. C	40. D	52. B
5. D	17. A	29. E	41. C	53. C
6. B	18. D	30. D	42. A	54. B
7. E	19. A	31. A	43. D	55. C
8. B	20. E	32. B	44. A	56. C
9. D	21. A	33. B	45. D	
10. A	22. B	34. A	46. B	
11. D	23. C	35. C	47. D	
12. B	24. E	36. A	48. C	

Ivy Global

CHALLENGE QUESTIONS (PAGES 63-68)

1. D	11. B	21. A	31. E	41. C
2. B	12. C	22. D	32. B	42. E
3. D	13. D	23. E	33. A	43. A
4. B	14. B	24. C	34. D	44. D
5. E	15. D	25. A	35. E	45. A
6. D	16. E	26. B	36. A	46. C
7. C	17. B	27. E	37. C	47. C
8. D	18. D	28. C	38. E	48. C
9. B	19. B	29. C	39. B	49. E
10. B	20. B	30. A	40. C	50. C

UPPER-LEVEL CHALLENGE QUESTIONS (PAGES 69-72)

1. B	9. B	17. B	25. C	33. B
2. A	10. C	18. E	26. C	34. A
3. C	11. E	19. B	27. D	35. C
4. D	12. D	20. C	28. B	36. D
5. D	13. E	21. A	29. C	37. D
6. B	14. C	22. E	30. E	38. B
7. C	15. A	23. D	31. C	
8. A	16. B	24. D	32. B	

TYPES OF ANALOGIES

EXERCISE #1 (PAGES 78-79)

2. Synonyms	5. Antonyms	8. Synonyms
3. Synonyms	6. Synonyms	9. Antonyms
4. Antonyms	7. Synonyms	10. Synonyms

EXERCISE #2 (PAGES 79-80)

2. Different, tornado is more intense
3. Same
4. Different, hatred is more intense
5. Same
6. Same
7. Different, jubilant is more intense
8. Same
9. Different, cataclysm is more intense
10. Different, livid is more intense

EXERCISE #3 (PAGES 80-81)

1. J	5. E	9. A	13. L	17. T
2. G	6. B	10. D	14. Q	18. K
3. H	7. C	11. P	15. S	19. N
4. I	8. F	12. M	16. R	20. O

EXERCISE #4 (PAGE 82)

1. C	5. I	9. G	13. R	17. K
2. H	6. J	10. D	14. L	18. O
3. A	7. E	11. M	15. Q	
4. F	8. B	12. P	16. N	

EXERCISE #5 (PAGES 83-84)

2. A stethoscope is used by a doctor to listen to hearts, lungs, etc.
3. A cleaver is used by a butcher to cut meat.
4. A chisel is used by a sculptor, mason, or woodworker to cut stone or wood.
5. A plow is used by a farmer to cut or turn over soil.
6. A scalpel is used by a surgeon to make incisions during surgery.

EXERCISE #6 (PAGE 84)

1. G	3. A	5. C	7. E
2. D	4. H	6. F	8. B

ANALOGY PRACTICE QUESTIONS

WARM-UP QUESTIONS (PAGES 100-101)

1. C	3. B	5. C	7. D	9. B
2. D	4. A	6. D	8. C	10. E

BASIC QUESTIONS (PAGES 102-105)

1. D	8. E	15. E	22. C	29. A
2. D	9. B	16. A	23. C	30. B
3. E	10. B	17. C	24. D	31. E
4. B	11. C	18. D	25. B	32. A
5. B	12. B	19. B	26. B	33. E
6. D	13. D	20. C	27. C	
7. A	14. B	21. D	28. C	

MEDIUM QUESTIONS (PAGES 106-111)

1. A	10. A	19. D	28. B	37. D
2. B	11. E	20. C	29. A	38. D
3. C	12. A	21. B	30. A	39. D
4. E	13. C	22. A	31. C	40. B
5. E	14. B	23. C	32. A	41. B
6. C	15. D	24. B	33. D	42. E
7. A	16. A	25. D	34. D	43. B
8. C	17. E	26. C	35. B	44. D
9. C	18. C	27. E	36. B	45. C

| 46. D | 48. C | 50. B | 52. D |
| 47. B | 49. C | 51. A | |

DIFFICULT QUESTIONS (PAGES 112-116)

1. C	9. A	17. D	25. A	33. B
2. C	10. A	18. B	26. E	34. E
3. B	11. B	19. A	27. B	35. E
4. B	12. C	20. B	28. D	36. E
5. D	13. A	21. A	29. A	37. E
6. B	14. B	22. C	30. B	38. A
7. D	15. E	23. E	31. C	39. A
8. D	16. A	24. A	32. A	40. B

CHALLENGE QUESTIONS (PAGES 117-119)

1. D	7. D	13. A	19. B	25. C
2. A	8. C	14. E	20. C	26. D
3. B	9. B	15. C	21. B	27. B
4. B	10. D	16. B	22. B	
5. A	11. C	17. E	23. D	
6. E	12. A	18. B	24. C	

UPPER-LEVEL CHALLENGE QUESTIONS (PAGES 120-122)

1. E	6. D	11. C	16. B	21. A
2. B	7. C	12. C	17. A	22. B
3. A	8. A	13. E	18. D	23. E
4. B	9. B	14. B	19. B	
5. C	10. D	15. E	20. A	

THE READING SECTION

CHAPTER 4

READING PRACTICE QUESTIONS

BASIC PASSAGES (PAGES 172-183)

1. C	7. E	13. B	19. B	25. D
2. E	8. B	14. E	20. C	26. B
3. B	9. D	15. C	21. B	27. B
4. A	10. A	16. D	22. E	28. C
5. E	11. C	17. B	23. A	29. E
6. C	12. D	18. E	24. B	

MEDIUM PASSAGES (PAGES 184-201)

1. D	9. E	17. E	25. A	33. B
2. E	10. B	18. C	26. C	34. A
3. B	11. A	19. C	27. D	35. E
4. B	12. C	20. B	28. B	36. C
5. D	13. C	21. C	29. C	37. B
6. C	14. A	22. A	30. C	38. D
7. B	15. D	23. B	31. B	39. A
8. A	16. D	24. C	32. E	40. D

DIFFICULT PASSAGES (PAGES 202-219)

1. C	9. E	17. C	25. D	33. D
2. A	10. E	18. C	26. C	34. D
3. E	11. A	19. E	27. C	35. E
4. D	12. D	20. D	28. B	36. B
5. A	13. B	21. B	29. B	37. D
6. C	14. C	22. B	30. A	38. E
7. D	15. E	23. B	31. E	39. D
8. B	16. A	24. C	32. C	40. A

CHALLENGE PASSAGES (PAGES 220-231)

1. B	7. E	13. D	19. C	25. B
2. C	8. C	14. C	20. A	26. C
3. B	9. C	15. E	21. D	27. A
4. D	10. B	16. A	22. B	28. B
5. D	11. A	17. D	23. B	
6. D	12. B	18. A	24. D	

UPPER LEVEL-CHALLENGE PASSAGES (PAGES 232-241)

1. A	6. C	11. D	16. C	21. E
2. E	7. E	12. A	17. D	22. B
3. C	8. C	13. A	18. A	23. C
4. B	9. B	14. D	19. E	24. A
5. C	10. C	15. E	20. D	

WRITING BASICS

EXERCISE #4 (PAGE 256)

1. Amanda ate the cookie.
2. My brother washed the dishes.
3. My dog ate my homework.
4. I made the mistake.

EXERCISE #5 - SOME POSSIBLE SOLUTIONS OUT OF MANY (PAGE 257)

1. I like to ski. It makes me happy.
2. When I ski, it makes me happy.
3. James went home, did his homework, and went to bed.
4. After James got home, he did his homework. Later, he went to bed.
5. Don't forget to bring your folder. It is important.
6. The strangest thing happened on my way to school. Our school bus broke down! They made us all get out through the back door, and we had to wait beside the road for another bus to pick us up. Because it took a long time to come, we were late.

EXERCISE #6 (PAGE 259)

1. "To Build a Fire" was written by Jack London.
2. Jack borrowed two pens. Then he went home.
3. They're coming to our house tomorrow.

4. You're waiting too long to answer.

5. My mother told me to wait there.

6. They're right here. Can't you see them?

7. My school has a great principal.

8. You're not serious!

9. The weather is nice outside.

10. I need to buy three binders to take to school. It's important.

EXERCISE #7 (PAGE 260)

1. Mike's dog is sweet.

2. The men's suits were elegant.

3. All the partiers' hats fell off.

4. Is this someone's pencil?

WRITING A SHORT STORY

EXERCISE #1 (PAGES 264-266)

2. First Person, Past Tense

3. First Person, Present Tense

4. Third Person, Present Tense

5. First Person, Past Tense

6. First Person, Present Tense

7. Third Person, Present Tense

8. Third Person, Past Tense

EXERCISE #2 (PAGE 266)

1. When she was two years old, she was playing in a garden, and she plucked a flower. She looked rather happy. Her mother wondered where she found the flower.

2. Marley is dead. There is no doubt about it. The death certificate is signed by the clerk, the undertaker, and the chief mourner. Even Scrooge signs it.

3. When I was left alone, I began to feel hungry. I went to the cupboard and cut myself some bread. I gave some to my dog and, taking a pail from the cupboard, I carried it down to the brook and filled it with clear sparkling water.

4. She opened the door and saw that it led to a small passage, no smaller than a rat-hole. She knelt down and looked into the prettiest garden she ever saw. She longed to wander through those flower beds! She could not get her head through the doorway.

EXERCISE #5 (PAGE 277)

1. Did Anne really say, "I don't know how to tie my shoe laces"?
2. "I know where to go," Mario said.
3. Marina said, "I will find the right book."
4. "Incredible!" exclaimed Ismaeel.
5. "Well," he said, "it makes sense."
6. I heard her say "go" but I didn't hear her say "stop."
7. "Where is the park?" asked Samuel.
8. Maria asked, "Can I borrow this book?"

THE ESSAY: INTRODUCTION

EXERCISE #1 (PAGES 287-289)

1. Informative
2. Creative Writing
3. Informative, but could also be Persuasive
4. Persuasive
5. Persuasive
6. Creative Writing
7. Informative

ROOTS, PREFIXES, AND SUFFIXES

EXERCISE #4 (PAGES 324-325)

2. in + aud + ible: not able to be heard (verb)

3. a + morph + ous: without shape (adjective)

4. syn + chron + ize: to occur at the same time (verb)

5. re + juven + ate: to make young again (verb)

6. in + cred + ulous: not believing, full of disbelief (adjective)

7. ambi + val + ent: valuing both sides of an issue, being undecided (adjective)

8. phil + anthrop + y: love of humanity, charity (noun)

9. vivi + sect + ion: cutting into a living animal (noun)

10. retro + spect + ive: backward-looking (adjective)